Sex

WITH THE QUEEN

ALSO BY ELEANOR HERMAN

Sex with Kings

Eleanor Herman

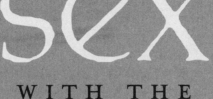

sex

WITH THE
QUEEN

900 YEARS
OF VILE KINGS,
VIRILE LOVERS,
AND PASSIONATE
POLITICS

 WILLIAM MORROW *An Imprint of* HarperCollins*Publishers*

SEX WITH THE QUEEN. Copyright © 2006 by Eleanor Herman. All rights reserved. Printed in the United States of America. No part of this book may be used or reproduced in any manner whatsoever without written permission except in the case of brief quotations embodied in critical articles and reviews. For information address HarperCollins Publishers, 10 East 53rd Street, New York, NY 10022.

HarperCollins books may be purchased for educational, business, or sales promotional use. For information please write: Special Markets Department, HarperCollins Publishers, 10 East 53rd Street, New York, NY 10022.

FIRST EDITION

Designed by Janet M. Evans and Shubhani Sarkar

Printed on acid-free paper

Library of Congress Cataloging-in-Publication Data has been applied for.

ISBN-13: 978-0-06-084673-2
ISBN-10: 0-06-084673-9

06 07 08 09 10 WBC/RRD 10 9 8 7 6 5 4 3 2 1

To my husband, Michael Dyment.
If all queens had been married to a prince like you,
they would never have committed adultery.

CONTENTS

ACKNOWLEDGMENTS

Putting a first book out there for the world to read is like standing on a podium naked and asking people to judge you, body and soul. This is because each book is a clear reflection of its author, her personality, her thoughts and experiences, her way of looking at the world. Judgment, therefore, will not only be about her writing, but about . . . *her soul*!

It is extremely frightening to take that step up to the podium, utterly exposed; the least bit of jiggle, cellulite, or sagging clearly visible to potentially cruel judges.

It is also an exhilarating experience when the judges agree the results are pretty good, and any minor jiggle can be forgiven. To a first-time author, this means not only that she did the right thing giving up her day job to write books, but also removes any lingering doubt in her mind as to whether she is a good human being worthy of inhaling air on this planet.

To all those who supported me in the roller-coaster ride of bringing out *Sex with Kings* while simultaneously working on *Sex with the Queen,* I thank you most heartily. On the personal side, this is my amazingly patient husband, Michael Dyment; my encouraging sister, Christine Merrill; and my supportive father, Walter Herman. I would also like to thank my friends Kitty Jensen and Steve Ledebur, who attended so many *Sex with Kings* book events with an entourage dressed in full Renaissance costume. The ladies-in-waiting on my European book tour—my friends Leslie

Harris of Noblesse Oblige costumes, and Lorraine Nordlinger—deserve special gratitude for wearing those tight corsets.

On the professional side I have been extremely fortunate to work with amazing women on both sides of the Atlantic. My editors Angelika Schwartz and Karin Herber-Schlapp at Fischer Verlag in Frankfurt, Germany, and my agent Barbara Perlmutter in New York, have been an absolute delight.

The ongoing laughter I have shared with my contacts at William Morrow has never reduced the high level of professionalism of our work. Many thanks are due to my editor Lucia Macro; her assistant, Kelly Harms; and my thick-skinned, hardworking publicists, Dee Dee Di Bartolo and Shannon Valcich.

INTRODUCTION

That wife alone unsullied credit wins
Whose virtues can atone her husband's sins.
Thus, while the man has other nymphs in view,
It suits the woman to be doubly true.

—RICHARD SHERIDAN

❋

VIRILE KINGS, CHASTE QUEENS

LUSCIOUS MISTRESSES GRACED THE BEDS OF MOST EUROPEAN kings for hundreds of years, pocketing eye-popping salaries and sometimes ruling nations. Indeed, between the sixteenth and eighteenth centuries, the position of royal mistress was almost as official as that of prime minister. She influenced the arts, charmed foreign ambassadors, and appointed ministers. Her rooms were often grander than those of the queen, her gowns more gorgeous, her jewels more dazzling.

While adultery was never lauded, judgment was often mute when the king took a mistress; he had been forced for political reasons to marry an unattractive, awkward foreign princess with whom he had absolutely nothing in common. In 1662 the tall, swarthy Charles II of England wed the tiny bucktoothed Princess

Catherine of Portugal. Much to his bride's chagrin, Charles refused to give up his highly sexed auburn-haired mistress, Barbara, Lady Castlemaine.

Charles explained that "he was no atheist but he could not think God would make a man miserable for taking a little pleasure out of the way."[1] Over the years, Charles took a great deal of pleasure out of the way—the darkly elegant Frenchwoman Louise de Kéroualle, the spunky actress Nell Gwynn, the sleekly bisexual Italian Hortense Mancini, and many more.

In 1660 the handsome Louis XIV of France married his first cousin, Princess Marie-Thérèse of Spain, the dwarfish byproduct of generations of inbreeding. Though spared the drooling insanity which had plagued many of her ancestors, Marie-Thérèse had a limited understanding and found herself adrift in the most witty, polished court in Europe. Louis placated himself first with the shy pretty Louise de La Vallière. After seven years he found himself racing into the arms of Athénaïs de Montespan, a magnificent tawny lioness who kept him ensnared for thirteen years. He enjoyed numerous lesser mistresses, however, including the tall redheaded princesse de Soubise, and the breathtaking blonde Marie-Angélique de Fontanges.

In 1725, at the age of fifteen, Louis XV married the dowdy twenty-two-year-old Polish princess Marie Leczinska for her family's renowned fertility. Her own father, King Stanislaus, proclaimed Marie to be one of the two dullest queens in Europe, the other dull queen being his own wife. Marie spent her mornings in prayer, her afternoons doing embroidery, and her evenings playing cards. Her husband, who grew into a witty and cultured bon vivant, remained faithful for eight years, after which he chose four sisters as his mistresses, followed by the cultured Madame de Pompadour, and lastly the talented prostitute Madame du Barry.

Princesses were raised to accept their future husbands' philandering with admirable nonchalance. When the heir to the French throne, Charles-Ferdinand, the duc de Berry, was assassinated in 1820, his wife, Duchess Marie Caroline, was pregnant. Visiting a certain city a few months after her husband's death, she was appealed to by twenty poor women, each one claiming also to be carrying the dead duke's child and asking for alms. Duchess Marie Caroline paused, considered, and replied, "It is quite possible. My husband spent a whole week in this neighborhood at the time in question."[2]

In 1717 Czar Peter the Great of Russia and his wife, the good-natured Empress Catherine, toured the European capitals. At the court of Prussia, Princess Wilhelmina wrote of the empress, "She had with her a retinue of four hundred so-called ladies. . . . Almost every one of these creatures carried a richly dressed child in her arms, and when asked if the child were hers, replied, bowing and scraping after the Russian fashion: 'The Czar did me the honor to give me this child.' "[3]

Where was the queen, we might wonder, as her husband laughed, and flirted, and planned political strategy with his mistress? Perhaps she was fulfilling her primary duty for the nation—belching forth as many royal children as her over-wrought uterus could bear. Most likely she was on her knees in prayer, interceding with God for the prosperity of her adopted country. Or she was carrying out the queen's traditional tasks of dispensing charity to the poor and mercy to the condemned. And when all else failed, there was always embroidery, an art at which neglected queens usually excelled. The majority of queens would never have dreamed of paying their straying husbands back in kind by jumping in the sack with a dashing courtier. If these queens never won their husbands' ardor, they at least earned their *respect.*

But not all European queens were dull and pious and married to handsome clever husbands. In dozens of instances, the exact opposite was true. Beautiful intelligent princesses were forced into marriage with royal ogres—sadistic, foaming at the mouth, physically repulsive, mentally retarded, or sexually impotent—and in some cases all of the above. Casting about a court bristling with testosterone in the most delectable shapes, many queens glanced quickly back at their embroidery and said a Hail Mary to ward off temptation. Many another stared hard and, heart racing, threw down her embroidery, dropped her rosary on the floor, and chose a lover.

The queen's choice often fell on a swashbuckling general, virility in boots, whose manly stride across polished parquet floors made her weak-kneed with desire. A witty courtier, his masculinity varnished with a sparkling layer of elegance, often won the queen's heart. Perhaps she would select a brilliant politician whose cunning insight would help her gain control of the nation; oddly, some of these politicians were draped in the robes of a bishop or cardinal. One empress found her lover in the church choir; she was thunderstruck by a young Adonis with the voice of an angel and quickly got him out of the house of God and into her royal four-poster.

VIRGIN AND QUEEN

While kings felt compelled to take mistresses to enhance their virile royal image, queens, on the other hand, were supposed to emulate the mother of Christ. Chastity, mercy, patience, and obedience—these were the qualities expected of a queen.

As early as the fifth century, the image of the Virgin, Mother of the Savior of the World, became blurred with the image of the queen, mother of the savior of the realm. Both Virgin and queen were often portrayed holding a baby. The Virgin morphed into the Queen of Heaven and was often painted wearing a crown and coronation robes—though it is safe to assume that Mary, wife of a Judean carpenter, never possessed any such luxuries. The earthly queen was often depicted bestowing the heavenly blessing of the Virgin, as if she were the Virgin herself.

To compound the parallel images, by the Middle Ages queens' marriages, coronations, and burials were made to fall on dates sacred to the Virgin Mary. Surely no queen personified the Virgin as closely as Elizabeth I of England (1533–1603) who was, ironically, Protestant. Elizabeth was truly a virgin—we think. It is possible she had an affair as a young queen with Robert Dudley, the Earl of Leicester, but those suitors of later years, Sir Walter Raleigh; Robert Devereux, the Earl of Essex; Sir Thomas Heneage;

and Sir Christopher Hatton, were admirers held firmly at arm's length.

This virgin queen replaced the dazzling images of Mary with dazzling images of herself. Courtiers, who a generation earlier had worshiped images of the Virgin Queen of Heaven, now bowed down before images of the virgin queen of England. Elizabeth even borrowed symbols traditionally associated with Jesus's mother in religious art—the moon, the phoenix, the ermine, and the pearl. English subjects felt it was no coincidence that Elizabeth was born on September 7, the eve of the Feast of the Virgin, and died on March 24, the eve of the Annunciation of the Virgin.

Though Elizabeth most closely resembled the Virgin Mary in her probable physical virginity as well as her iconography, her single state confounded all of Europe. The ideal was to be *like* the Virgin, not *be* a virgin. Many didn't fall for the virgin story at all; they said the queen did not marry because she refused to confine her lusts to one man. While some protested a bit too much about Elizabeth's insatiable desires, claiming she even had sex with certain foreigners who were known to have enormous private parts, others declared the poor queen never married because she suffered from a genital deformity which prevented sex and childbearing. The Venetian ambassador in France heard that her menstrual cycle flowed out of one of her legs rather than the usual place.

Most likely, the queen's single state was due neither to frigidity nor nymphomania nor deformity. The tragic fates of her mother and stepmothers at Henry VIII's hands must have nurtured a horror of marriage that grew like a cancer in her belly. She once told the ambassador to the duchy of Württemberg, "I would rather be a beggar and single than a queen and married."[4] To the French envoy she stated, "When I think of marriage, it is as though my heart were being dragged out of my vitals."[5]

By the time of Elizabeth's death in the early seventeenth century, virgin worship was less prominent in those countries which remained Catholic after the Reformation. The result was a more secular, relaxed lifestyle, in which the queen was viewed as a flesh-and-blood woman with faults and foibles, not as a chiseled stone statue interceding with God. But the intertwined images of Virgin Mary and queen had been hammered into the social subconscious for a thousand years and, though less pivotal in daily life, still existed. As both Virgin and queen had borne a princely savior with a sacred father, a queen whose behavior cast doubt upon the paternity of her son must have left a sour taste in the mouth of many a good Christian.

THE SANCTIFIED SUBSTANCE

Royal blood was almost always passed down from kingly father to princely son—via a uterus where the child incubated for nine months. The strict refusal of that uterus to harbor any but royal seed was of the utmost importance to keeping the bloodline pure. It was the myth of royal blood that kept kings seated firmly on their thrones, prevented civil war, held foreign invaders at bay, and kept a superstitious people groveling before their monarch and paying the exorbitant taxes he required.

The myth started long ago when, shrouded by the mists of time, a bold warrior rode into battle swinging his sword and conquered his enemies. Chosen king by his grateful admirers, he continued to destroy adversaries, appease a wrathful deity, and rule with wisdom—sure signs that he was God's chosen. Grasping at the mirage of immortality on earth, the aging monarch wanted to ensure that a part of him—his own flesh and blood—would rule after his death. But what if the king's son was sickly, effeminate, weak-minded? How to convince the people that they must accept this poor specimen of manhood as their king rather than choosing instead a fearless warrior from a rival family?

And so the myth was born which declared that the king's connection with God, his divine right to rule, was manifested in his blood—rather than his intelligence, looks, or temperament—and could be passed on to future generations. True, the myth of royal blood often ensured a stable transition of power from father to son instead of a bloody fracas of maces and battle-axes to determine who would be the new king. But it also resulted in countless insane monarchs, dribbling onto their chins and cackling, while millions of subjects bowed down to them in worshipful reverence. Insane they might be, but that sacred stuff coursing through their veins, the mystical royal blood, made them better than anyone else, made them God's chosen to rule.

A scientific means of establishing paternity was not developed until the blood test of 1927. Until then, to ensure that the next generation of royals possessed the sanctified substance, the queen had to maintain strict fidelity to her husband. The ancient double standard—men rutting with mistresses while their wives sewed altar cloths—was rooted not in misogyny, but in biology.

"Consider of what importance to society the chastity of women is," said the renowned wit and scholar Dr. Samuel Johnson, who wrote the first English dictionary in 1757. "Upon that all the property in the world depends. We hang a thief for stealing a sheep, but the unchastity of a woman transfers sheep, and farm, and all from the right owner."[6]

In 1695 Louis XIV's sister-in-law, Elizabeth Charlotte, the duchesse d'Orléans, wrote, "Where in the world is a prince to be found who loves his wife only, and has no one else? If their wives on that account were to lead the same kind of life that they do, no one could be sure that their children were the true heirs." Referring to a young relative who had committed adultery, she added, "Doesn't this Duchess know that a wife's honor consists in giving herself to nobody but her husband, whereas for the husband there is no shame in having mistresses but only in being made a cuckold?"[7]

Considering the emphasis on the royal bloodline, it is ironic that courts were littered, not just with the king's bastards, but with the queen's bastards as well; in her case these were children who bore the name of the kingly house, children who married into other royal families based on ancestry they did not, in fact, possess. With regard to royal children, the only consideration more important than their kingly blood was the monarch's self-interest. Many kings acknowledged children they knew had been fathered by someone else. Often, kings did not want to cast doubt on the paternity of older children they knew to be their own. In the case where the king could not father children, sometimes court factions heartily desired the queen to bear bastards in order to stabilize the throne and cement their own interests.

Fortunately, the queen's complete and utter disillusionment with her husband usually set in after the birth of the heir. And so it was not deemed worthwhile to lose international prestige, throw the nation into tumult, and question the paternity of all royal children, simply to deny the one cuckoo in the robin's nest. In the early nineteenth century, the last son of King John VI and Queen Carlota Joaquina of Portugal was extremely good-looking and slender—unlike either of his parents—and happened to be the spitting image of the handsome gardener at the queen's country retreat. Other than a few snickers behind painted fans, no one said a word.

More recently, the love affairs of Diana, Princess of Wales, created doubt about the paternity of her second son, Prince Harry, born in 1984. When Prince Charles first glanced at his newborn, he expressed alarm at the child's red hair. Diana often spoke of this moment as the point where her marriage was over. Charles, who had been hoping for a daughter, was disappointed that his wife had presented him with another boy, and worse, that the child had red hair, which Charles disliked. There is, however, a different way of interpreting Charles's irritation at his son's hair color. If he had suspected that Diana had been having an affair with a red-haired man, then his reaction would have been quite understandable.

Fingers often point to Captain James Hewitt, the charming carrot-topped lady-killer who confessed to having a five-year affair with the princess starting in 1986, a year and a half after Harry's birth. Yet there are rumors that the two met each other before Diana's 1981 wedding and denied the earlier date to protect their son, poor illegitimate Harry.

If Prince Harry had slipped into the world blessed with blond or dark locks, there probably would have been no unflattering speculation about his paternity. Red hair pops up unexpectedly in families, often skipping several generations. Diana's brother, Charles, Earl Spencer, has red hair and freckles. Moreover, if we get beyond the hair color and youthful good looks of Prince Harry, we can detect small narrow eyes, large flapping ears, and a wide mouth, the unfortunate hereditary traits of the Windsors.

But the rumor is just too good for tabloids to ignore. In December 2002 two newspapers reported that a competing paper had hired a pretty girl, a "honey trap," to seduce Harry and pluck a hair—we can assume from his head—to be sent for DNA analysis. Stories abound of tabloid investigators taking sheets off the hotel beds of Prince Harry and James Hewitt, of fishing used tissues out of public trash cans, of stealing coffee cups with minute particles of lip detritus, of swabbing drops of sweat from polo gear in a locker room.

The British antimonarchy group ThroneOut is calling for all members of the royal family, who occupy their positions based solely on heredity, to take DNA tests. The royal family's response to these requests has been dignified silence, and reports indicate they are guarding their DNA more jealously than the crown jewels themselves.

Yet it is only a matter of time before a servant or acquaintance does acquire a hair, a coffee cup, or a bedsheet and hands it over for analysis. Modern science is now able to provide answers to the question marks of paternity that have punctuated history from the dawn of time. And the truth may not be what royal families want to hear.

ACCUSATIONS OF ADULTERY—
A POWERFUL WEAPON

It was never adultery alone that did in a queen, or the fact that she did not resemble the Virgin Mary, or that she had polluted the royal bloodline. It was politics.

If the queen followed the traditional pattern of bearing children, embroidering altar cloths, and interceding for the poor—pious duties that the Virgin Mary would likely have approved of—even if she took a lover she was usually left in peace. There was rarely reason to shoot down a political nonentity at court. But an intelligent ambitious woman who spoke her mind and built up a faction was always open to the accusation of adultery by her political rivals, whether the accusation was true or fabricated.

Adultery charges offered the accuser many benefits. The very mention of adultery suddenly cast doubt upon the legitimacy of the offspring of a suspected queen, possibly rendering them unfit for the throne and opening the door to other ambitious candidates—usually the accusers themselves.

In 830 Queen Judith of the Franks, the second wife of King Louis the Pious, found herself accused of adultery with a handsome court chamberlain. The accusers were her husband's three sons by his first marriage who feared that Judith would influence their aging father to name her son, Charles, as his heir. Bristling with weapons, the three brothers forced their father to abdicate and imprisoned Judith in a convent. We don't know if the queen committed adultery or not; we do know that the missiles of her enemies hit their mark and she was removed.

In those cases where a powerful man was accused of being the queen's lover, we must assume that he and the queen had formed a faction that threatened other groups at court; whether or not the pair was in fact committing adultery was not the crucial question. In such a case, the powerful queen could be imprisoned in a convent, and her threatening lover executed, exiled, or imprisoned, his friends and relatives collapsing in the wake of his own disgrace. Very neatly, aiming only one poisoned dart at the queen, her enemy could remove the entire rival power base at court.

In 887 Queen Richardis of the East Franks, wife of King Charles the Fat, was accused of adultery with Bishop Liutward of Vercelli, the king's powerful archchancellor. It was the custom at the time for an accused woman to defend her honor by walking over burning plowshares. If she emerged unharmed, God was protecting her because she was innocent. Only the guilty, it was assumed, would be burned to a crisp. Richardis came through the ordeal unscathed, retired to a convent, and was later made a saint. But her enemies had successfully removed her.

Character assassination which had proved so effective in the ninth century was alive and well a thousand years later. Napoleon, who hated the virtuous and beautiful Queen Louise of Prussia for egging her apathetic husband on to defend his country against the French, twisted her admiration for Czar Alexander of Russia into a slanderous story. The handsome blond czar had visited Prussia in 1805 and an instant bond sprang up between the czar and the queen. When French troops marched into the vacated royal palace in Potsdam, Napoleon was delighted to find Alexander's portrait hanging in the queen's bedroom. He did all he could to tarnish the lady's unblemished reputation and make her bumbling husband, King Frederick William III, look like a cuckold. Stories of the pious queen's sordid affair with the czar haunt her memory to this day.

It was harder for Napoleon to blacken the reputation of Louise's aunt, Queen Maria Carolina of Naples, who had had numerous affairs with courtiers and a decades-long affair with her top minister. What outraged the prudish French emperor received only a shrug and a wink from the rowdy Neapolitans.

Stymied in his efforts to ruin the queen's reputation, Napoleon invented the story of a lesbian affair between Maria Carolina and her friend Emma, Lady Hamilton, the wife of the British ambassador and later the mistress of Admiral Horatio Nelson. Emma, the conqueror learned, would tiptoe up a secret stairway to the queen's apartments, probably to deliver dispatches from British allies or perhaps just to avoid palace protocol and enjoy a cup of coffee. But Napoleon saw the secret staircase as proof of unnatural vice. Unfortunately for the French emperor, his dart did not hit home; the raucous Neapolitans were equally undisturbed by rumors of the queen's lesbianism.

Some Italians gladly strangled erring wives with silken ribbons, but many more were cavalier about sexual escapades. When the theocrat Savonarola, who had held a moral stranglehold over the sex lives of Florentines, was burned at the stake in 1498, one high-level magistrate, eyeing the rising flames of the pyre, heaved a heavy sigh of relief. "Thank God," he grunted. "Now we can return to our sodomy."[8]

Indeed, of all European nations, the king, court, and country of Naples was the least disturbed by stories of queenly adultery. When a stroke felled the sixty-one-year-old queen Maria Carolina in her sleep in 1814, her husband, King Ferdinand, loudly proclaimed that his forty-four years of marriage had been nothing short of martyrdom, and within two months he married his young mistress. Ferdinand's son, the hereditary prince, sharply rebuked him for marrying a woman known to have enjoyed so many lovers. But the king, laughing, replied, "Think of your mamma, my boy!"[9]

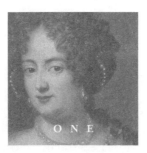

ONE

LIFE BEHIND PALACE WALLS

In love the heavens themselves do guide the state;
Money buys lands, and wives are sold by fate.

—WILLIAM SHAKESPEARE

PRINCESSES WERE RAISED TO BE DEVOUT, OBEDIENT, AND
faithful. When sent to meet their new husbands, they set off with
every intention of retaining these vital qualities in their new
lives. What happened over the years that made so many of them
lose their religion, their obedience, and their fidelity?

When imagining the life of a princess bride, we envision opulent rooms boasting every comfort, efficient servants carrying
out her every whim, a wardrobe of luxurious gowns, and a jewel
box bursting with sparkling gems. We can hear the sweet strains
of violins at a candlelit ball, smell the aroma of succulent roasted
meats at the banquet table. We picture her handsome loving husband, her growing brood of healthy children, and envy her.

And yet the queen was often chained to a husband who didn't

want her, didn't even want to sleep with her. Her children were taken out of her control and raised by palace officials as property of the state. She was forced to stand by patiently while doctors killed her children by bleeding them to death.

Her servants were often spies in the pay of her enemies. Nor was her life what we would call physically comfortable, let alone luxurious. For several months a year, drafts sliced through palace rooms like knives. Rats and insects nested behind gilded walls. Nor was the queen consort necessarily rolling in money; she possessed only the funds which her husband chose to bestow upon her—in some cases, nothing.

Until the mid-nineteenth century when travel became easier, the princess sent off to wed a foreign monarch would likely never see her family again. The childhood friends and devoted servants she brought to her new country caused jealous intrigues and were often sent home as meddling intruders, leaving the princess alone and friendless.

Perhaps we will begin to comprehend why a decent God-fearing woman, cast upon a foreign shore bereft of family and friends, might jump into an adulterous affair, might seek a little love and understanding in the midst of her misery.

PALATIAL LUXURY

The beauty of royal lodgings increased with the centuries. The medieval queen spent most of her time in the great hall, a large dark chamber with slits for windows and an enormous hearth. Meals were served here, and in between meals the queen sewed with her ladies and met with subjects seeking mercy or justice. But she was not alone in the hall; also present were the rest of the royal family, the entire court, bustling servants, and flea-bitten dogs hunting for food scraps on the rush-covered floor. There was scant furniture, and that was uncomfortable—tables, benches, and, for the queen, a stiff high-backed chair. Vivid tapestries covered the stone walls but did little to dispel the gloom.

By the Renaissance, a European queen had her own suite of

small, cozy wood-paneled rooms with large windows and heavy ornately carved furniture. In the baroque period, royal rooms boasted high ceilings painted with mythological scenes, gilded walls, silver-framed mirrors, and gleaming parquet floors. The dainty furniture was covered in silk or satin. Yet despite the ever-increasing grandeur of royal suites, life in the palace remained profoundly uncomfortable.

Catherine the Great, who arrived in Russia in 1744 as a German bride for Empress Elizabeth's nephew and heir, suffered terribly from the cold. Russian winters, so hard on peasants, were often not much easier on royalty. Churches were unheated, and many of the palace rooms were drafty and cold despite the presence of a crackling fire. Windows did not close properly, letting icy arctic winds howl through the rooms. Many days Catherine was "blue as a plum" and numb from the cold.[1] She frequently suffered colds and fevers.

At night she was often kept awake by the sounds of rats scuttling behind the walls. Once, when a palace caught fire, Catherine stood outside in the street watching thousands of black rats evacuating the palace in an orderly fashion, followed by thousands of gray mice. She was not sorry to see that palace go; in addition to the rats and mice it had been "filled with every kind of insect."[2]

In the 1660s, utilizing daring feats of engineering, experts transformed a hunting lodge in a swamp into glorious Versailles Palace with an impressive system of fountains and canals. Yet for all the engineering advances of the time, no one had come up with the simple idea of window screens. Open windows allowed in a pleasant breeze, to be sure, as well as birds, squirrels, bats, and insects.

"The confounded gnats here do not let me have an hour's sleep," opined Elizabeth Charlotte, duchesse d'Orléans, from her gilded Versailles apartments in 1702. "They have chewed me up so much that I look as if I had smallpox again. We are also plagued with wasps," she added. "Not a day goes by that someone is not stung. A few days ago there was tremendous laughter: one of these wasps had flown under a lady's skirt; the lady ran around like mad because the wasp was stinging her high up on the thigh, she pulled up her skirt, ran around, and cried, 'Help! Close your eyes and take it off!' "[3]

Elizabeth Charlotte also suffered from the extremes of weather. "The heat is so great that the oldest people cannot say they have ever experienced anything like it," she reported in July 1707. "Yesterday everyone kept to his room in his shirt until seven at night; one constantly had to change shirts; I changed mine eight times in one day, and it was as if they had been dipped into water. At table too people keep mopping their faces."[4]

"The cold here is so fierce that it fairly defies description," she wrote in January 1709. "I am sitting by a roaring fire . . . and still I am shivering with cold and can barely hold the pen. . . . The wine freezes in the bottles."[5]

Nor had palace sanitation evolved to a high level. In the early eighteenth century, the duc de Saint-Simon wrote, "The royal apartments at Versailles are the last word in inconvenience, with back views over the privies and other dark and evil smelling places."[6]

"How would it be possible to prevent men from pissing in the streets?" lamented Elizabeth Charlotte in 1720. "In fact it is a wonder that there are not entire rivers of piss, considering the huge numbers of people living in Paris."[7] But hygiene inside the palace was no better than in the streets. English visitors to Versailles were shocked to find the most elegant courtiers spitting on the floor and urinating in the corners.

Even life in a modern palace is not what we would imagine. The British royal family insists on cost-saving measures that would be laughed at by a middle-class family. In 1981 Diana, Princess of Wales, was baffled to find Her Majesty Queen Elizabeth II of Great Britain wandering around Buckingham Palace at night turning off lights to save on the electric bill. When the princess complained of the chilly rooms in the Scottish estate of Balmoral, the queen politely suggested she put on another sweater. When royal toes poke through socks, servants darn them rather than throwing them out and buying new. Dirty bedsheets are reversed to get both sides soiled before being laundered. And when Paul Burrell, who later became Princess Diana's butler, started working at Buckingham Palace, he was given a musty uniform that had first seen service under George III, when he was fighting the American Revolution.

THE BRIDEGROOM

A princess usually discovered that her greatest discomfort was not the weather, or the insects, or the smell of human waste, or the puzzling thriftiness of her royal in-laws, but the husband she was forced to wed. The purpose of a royal bride was to produce royal babies. "I want to marry a womb," said Napoleon.[8] Other monarchs, though shuddering at the little Corsican's indelicacy, would have agreed with his sentiments. A princess was valued primarily not for her education, her personality, her good works, or even her beauty, but for her uterus.

Because she was regarded as a body part rather than a person, a princess found that her feelings were usually disregarded. Politicians, pushing their candidates for groom sight unseen, tried to cram their selections down a princess's throat. A Prussian minister, hoping to persuade Frederick the Great's sister, Princess Wilhelmina, to accept a marriage candidate in 1727, grandly declared, "Great princesses are born to be sacrificed for the welfare of the state."

When the princess objected that she had never met the proposed bridegroom, the minister gravely replied, "As you are not acquainted with him, Madam, you cannot possibly have any aversion for him."[9]

Until the mid-nineteenth century, most princesses never met their husbands until *after* they were married by proxy, ceremonies held in two locales, the home cities of the affianced pair. In each ceremony, a person of honorable character stood in for the missing bride or groom and went through a church wedding, giving or receiving a ring.

Oddly, the proxy wedding ceremony was followed by a proxy bedding ceremony, in which the bride and her stand-in groom would meet in the royal four-poster bed, with all the wedding guests crowding around to watch. Wearing an ornate ruffled nightdress, the bride would lie down. The stand-in groom, fully clothed, would remove his boots and stockings, lie down beside the bride, and touch her bare foot with his. And in this way was a proxy marriage consummated.

A proxy wedding offered many advantages. It ratified the dowry, trade agreements, military alliances, and treaties before the bride set out. Moreover, the honor of the princess was assured: she would be traveling out of her native land as a married woman to meet her husband. It held the added benefit that the groom, should he be revolted by the first sight of his new wife, or the bride, disgusted by the looks of her husband, could not return the goods. A second marriage ceremony was held with both bride and groom taking part, but after the proxy wedding it was too late to get out of the marriage without legal difficulty.

In 1672 the twenty-year-old Princess Elizabeth Charlotte of the Palatinate set off from her home in Heidelberg to meet the husband she had already married by proxy, Philippe, duc d'Orléans, the transvestite brother of Louis XIV of France. Throughout the journey, the bride wept bitterly. She had heard of her husband's proclivity for young men, and the rumor that one of his lovers had poisoned his first wife in a fit of jealousy.

When the bride and groom met, they took one look at each other and gasped. She saw a long aristocratic nose emerging from a huge frizzy black wig, diamond earrings, cascading rows of lace and ruffles, dozens of clanking bracelets, beribboned pantaloons, and high-heeled shoes. The prince saw a flat broad face, freshly scrubbed from her journey, tiny blue pig eyes, and a broad German rear end. He whispered to his gentlemen, "Oh! How can I sleep with that?"[10]

Once lodged in Versailles, Elizabeth Charlotte found that the golden magnificence of her new home did nothing to assuage her raw pain. "Between ourselves I was stuck here against my will," she lamented to her beloved aunt, Duchess Sophia of Hanover. "Here I must live, and here I must die, whether I like it or not."[11]

On occasion, over the decades, she thought of "simply running away" from her horrible husband and the vicious malice at court.[12] Though sometimes she grew feisty and, squaring her shoulders, resolutely declared, "He who dies of threats must be buried with donkey farts."[13]

As Elizabeth Charlotte and her husband, who was called Monsieur, grew older, he alienated her by giving her gowns and jewelry to his male lovers. Away from court rituals, in the privacy of their elegant Versailles apartment, they often found they had nothing to say to each other. She wrote Duchess Sophia about an evening she had spent with her husband and their grown children. "After a long silence," she recalled, "Monsieur, who did not consider us good enough company to talk to us, made a great loud fart, by your leave, turned toward me, and said, 'What is that, Madame?' I turned my behind toward him, let out one of the selfsame tone, and said, 'That's what it is, Monsieur.' My son said, 'If that's all it is, I can do as well as Monsieur and Madame,' and he also let go of a good one. . . . These are princely conversations. . . ."[14]

In 1768 Archduchess Maria Carolina of Austria boarded the gaily bedecked vessel that would transport her to reign over Naples with the husband she had already married by proxy. Looking out across the sea, the fifteen-year-old declared she would be far better off if someone would only throw her in.

King Ferdinand IV, her seventeen-year-old groom, was often covered with herpes lesions which his doctors considered to be a sign of rude good health. He had received almost no education; his brothers were incurably insane, and his tutors feared that any mental effort would topple Ferdinand over the edge as well. The king loved to pinch his courtiers' rear ends and put marmalade in their hats when they weren't looking. He would go to sea with the fishermen of Naples and sell his catch at a market stall, haggling with buyers over the price and loudly cursing them.

On the morning after his wedding to Maria Carolina, King Ferdinand was asked how he had enjoyed his bride. Shaking his head, the king reported, "She sleeps as if she had been killed, and sweats like a pig."[15]

After eating a meal in public—a special event where the monarch sat alone on a platform surrounded by gawking spectators of all classes—Ferdinand would then call for his chamber pot and, to the delight of his audience, defecate proudly. Aside from public meals, the king insisted on company whenever he heeded the call of Nature. In 1771 Maria Carolina's brother Joseph II of Austria visited the Neapolitan monarchs and was perplexed to receive an invitation to accompany the king to his chamber pot after dinner.

"I found him on this throne with lowered breeches," Joseph wrote to his family in Vienna, "surrounded by five or six valets, chamberlains and others. We made conversation for more than half an hour, and I believe he would be there still if a terrible stench had not convinced us that all was over. He did not fail to describe the details and even wished to show them to us; and without more ado, his breeches down, he ran with the smelly pot in one hand after two of his gentlemen, who took to their heels. I retired quietly to my sister's, without being able to relate how this scene ended, and if they got off with only a good scare."[16]

The luxurious trains and opulent steamboats of the Victorian era resulted in young royals at least meeting each other before agreeing to marry. Even so, most marriages were unhappy. In 1891 Princess Louisa of Tuscany married Prince Frederick Augustus, the heir to the Saxon throne. The prince won Louisa over with his gentle manner and striking blond good looks. Yet years later, disenchanted, she wrote in her memoirs, "Although every princess doubtless at some time dreams of an ideal Prince Charming, she rarely meets him, and she usually marries some one quite different from the hero of her girlhood's dreams."[17]

SEX WITH THE KING

While palace life was no bed of roses, a queen's sex life, that most intimate aspect of a woman's relationship with her husband, was sometimes downright horrifying. Many a princess was completely unacquainted with her wedding-night duties and surprised when the strange man she had just married climbed on top of her and started to poke her painfully.

In 1797 the eighteen-year-old Princess Frederica Dorothea of Baden married the nineteen-year-old King Gustavus IV of Sweden. She was ceremoniously placed in bed with her new husband, and the guests withdrew. But a few moments later the bride raced out of the bedroom screaming and flew into the arms of her ladies-in-waiting who were assembled in an outer room. She had just learned what would be required of her and refused to take part in it. It took several weeks before the bride could be persuaded to return to the rough embraces of her husband.

When thirteen-year-old Margaret Tudor bedded the thirty-year-old James IV of Scotland in 1503, she found to her horror not only that her husband jumped on top of her and poked her, but that he wore an iron chain around his waist, which he never took off, and to which each year he added another link for his sins. We can imagine how the rusty links felt on her tender flesh.

In 1893 the seventeen-year-old Marie of Edinburgh, Queen Victoria's granddaughter, was flummoxed by what her husband the crown prince of Romania did to her on her wedding night. "In my immature way I tried to respond to his passion but I hungered and thirsted for something more," she wrote years later in her memoirs. "There was an empty feeling about it all, I still seemed to be waiting for something that did not come." She cried for weeks afterward. "Often I had to smother my mouth in my pillow not to call out with grief and longing—Mamma . . . Mamma . . . Mamma!"[18] When she started to throw up in the mornings, she thought she was dying. No one had told her how a woman became pregnant.

Undoubtedly the worst case of undesired sex endured by a queen occurred in 1714 when the twenty-six-year-old Maria Luisa of Savoy lay dying of tuberculosis, her tortured lungs rasping as blood trickled from her lips. Her husband, King Philip V of Spain, was devastated at the thought of her death—not because he would miss his beloved wife, but because he would miss sex. The king was a devout Catholic who thought he would go to hell for having sex outside of marriage. He knew that after his wife died he would have to remain celibate for a decent amount of time before he could remarry.

So instead of mourning his wife's passing in prayer at her bedside, as her illness worsened he jumped in bed with her and humped her several times a day. The queen endured his exertions with admirable patience, probably because she knew she wouldn't have to put up with them much longer. Finally, after the priests administered last rites, and the death rattle rose in her throat, the king tried to jump in bed one last time and was only with difficulty restrained.

ROYAL IMPOTENCE

Many royal wives, steeling themselves for the duties of their wedding night, were surprised to find they had no bedtime duties at all; their husbands were hopelessly impotent.

In 1615 the nervous twitching fourteen-year-old King Louis XIII of France married his cousin, a beautiful hazel-eyed Spanish princess. The daughter and granddaughter of Austrian archduchesses who had married Spanish kings, the princess was known as Anne of Austria. After the wedding banquet, the king, to the utter astonishment of the guests, ambled out of the dining hall back to his own chambers. His mother had to convince him to leave his bed and sleep in that of his wife. "My son," she pleaded, "it is not sufficient to be married; you must come and see the queen your wife, who is waiting for you."[19]

The king obediently stayed for two hours in bed with his wife, and then stood up, put on his slippers, and shuffled back to his own room. The years passed, and both king and queen remained virgins. To all advice upon the subject, the king replied that there was no reason to be in a hurry, and that he could not take too much care of his health. Yet the royal marriage, which ratified a precarious treaty between France and Spain, was not valid until consummation. Both nations and the Vatican—which wanted a strong alliance between the two most powerful Catholic countries in Europe—fretted over the situation. In 1618 Cardinal Guido Bentivoglio wrote the pope that he had advised the king to take up masturbation as a means of preparing himself for marital sex, but the king's confessor prohibited him from committing such a sin.

Finally, when the king was eighteen, late one night his adviser the duc de Luynes begged him to go to the queen and finally consummate the marriage. When the king began to cry, the duke picked him up and carried the sobbing monarch to the queen's chamber, with the royal valet solemnly holding a candle to light the way. Once in bed, Louis stayed for three hours and did his royal duty. But still, sex was intermittent over the years and the king did not seem to particularly enjoy the business.

In December 1637 the king, setting out from the Louvre for his palace of Saint-Maur, was delayed by a terrible storm. As his bed and bed linens had been sent ahead, he found himself in the embarrassing position of returning to the Louvre and unexpectedly dropping in on his wife, who possessed the only bed fit for a king. Given a choice between the freezing rain and howling wind, or the horrors of the queen's bed which he had not shared for seven years, Louis resolutely chose the storm, but his bedraggled valets finally convinced him to take shelter. It was a fortuitous rainstorm for France. Nine months later, after twenty-three years of marriage, the future Louis XIV was born. Perhaps it is no surprise that as soon as Louis XIII died in 1643, his merry widow, deprived of sex for the greater part of three decades, took the polished, virile Cardinal Jules Mazarin as her lover for the greater part of the following two decades.

In 1769 the sixteen-year-old crown prince of France, the future Louis XVI, married the most beautiful princess in Europe, the fourteen-year-old Marie Antoinette of Austria. Heavy, clumsy, and painfully shy, on his wedding night Louis found himself in bed with a dazzling blue-eyed blonde—all golden curls and golden curves—and froze with fear. But the prince's impotence was not completely psychological in nature. Louis suffered from phimosis, an unnatural elongation of the foreskin which permitted erections but prevented intercourse.

Three years after the wedding, Louis's exasperated grandfather King Louis XV—who had rarely gone a day without sex since he was fifteen—ordered the court physician to give the couple sex education lessons. Louis was put on diets to render him more virile, but they only made him fatter. In a desperate attempt to arouse the prince, advisers lined the corridor leading to his wife's bedroom with pornographic prints and obscene paintings. But all such steps were futile, as were efforts to persuade the prince to undergo circumcision. In a day and age when anesthesia was a stiff glass of whiskey, and some 25 percent of wounds resulted in infection and death, surely we cannot blame him.

Marie Antoinette's mother, the Austro-Hungarian empress Maria Theresa, who had borne no less than sixteen children, was so alarmed at her daughter's situation that she sent her son and coruler, Joseph II, to talk to Louis. From Versailles on June 9, 1777, Joseph wrote home, "Her situation with the king is very odd; he is only two-thirds of a husband, and although he loves her, he fears her more. . . . Just imagine, in his marital bed— here is the secret—he has strong, well-conditioned erections; he introduces the member, stays there without moving for perhaps two minutes, withdraws without ejaculating but still erect, and says goodnight; this is incomprehensible because with all that he sometimes has nightly emissions, but once in place and going at it, never, and he's satisfied. He says plainly that he does it all purely from a sense of duty but never for pleasure; oh, if only I could have been there, I would have taken care of him; he should be whipped so that he would ejaculate out of sheer rage like a donkey."[20]

In 1778 Louis submitted to circumcision for the good of the realm. His physician must have washed his hands and instruments thoroughly before the operation because the prince sailed through it. He was able to have sex with his wife a few weeks later, though he never got the hang of lovemaking. Marie Antoinette found him physically repulsive and, after giving him a daughter and son, began a torrid affair with an elegant young Swedish nobleman, Count Axel Fersen.

The queen's son with Louis died young, and it is likely that her second son, who later became known as Louis XVII, was actually the child of her lover, born exactly nine months after Fersen visited Versailles. "The Queen was delivered of the Duc de Normandie at half-past seven," Louis reported in his diary. "Everything happened just as to my son (the Dauphin)."[21] The entry seemed to indicate that Louis did not believe the child was his. "One of the most handsome children one could ever see," said one courtier about the queen's third child, which in and of itself cast doubt as to his paternity.[22]

GAY KINGS

Many European princes were gay, yet this did not prevent them from fulfilling their marital duties. Married in 1308 to a French princess, the English king Edward II fathered four royal children, although he spent most of his life in love with other men.

The transvestite Philippe, duc d'Orléans, launched six children into the world with two wives, although the clanking saints' medallions he tied to his private parts before the act may have helped. In 1614 James I of England fell head over heels in love with young George Villiers; the king made him master of the horse, an earl, a marquess, a duke, and lord high admiral. Yet James could proudly point out that he had made his wife, a Danish princess, pregnant no less than nine times.

But not all gay princes could force themselves to have sex with their wives. Gustavus III of Sweden was so disgusted at the thought of sex with a woman that he didn't even want to try. "This prince did not pay homage at the shrine of Venus" was the polite explanation of a contemporary.[23] Nonetheless, he married Princess Sophia Magdalena of Denmark in 1766. When a Swedish artist visited the Copenhagen court of Christian VII in 1769, the king asked after the health of his sister. "She was as happy as any woman who had been married nearly three years and yet remained a virgin" was the reply.[24]

Yet the queen's barrenness was a perplexing problem to Gustavus who urgently needed an heir to stabilize his tottering throne. Powerful nobles, stripped of their rights by the king, threatened rebellion, and it was easier to topple a monarch without an heir. Rumor had it that after eleven years of marriage, the king hit upon an excellent idea.

He had seen his neglected virgin queen exchanging glances with a sophisticated courtier, Count Adolph Frederick Munck. According to the story that raced like wildfire through the Swedish court—the king insisted that the two begin an affair. When they hesitated—such treason could result not only in dishonor but also in dismemberment—Gustavus wrote down his request in his own hand and gave both his wife and the count a copy. It was also rumored that his wife, though acting the role of queen until her death, insisted upon a quiet divorce and immediately married Count Munck so no charge of treason could be preferred against her if the king changed his mind.

Within a year after her reported liaison with Count Munck began, Sophia Magdalena gave birth to the future Gustavus IV. The king was absolutely delighted to have an heir—apparently without soiling himself in bed with a woman—and attended council meetings with his wife's illegitimate child sitting on his shoulders.

Frederick the Great of Prussia, the most renowned warrior king of Europe, was haunted by rumors of his bisexuality after his father chopped off the head of the man who supposedly seduced him as a teenager. Whether Frederick had sex with men is not entirely certain. What is certain is that in 1733 the nineteen-year-old prince was horrified to learn that his father insisted he marry a dumpy German princess, Elizabeth of Brunswick-Bevern. "I have always wanted to distinguish myself by the sword and have not wanted to obtain royal favor by any other means," the crown prince huffed. "Now I will have only the duty to fuck. I pity this poor person, for she will be one more unhappy princess in the world."[25]

"I believe that anyone who allows himself to be bossed by a woman is the biggest asshole in the world and unworthy of being called a man," he added. "Love can never be forced. I love sex but in a very fickle way; I like the immediate pleasure, but afterward I despise it. Judge then if I am the stuff from which one makes good husbands. . . . I shall marry, but after that, goodbye and good luck."[26]

After a few halfhearted attempts at lovemaking produced no pregnancy, when Frederick became king he stuck Queen Elizabeth in a country house where she grew fat, raised dogs, and tried to make do with the pitiful allowance he sent her; for his part, he returned to his favorite pastimes of waging war and playing the flute. Out of respect, however, Frederick kindly arranged to have dinner with his wife once a year.

THE JOYS OF CHILDREN

Royal children belong not to their parents but to the state. Until the twentieth century, a royal mother was not permitted to nurse her children or to have much say in their education or even in their marriages.

In September 1754 the future Catherine the Great finally gave Russia its longed-for heir, Paul. Empress Elizabeth scooped up the infant gleefully and raced away with him, courtiers running behind her. Catherine was left alone with a servant woman who refused to change her sticky bloody sheets or get her a glass of water, fearing the empress might disapprove. Catherine was not permitted to see her child or even ask after him, as that would imply she did not trust the empress to provide adequately for him. By the time Catherine became empress in her own right in 1762, she and Paul were strangers and soon found they heartily detested each other.

Marie, crown princess of Romania, was forbidden by her husband's uncle, King Carol I, to nurse her first child, Prince Carol, despite her repeated pleas. Carol's wife, Queen Elizabeth, who despised Marie, hired a bone-dry German governess named Miss Winter to turn young Prince Carol against his mother. Miss Winter forced the prince to drop his mother from his nightly prayers and even barred the door to Carol's sickroom when he was deathly ill until Marie rudely shoved her out of the way. When Carol was in his early teens, his tutor had homosexual designs on him and may have seduced him. His mother could do nothing. "I could never get my own child without scenes and explanations," Marie lamented to a relative.[27]

Similarly, Elizabeth Charlotte, duchesse d'Orléans, had no control over her children's education. In 1689 her husband wanted to appoint one of his lovers, the marquis d'Effiat, tutor to their thirteen-year-old son Philippe. But Madame, as she was called, howled in protest, "For there is no doubt that there is no greater sodomist in France than he, and that it would be a bad beginning for a young prince to start his life with the worst debauchery imaginable." To which her husband gravely replied "that he had to admit that d'Effiat used to be debauched and loved the boys, but that he had corrected himself of this vice many years ago."[28]

Neither did Elizabeth Charlotte have any say in her son's marriage. In 1692 Louis XIV betrothed her son to Françoise-Marie, Mademoiselle de Blois, his bastard daughter with a mistress. Bristling with pride in her royal birth, Elizabeth Charlotte was devastated at such a misalliance for her only son. "Her figure is all askew," she reported of her future daughter-in-law, "her face is ugly, and she is unpleasant in everything she does."[29]

The duc de Saint-Simon related that after hearing the news of the betrothal, Madame "was walking briskly, handkerchief in hand, weeping without restraint, speaking rather loudly, gesticulating, and giving a fine performance of Ceres after the abduction of Proserpina. . . . [The next day Madame's] son approached her, as he did every day, in order to kiss her hand; at that moment Madame slapped his face so hard that the sound was heard several paces away, which, in the presence of the entire court, deeply embarrassed this poor prince. . . ."[30]

Elizabeth Charlotte despised lowborn individuals seeking to ally themselves to those of better birth. For years after her son's marriage, casting sidelong glances at her daughter-in-law, she muttered, "Mousedroppings always want to mix with the pepper."[31]

Royal children have always belonged to the state and still do. Though modern customs are not nearly as draconian as those of centuries past, even in the 1990s Diana, Princess of Wales, was unable to take her sons on a holiday outside of Britain without the queen's explicit permission. Indeed, the events that led to her August 1997 death started when she asked to take the boys to visit friends in the United States. Royal permission was withheld for such a distant locale, but it was granted to take her sons on a Mediterranean cruise on a yacht owned by Mohammed Fayed.

THE FOREIGN RETINUE

It would have been a great consolation for a royal bride trapped in a loveless marriage, with no control over her children, to have at her new court beloved childhood friends from her old one. But in many cases such friends were abruptly sent home or were not permitted to come in the first place.

The princess bride usually arrived with a large retinue of servants all hoping to take up plum positions at her new court. And, indeed, her home court was eager to surround her with as many compatriots as possible to influence her on behalf of her native land. As for the bride herself, she was glad to see familiar faces and speak her mother tongue. But this influx of outsiders caused ill will in her new country from courtiers unwilling to see their remunerative positions go to babbling foreigners.

In 1600 Princess Marie de Medici of Tuscany, the bride of Henri IV, arrived with a throng of Italians itching to be awarded positions at the French court. But the king's minister, the duc de Sully, vowed he would recommend "neither a doctor nor a cook." Those already holding offices at court protested that "the bread would be taken from their mouths," he said, citing that "in France there are vested interests."[32]

When the fourteen-year-old French princess Elizabeth of Valois married thirty-two-year-old Philip II of Spain in 1559, she arrived in Madrid with a large flock of noble ladies who expected to serve as her ladies-in-waiting. They squabbled constantly with the queen's Spanish ladies-in-waiting, who felt threatened by the intruders. The king wanted to send home all the arrogant French ladies but had a hard time dealing with his young bride's tears. Finally, he allowed them to stay as her friends, but announced that French subjects could not hold official positions at the Spanish court. Her ladies erupted in a flurry of complaints and reproaches, and some indeed went back to France. Those who remained were accused of alienating the queen from her new country; they kept her surrounded by French language and customs so she did not learn Spanish words and ways; furthermore, they prevented her from becoming close to her Spanish ladies.

The duque de Alba, majordomo of the queen's household, looked at her French ladies as vile interlopers and hoped to insult them so irrevocably that they would all leave voluntarily. He assigned one lady in delicate health, Mademoiselle de Montpensier, a French princess of the Blood Royal, a cheerless chamber without a fireplace so she suffered dreadfully from the cold. There were stories that he tried to prevent her from riding in the queen's coach, that he even grabbed the train of her gown and dragged her from the carriage as she fought him off with punches and kicks. On another journey he pulled the cushions from under her in the royal litter to make her ride intolerably uncomfortable. The government of France was furious.

Such disputes convinced many courts that, in the interest of international relations, no foreign bride should be permitted to bring with her a single lady. No childhood friends, no familiar faces, no one to speak her own language in a familiar accent. In 1893 Crown Princess Marie of Romania was not allowed to bring ladies from her native England. Neither was she permitted to make Romanian friends. The curmudgeonly King Carol was afraid that she might ally herself to one political faction or another at court, and therefore forbade her any society at all.

Living in a kind of prison in her rooms, Marie described her life as "cramped, lonely, and incredibly dull."[33] Rarely permitted to attend state functions, balls, operas, or parties, Marie found herself bored to death, surrounded by hawkeyed servants who spied at keyholes, fished papers out of her trash bin, and reported her every word and action to the king. When Marie complained, old King Carol informed her that members of a royal family should have no expectation of personal happiness.

If the princess bride felt lonely and unhappy at her new court, she was in no position to visit her family back home. Travel was strenuous and often dangerous. Carriages, without benefit of springs, jolted mercilessly over rutted roads. When it rained, wheels stuck in morasses of mud; when it didn't, dust coated passengers from head to toe. Many roads were too atrocious to permit the use of carriages, and travelers, even the old and ailing, were forced to mount mules. Roadside inns were so riddled with filth and insects that well-heeled travelers carted their own beds, sheets, and armchairs with them.

Even sea travel had its difficulties. Sailboats were pitched about by storms which strained the rigging and sometimes snapped the masts. Even the noblest travelers heaved up their meals into the deep blue sea. Periodically the lack of wind was a problem—ships were becalmed for weeks on end while passengers cooled their heels. Pirates cruised the ocean blue ready to swoop down upon unsuspecting vessels. In 1149 Eleanor of Aquitaine, queen of France, was captured by Byzantine pirates on her return from the Crusades and held prisoner until warships came to her rescue. In 1784 Aimée de Rivery, a cousin of Josephine, the future empress of France, was captured by North African pirates and sold into the Sultan's harem in Istanbul from which she never emerged.

Pirates aside, even legitimate navies posed a threat. The shifting balance of European power often meant war or threats of war, and royalty would make valuable hostages. In 1795 French warships hoped to capture Princess Caroline of Brunswick on her way to marry George, Prince of Wales. When the British squadron sent to defend her became stuck in the ice, Caroline had to backtrack and wait for warmer weather. Her weeks of boredom were punctuated by the booming of cannon fire in the distance.

Not only was travel difficult and dangerous, but those willing to endure the hardships of the road or sea usually found that the demands of royal protocol were more aggravating than the trip was worth. For several years after her 1559 marriage to King Philip II of Spain, Elizabeth de Valois longed to visit her mother, the French queen regent Catherine de Medici, and her younger brother, King Charles IX, who were, after all, just across the border.

After much wrangling among diplomats, ministers, and both royal families, it was decided that the reunion of mother and daughter would be held in June 1565. The first debate centered on the location. The French did not want to demean themselves by crossing the Spanish border, using the excuse that out of respect the daughter should travel farther to visit her mother. Similarly, the Spanish believed that their nation's prestige was far greater than that of France, so the French court should cross the border into Spain. The town of Bayonne, just over the Spanish border, was finally agreed upon.

On both sides, the selection of courtiers for the voyage was hotly contested; men unsheathed their swords to win this great honor; women unsheathed their claws. In both Spain and France, there was much slashing and shredding. Ladies pleaded the honorable positions they held in the royal household, while men trumpeted the battlefield feats of their ancestors. Tears were shed, sobs erupted, and finally a list was assembled that delighted some and outraged others.

The next question was one of wardrobe. Each court wanted to outdo the other in its magnificence. But Philip told the queen's ladies that Elizabeth "deprecated foolish and extravagant expenditure on the occasion, and that she considered the robes, which the ladies of the household ordinarily wore, were costly and magnificent enough, and ought to be worn full nine months longer." He prevented his courtiers from ordering new gold and silver embroidered equipment for their horses, and "hoped that in France they would act on the same principle, in order that a meeting, which was planned for pleasure, and not for ostentatious display, might not give occasion for grievous expenses."[34]

The French court, however, saw this as the perfect opportunity to outshine their Spanish rivals and ordered opulent carriages and lavish clothing. The queen mother emptied the national treasury and then went headlong into debt to impress the Spanish with the magnificence of France. When her ministers reproached her, she replied that "the reason wherefore she sanctioned so great an outlay of money, for the reputation of the kingdom must be maintained, at least in outward matters, the more especially as the national funds were failing."[35]

Hearing of this, Philip sadly agreed that his court must not be outdazzled by the French, and he allowed the Spanish entourage the same expenditures. When Philip heard of the large number of courtiers accompanying King Charles, he reluctantly tripled the number in Elizabeth's retinue. In addition to new wardrobes and carriages, both sides would bring with them their own furniture, drapes, tapestries, tables, beds, bedsheets, and silverware, on pack mules and in carts, crossing plains and mountains in biting rain and broiling sun. These items, too, must impress with their magnificence.

On April 9 Elizabeth set out for Bayonne. But the Spanish queen could not take a speedy, direct route. Cities and towns along the way clamored for her visit. Townspeople organized parades; artisans crafted triumphal arches for her carriage to pass through. Mayors and city councilmen gave lengthy speeches praising their queen and arranged long banquets in her honor. Churches insisted that she pray at their altars, worship their saints, and march in their processions. Poorhouses and orphanages begged her to stop by with alms. By the time the exhausted Elizabeth reached Bayonne, the journey had taken her almost nine weeks and her mother had been stewing for a fortnight in a heat wave.

Notified of the imminent arrival of the Spaniards, on June 14 King Charles and Queen Catherine waited in the royal pavilion for two hours. Six soldiers assigned to stand guard outside died of sunstroke. It is likely that Elizabeth's vicious majordomo, the duque de Alba, who hated Catherine, indulged in a little revenge by making the queen of France sweat beneath her gold embroidered velvets. When the Spanish entourage approached, thirty-five of the noblest ladies rode sidesaddle on mules, to the hearty guffaws of French courtiers who thought the sight ridiculous. During the heartwarming reunion of mother and daughter, hundreds of courtiers were roaming the nearby villages seeking food and shelter. Catherine was forced to step in to prevent famine and pestilence; she unceremoniously ejected the villagers from their houses, which she assigned to courtiers.

In between the jousts, pageants, feasts, masked balls, artificial combats, fetes, and galas, the several political conversations between mother and daughter proved fruitless; Catherine exerted pressure on Elizabeth to influence Philip on issues that would benefit France, and not necessarily Spain. The duque de Alba, furious at Catherine's misguided political efforts, informed her that her daughter must return forthwith to Spain, as her husband could no longer live with her absence.

Catherine's parting instructions to Elizabeth were oddly impossible—that she was to "follow the humor of the king her husband in all matters, and above all, never to forget or to slight the interests of her brother's crown."[36]

The expense, the wrangling, and the wasted months and futile political negotiations of this visit served as an example to future generations of royals. Family reunions would be few and far between, if ever. In 1699 Elizabeth Charlotte, duchesse d'Orléans, hoped to visit her pregnant daughter who had married the ruler of the duchy of Lorraine. Because no one in either party was a king—her husband, Monsieur, was a duke, as was her daughter's husband—she hoped the visit would not be prevented by the fractious demands of protocol.

But the duc de Lorraine insisted on sitting in an armchair in the presence of the duc d'Orléans, an honor he was accorded by the Holy Roman Emperor. The duc d'Orléans, however, citing French etiquette, replied that the duc de Lorraine would only be given a stool to sit upon. When the duc de Lorraine flat-out refused to sit on a stool, the duc d'Orléans generously suggested that he be given a high-backed chair with no arms. But the duc de Lorraine stubbornly insisted on having a chair *with* arms.

Louis XIV himself became involved and forbade the duc de Lorraine to sit on a chair with arms, signaling a dignity equal to that of Monsieur, whose dignity as a son of France was incomparably greater. However, the duc de Lorraine refused to admit he was worthy of less dignity than that given him by the emperor. And so the visit was called off, and Elizabeth Charlotte did not see her daughter for nearly two decades.

QUEENLY FINANCES

While commoners envied the luxuries of royal women, the fact was that many princesses had less spending money than a farmer's wife. In 1666 King Alfonso VI of Portugal denied his French-born queen money for her household expenses and refused to give her the fifty thousand francs she had been promised as her wedding portion. Unable to pay her servants or buy herself a new gown, Queen Maria Francisca was often seen sobbing loudly into a handkerchief.

In the 1840s the thrifty King Ludwig I of Bavaria made his wife, Queen Therese, wear threadbare dresses to the opera, the same opera where his greedy mistress, Lola Montez, arrived shining in a diamond tiara, necklace, brooch, earrings, bracelets, and rings—gifts from the king.

Despite her exalted position as the highest-ranking woman in France after the death of Louis XIV's queen in 1683, Elizabeth Charlotte suffered for decades from her husband's stinginess. "All he has in his head are his young fellows," she wrote, "with whom he wants to gorge and guzzle all night long, and he gives them huge sums of money; nothing is too much or too costly for these boys. Meanwhile, his children and I barely have what we need. Whenever I need shirts or sheets it means no end of begging, yet at the same time he gives 10,000 *talers* to La Carte [a lover] so that he can buy his linens in Flanders."[37]

Not only did Monsieur refuse to give his wife spending money, he even raided her rooms and took the wedding gifts she had brought from Germany. "One day he came in," Elizabeth Charlotte huffed in a letter to her aunt, "and, despite my urgent pleading, gathered up all the silver dishes from Heidelberg and some other silverware that decorated my room and looked quite pretty, had them melted down and pocketed all the money himself; he did not even leave me one poor little box in which to put my kerchiefs."[38]

In 1697, desperate for funds, she asked the king if the money she had brought as dowry from the Palatinate twenty-five years earlier was hers. The king replied "that, yes, it is, but that Monsieur is *maître de la communauté*, who as long as he lives can dispose of it as he sees fit and that there is nothing I can do about it. . . . What annoys me most is that I see with my own eyes that my money is being spent so badly and on such despicable people."[39]

STATE-OF-THE-ART HEALTH CARE

While today's wealthy can afford health care unimaginable to the poor and uninsured, in centuries past the exact opposite was true. State-of-the-art health care involved frequent bleeding, and the administration of pukes and purges—medicines resulting in violent vomiting and diarrhea. Many patients were killed not by the original illness but by the expensive ministrations of a highly respected doctor. The poor, on the other hand, could not afford doctors. Rest, hot soup, and fresh air often revived them.

Anne of Austria, the mother of Louis XIV, was diagnosed with breast cancer in 1665. Over the period of a year, with no painkillers and no antibiotics to prevent infection, her breast was removed one slice at a time with a knife and fork, as if it were a roast being carved. Perhaps it was a mercy when, after suffering untold agony, she finally died.

One day as a teenager, after suffering weeks from a decayed tooth, the future Catherine the Great agreed to have it pulled. A "surgeon" came to her room armed with a pair of pliers and yanked out the offending tooth—and a chunk of jawbone as well. Blood gushed all over her gown. The swelling and pain were so shocking that Catherine did not leave her room for a month, and even when the swelling went down, the dentist's five fingers were imprinted in blue and yellow bruises at the bottom of her cheek.

Elizabeth Charlotte, duchesse d'Orléans, came from hearty German stock and hated the Versailles doctors. Whenever she heard that Louis XIV was sending doctors to attend her, she bolted the gilded doors to her room and refused to emerge until she was well. She believed the best antidote to illness was a vigorous two-hour walk in her gardens regardless of the weather, followed by a stout German beer and some spicy sausages.

"Here no child is safe," she wrote a friend back in Germany in 1672, "for the doctors here have already helped five of the Queen's to the other world; the last one died three weeks ago, and three of Monsieur's, as he says himself, have been expedited in the same way."[40] In 1683 she accused palace doctors of killing the wife of the heir to the throne. The princess expired "through the ignorance of the doctors, who killed her as surely as if they had thrust a dagger into her heart."[41]

When royal physicians succeeded in killing almost the entire French royal family in 1712 by bleeding them to death during a measles epidemic, the nurse of the youngest prince, the two-year-old Louis, hid with him in a closet for three days until the doctors stopped their search. By the time she emerged, all other heirs to the throne were dead, and the entire future of France rested on the slender shoulders of the future Louis XV.

Though the field of medicine made tremendous strides in the second half of the nineteenth century—germs had been discovered under a microscope, hygiene was greatly improved, and chloroform was used as an anesthetic—some royal women were not permitted to enjoy the benefits. When Marie of Romania was due to deliver her first child in 1894, her grandmother Queen Victoria sent an English physician with instructions to administer chloroform as the pain became intense.

The Romanian priests objected heatedly, citing the Bible's statement that women must pay for Eve's sin by bringing forth children in pain. Romanian doctors agreed. Forcing the priests and local doctors from the room, the British doctor administered the anesthetic, anyway, much to the relief of the pain-stricken princess. But for her second delivery a year later, the Romanian royal family and the attending doctors absolutely forbade painkillers. Marie suffered horribly.

Perhaps Louis XIII best summed up royal health care in 1643 when the forty-one-year-old monarch lay dying of a stomach complaint. Those at his deathbed marveled at the king's admirable resignation to God's will. The king's calm acceptance of his fate, however, vanished the moment his chief physician walked in the room. Scowling at his doctor, Louis snapped, "I would have lived much longer if it had not been for you."[42]

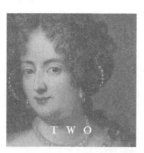

TWO

THE QUEEN TAKES A LOVER

Women are as roses, whose fair flower
Being once displayed, doth fall that very hour.

—WILLIAM SHAKESPEARE

❀

BEFORE WE EMBARK ON OUR JOURNEY THROUGH NINE CEN-
turies of queenly adultery, we must first understand that there
were two kinds of queens—a ruling queen and a queen consort.
If she had power in her own right—as a hereditary queen or
queen regent—some at court might grumble about her love affairs but there was no chance of beheading or divorce. Queen Isabella II of Spain had numerous lovers, and her poor little
consort Don Francisco was in no position to say a word. Peter the
Great's daughter Empress Elizabeth, who never officially married, had four lovers at once. The spinster Queen Elizabeth I of
England had passionate flirtations with courtiers, and the widowed Queen Victoria fell in love with her groom. But no one at

these courts dared utter a word of reproach to the hereditary monarch.

Widowhood often bestowed great power on a formerly power-less queen consort. Having suffered thirty years of malice and neglect as the wife of Louis XIII of France, the widowed Anne of Austria ruled for her young son, Louis XIV, together with her politically brilliant lover Cardinal Mazarin. Catherine the Great of Russia—who hastened herself into an early widowhood by hav-ing her husband murdered—grabbed power in her own right and took as many lovers as she wanted without fear of reprisals.

Some queen consorts were married to complacent husbands who permitted them not only political power in their own right, but love affairs as well. For thirty years starting in 1788 the odd ménage à trois of King Carlos IV of Spain, Queen Maria Luisa, and her lover, Manuel Godoy, lived happily together, calling themselves "the earthly trinity."[1] The king went out hunting every day, while the queen and her lover—whom the king oblig-ingly named prime minister—made love and policy. Carlos was grateful to Godoy for taking the burdens of statecraft off his shoulders so he could chase rabbits. Carlos was so devoted to hunting that one day, when he was informed that one of his chil-dren lay dying, he said, "Well, what can I do about it?" and jumped on his horse.[2]

Carlos had inherited his passion for the hunt from his father, Carlos III who, whenever he passed a tapestry with the figure of a horse, could not restrain himself from lifting one leg as if he were going to mount the animal and ride off. His son Ferdinand IV of Naples, brother of Carlos IV of Spain, shared the family's genetically predisposed mania. Ferdinand permitted his wife, Queen Maria Carolina, to rule his nation with her lover Sir John Acton, readily nodding agreement to most of their political recommendations so that he could race back to the fields.

When Carlos was visiting Ferdinand in 1821 and fell deathly ill, a messenger was sent to recall Ferdinand from the hunt. The king refused. "Either my brother will die, or he will recover," he said. "In the first case, what will it matter to him whether I amused myself hunting or not? In the second, being a crack sportsman himself he will be delighted to see me return with a good bag of game to cheer his convalescence."[3] Carlos died without his brother, but with Ferdinand's name on his lips.

Those royal women who possessed power—whether by birthright, widowhood, or as a gift from husbands who wanted to go hunting—flaunted their love affairs. These women rewarded their lovers as generously as kings rewarded their mistresses. But powerless royal women were forced to hide their affairs. Their lovers not only received no financial benefits; far worse, they lived under the threat of torture and execution if the affair became public.

THE SKILL OF SUBTERFUGE

Fed up with her husband and palace life, the powerless queen consort who decided to take a lover could resort to tried-and-true stratagems to hide the affair.

We must bear in mind that royalty almost never had a moment alone. Even on the chamber pot, servants would be in attendance to lift up the heavy skirt or knee-length jacket, and hand the soft piece of cotton used for cleaning the body. At night, if a royal couple desired intimacy, they might send their servants to sleep in the antechamber or in front of the door. But royal husbands and wives had—and still have—their individual suites and often didn't sleep together. When the king slept alone, he usually had bodyguards in the room for his protection and servants to summon a doctor if he became ill or to bring him food or drink if requested.

Less likely a target of assassination, the queen, if sleeping without her husband, required waiting women in her room to provide an alibi for her virtue. A lady-in-waiting would sleep on the floor next to the royal bed or, if the queen wished another human body to warm the frosty sheets, in bed with the queen herself. Whether the queen went walking or stayed in her room reading by a crackling fire, a bevy of ladies always danced attendance.

A sure sign of a love affair was when the queen became partial to just one female servant at the expense of the others. Only this particular lady slept in the queen's room at night, only she walked with her in the gardens, dressed her and bathed her and embroidered with her before the fire. If the queen reduced her retinue to just one for her private time, it usually meant that this servant was her accomplice in a love affair. Indeed, without a lady-in-waiting accomplice, a queen or princess would have found it impossible to have a lover. And if her virtue was challenged, her servant would swear that she had been with the queen the entire time in question, reading the Bible.

When Henry VIII's fifth wife, the silly teenaged Catherine Howard, had a sizzling love affair with the handsome courtier Thomas Culpeper in 1542, the assistance of her lady-in-waiting Lady Jane Rochford was invaluable. The court was frequently changing lodgings, and when the queen arrived at a palace, Lady Rochford would first spy out which apartments were connected to back doors and secret staircases. These were the apartments she would choose for the queen. Lady Rochford took messages back and forth between the lovers and sneaked Culpeper in and out of Catherine's apartments.

In the 1690s Hereditary Princess Sophia Dorothea of Hanover relied entirely on her devoted lady-in-waiting, Eleonore de Knesebeck, to facilitate her love affair with the Swedish count Philip von Königsmark. Knesebeck wrote many of Sophia Dorothea's love letters to the count in her own hand and received the count's letters addressed to her. That way, if they were intercepted, it would look as if the count and Eleonore had been having the affair. When Königsmark was bold enough to venture into Sophia Dorothea's rooms in the palace, Eleonore de Knesebeck waited by a little door leading from the palace to the garden and opened it when she heard him whistling a tune called "The Spanish Follies." She then led him up a hidden staircase directly to the princess's bedchamber.

It was easier for a royal woman to have lovers when she was not under the intense scrutiny of thousands of eyes at the palace. Napoleon's sister Pauline, Princess Borghese, evaded her brother's prudish gaze by claiming ill health and rumbling about the health spas of Europe looking for a cure. Though she never found a cure, she did find vigorous sex from numerous lovers.

In 1807 at the health spa of Plombières, Pauline fell head over heels in love with the aristocratic comte Auguste de Forbin. The intensity of her passion seemed to consume her very flesh; she fell ill from the violence of it and could not eat or sleep. A gynecologist was sent for who made the following report: "Her habitual and constant state is one of uterine excitement and if this state is continued and prolonged it can become alarming."[4] To calm down her uterus, Pauline was forced to give up her lover, at least officially.

Clucking loudly about her need for improved health, she sent away most of her servants and rumbled over rutted roads nearly five hundred miles to the tiny spa town of Gréoulx, where the comte de Forbin had a castle. For months they lived quietly, spending most of each day in bed. But Napoleon's eagle eye turned for a moment from the field of war and searched out his rebellious sister. He forced the poor count to join the French army.

A century later Crown Princess Marie of Romania visited her mother at various locales throughout Germany, including health spas, her lovers secretly following her. Here were no spies paid by grouchy King Carol to report her every move, as there were at her palace in Bucharest. Twice Marie became pregnant during long visits to her mother, with her husband hundreds of miles away in Romania. The first pregnancy likely ended in a miscarriage, and the second pregnancy resulted in her third child, Princess Marie.

Taking the waters was a much-used strategy not only for lovers' trysts, but also when the result of a tryst was due to arrive nine months later. A woman in her third trimester of pregnancy would announce she was unwell—suffering from dropsy, perhaps, an illness which resulted in swelling—and needed to drink the restorative waters of a particular spa. She would choose one conveniently far from home, where she would be less likely to run into acquaintances. The journey there, in easy stages, might take a month. Once at the spa—where she would go incognito—

she would have the child and arrange to give it away. If she was fortunate, her lover's relatives would agree to take the child and raise it as their own. After the birth, she would socialize more, take the waters, and return home slender and radiating good health. The magical waters had worked.

In 1811 Hortense de Beauharnais, daughter of Empress Josephine, found herself pregnant by her lover, a handsome soldier named Charles de Flahaut. Hortense had not lived with her husband, Louis Bonaparte, Napoleon's brother, for years. Though Napoleon had made them king and queen of the Netherlands in 1806, Hortense reaped little benefit from her exalted status. King Louis forced his wife to remain in her rooms—which smelled of sewage and overlooked a graveyard— while he enjoyed palace entertainments.

Exposure of her pregnancy would have meant a public divorce, a shattered reputation, and the loss of her children with Louis. Luckily, the fashions of the times hid her expanding belly. In a high-waisted gown, with a large shawl draped around her, she hosted a party to celebrate Napoleon's birthday two weeks before her child was born, and no one guessed her condition. Right before the birth, Hortense visited a health spa with Charles where she had the child. Her son was whisked away to Charles's accommodating mother, so at least Hortense obtained news of him as he grew up.

Visiting a health spa was an alibi so frequently used by women with inconvenient pregnancies that the invalid visitor who really did hope for improved health was often credited upon her return home with having given birth to a bastard. Sometimes even a long illness inside the palace itself gave rise to rumors of pregnancy. When George III's daughter Princess Amelia died in 1810 of tuberculosis, it was said she had given up the ghost bearing twins.

Elizabeth I's 1562 smallpox attack—which almost killed her— led to stories that she had been not ill, but had given birth to a love child with her virile suitor Robert Dudley. Foreign courts, hearing stories of Elizabeth's daughter, were eager to arrange a marriage with her; even though illegitimate, the child would likely be named heir to the English throne. In 1575 the bishop of Padua heard that the queen had "a daughter, thirteen years of age, and that she would bestow her in marriage to someone acceptable to His Catholic Majesty (Philip II of Spain)."[5] When the Spanish ambassador politely brought up the subject of betrothing Elizabeth and Dudley's illegitimate daughter to a Hapsburg prince, however, his request was met with howls of laughter.

In 1802 Princess Sophia, the unmarried daughter of King George III of Britain, gained a great deal of weight and claimed she was terribly ill. At the royal residence of Weymouth one night, she gave birth to a boy. The following morning her doctor brought a baby boy to the wife of the village tailor who had also delivered a son in the night. The tailor proudly announced that his wife had actually delivered twins. Oddly, the twins looked nothing alike, and one of them was wrapped in a gorgeous palace blanket embroidered with a coronet. Word got out in the village about the tailor's royal twin, and dozens of curious people from all walks of life stopped by with alterations, offhandedly asking to see the boy and his regal blanket. When the crowds grew too large, the boy's supposed father, General Thomas Garth, took him away from the tailor and raised him as his own.

It was difficult for many to believe that the lovely twenty-five-year-old princess had had sex with an unattractive fifty-six-year-old palace official, disfigured by a huge red birthmark across half his face. Ironically, George III and his wife, Queen Charlotte, fiercely guarded the virtue of their six daughters, so much so that they didn't want them even to marry. They kept their grown daughters in a kind of harem, with only a few male servants, all of whom were old and repulsive.

The political diarist Charles Greville reported, "The only reason why people doubted Garth's being the father was that he was a hideous old devil, old enough to be her father, and with a great claret mark on his face—which is no argument at all, for women fall in love with anything. . . . There they (the princesses) were secluded from the world, mixing with few people, their passions boiling over, and ready to fall into the hands of the first man whom circumstances enabled to get at them."[6]

The morning after the birth, Princess Sophia's medical attendant announced that his patient had had a sudden remarkable recovery and "would be completely restored to health after a short period of rest and quiet retirement."[7]

"The old King never knew it," Greville continued, and indeed for decades the king had slipped into and out of madness, often enjoying impassioned conversations with trees and politely shaking their branches as if they were hands. "The Court was at Weymouth when she was big with child. She was said to be dropsical, and then suddenly recovered. They told the King that she was cured by *roast beef,* and this he swallowed, and used to tell it to people, all of whom knew the truth, as 'a very extraordinary thing.' "[8]

"It Is Dangerous to Love Princesses"

An amorous courtier, if he carefully considered the risks before making love to a queen consort, may have found his interest in the lady shrinking. Possible penalties included exquisitely slow torture and a lingering death.

In the early thirteenth century King John of England, fearing that his wife, Isabella, was having affairs, supposedly hanged the suspected lovers from her bedpost and allowed her to find them dangling there.

In the early fourteenth century three knights seduced the wives of the three royal princes of France, sons of King Philip the Fair. The princesses were imprisoned, but their lovers were strapped to huge wheels which were spun while executioners shattered their limbs with iron bars.

Catherine Howard was merely beheaded with one swift stroke in 1542, but her lover Francis Dereham was hanged until nearly unconscious, cut down, and his private parts lopped off and burned before his eyes. He was then cut open and his intestines pulled out as he watched. Finally, he was beheaded. His rotting head adorned Tower Bridge; his body parts were nailed to other buildings.

Even when the husband didn't mind his wife conducting

amorous intrigues, a queen's lover sometimes faced mortal danger. After marrying the beautiful dark-haired Margot de Valois in 1572, Henri, king of Navarre, welcomed her love affairs, as it allowed him ample opportunity to pursue his countless mistresses. But if Margot's husband didn't mind her behavior, her brother, King Henri III of France, minded very much indeed, and had some of her lovers beheaded, hanged, ambushed, and wounded. In addition, some of Margot's lovers killed one another in fits of jealous rage. Margot reportedly collected the embalmed hearts of her lovers and put them into small silver boxes, which she hung inside her hoopskirt on chains. Over the years, she built up quite a collection.

After twenty years of estrangement, separation, and an eventual divorce, by 1605 Margot and Henri had become good friends. No longer just king of tiny Navarre, Margot's former husband had inherited the crown of France and become King Henri IV. Moving to Paris to live off her ex-husband's largesse, the fat, aging fifty-three-year-old queen took men into her bed who were barely out of their teens. Alighting from her carriage one day with her lover the sieur de Saint-Julien, another admirer called Vermont shot his rival in the head and killed him. Vermont was hanged, and the queen collected two more hearts for the tin boxes rattling beneath her petticoat. She also insisted that the king buy her a new house, as she couldn't possibly remain in the one where the murder had been committed.

Soon after Margot moved to a house with less murderous memories, a jealous suitor ran her lover Bajaumont through with a sword in church. Visiting his ex-wife one day, the king saw her waiting women and asked them to pray for the recuperation of Bajaumont, for which he would reward them with New Year's gifts. "For, if he were to die," said the king, "*ventre Saint-Gris!* It would cost me a great deal more, since I should have to buy her a new house in place of this one, where she would never consent to remain."[9]

Though Henri shrugged off his ex-wife's love affairs with a joke, when Peter the Great found out his former spouse had a lover, the czar was not amused. Peter had divorced his pious aristocratic wife, Queen Eudoxia, in 1698 and put her in a convent. Allowed to come and go as she wished, and to receive visitors, by 1718 Eudoxia was having a love affair with Stefan Glebov, a Russian military official.

When Peter found out about the affair, he prepared a special punishment for Glebov. He was beaten and burned; his ribs were broken and his flesh torn out with red-hot pincers. But even that wasn't a sufficient expression of Peter's wrath. The czar had Glebov impaled through the rectum on a stake several feet high. Because the weather was bitterly cold, it was feared that Glebov would freeze to death mercifully quickly. So he was dressed in a fur hat, coat, and boots. He was impaled at three o'clock in the afternoon and lasted in excruciating pain until 7:30 the following evening. His corpse remained on the stake for months.

"It is dangerous to love princesses," said Laure d'Abrantès, a good friend of Napoleon's promiscuous sisters.[10] And indeed the emperor, seeing handsome admirers dancing attendance on Queen Elise of Tuscany, Queen Caroline of Naples, and Princess Pauline Borghese of Rome, routinely sent the amorous young men to the front. Though it was a gentler punishment than impalement, beheading, or hanging, many never returned.

Penalties still exist today. In 1991 James Hewitt, who was the lover of Diana, Princess of Wales, was drummed out of his army career for failing three exams by 1 percent each. "I was not so naïve as to think that the authorities didn't discuss my situation with regard to the heir to the throne," he huffed in his biography *Love and War.* "It would be much more convenient for all concerned if I simply resigned my commission."[11] Though, looking back on the fates of other men diving into forbidden royal beds, it could have been worse.

"Oh, What an Ass Is Man without Money!"

Not all royal lovers risked torture and death. It was far safer—and more profitable—to love a queen who ruled in her own right, or a consort who boasted a complacent husband.

The background of Manuel Godoy, lover of Queen Maria Luisa of Spain, was modest; he came from a rural area of Spain known for its swineherds, which earned him the nickname El Choricero—the Sausage Man. Given the titles duque de Alcudia, grandee of Spain, and Prince of the Peace, Godoy took precedence over every man in the country except his good friend King Carlos and the heir to the throne. Godoy was given large estates in Granada and the shocking income of one million reales a year. Suddenly the Sausage Man was the richest private individual in the country.

One day in the 1620s a young Roman named Giulio Mazarini—the future Cardinal Mazarin of France—was losing money at cards and cried out, "Oh, what an ass is man without money!"[12]

But when in 1643 he became the lover of the widowed queen regent Anne, mother of the young Louis XIV, Mazarin was never again an ass, at least in financial terms. He possessed a library of forty thousand books—the king himself had only ten thousand. The cardinal had the finest horses in his stables and rare breeds of dogs in his kennels. His palace in Paris had a grand double staircase, three huge entrances, several inner courtyards, a beautiful garden, and the best collection of art in France. With exquisite taste, he had brought the color, warmth, and elegance of Rome to the chill of Paris. He sent to the Vatican for artists to make frescoes and imported the finest carriages from Italy. His furniture was made of lapis lazuli, mother of pearl, gold, silver, ebony, and tortoiseshell. His statues were of alabaster, his bed of ivory. He wore only the finest linen, the most costly perfumes.

By applying clever cost-cutting measures, by 1648 he had saved the government of France the eye-popping sum of forty-two million livres, but reportedly rewarded himself with half that amount. In addition, he received 60,000 livres for taking charge of the king's education, 20,000 for the post of minister, 6,000 for being a council member, 18,000 as a cardinal, and 110,000 as a pension from the queen. He owned twenty-one abbeys, which were worth 468,330 livres. On his deathbed in

1661, the cardinal, looking about his magnificent possessions, cried, "I must leave all this! I'll never see these things again!"[13] He didn't seem to object to never seeing the queen again, however.

The widowed Catherine the Great was the most generous monarch to her lovers. Over a period of thirty-four years she doled out the equivalent of more than two billion dollars in cash, pensions, palaces, works of art, fine furnishings, and serfs. In the early 1790s, an English visitor to St. Petersburg—known as the Venice of the north because of its interconnecting waterways—reported, "A party was considering which of the canals had cost the most money; when one of them archly observed there was not a doubt about the matter; Catherine's Canal (this is the name of one of them) had unquestionably been the most expensive."[14]

GOVERNMENT AND MILITARY POSITIONS

Unlike the royal mistress who, even if she wielded significant political power behind the scenes, had no official political title, certain royal lovers were made prime minister, some of them with excellent results. For thirty years starting in 1777 the British naval officer Sir John Acton ran Naples efficiently for his mistress, Queen Maria Carolina. During World War I one of Europe's most capable politicians was Barbo Stirbey, lover of Queen Marie of Romania. Her husband, the weak and vacillating King Ferdinand, relied on Stirbey to steer his nation through the turmoil of war and into a golden age in the 1920s. When Ferdinand died in 1927, Stirbey ruled Romania as prime minister for Marie's young grandson, King Michael.

But not all royal lovers were suited for the position of prime minister. With the acquiescence of her mentally deranged husband, King Christian VII of Denmark, in 1771 Queen Caroline Matilda made her lover, Johann von Struensee, prime minister. Though possessed of great social vision, Struensee made so many new laws so quickly that Denmark erupted in rebellion and conspiracy.

In 1792 Queen Maria Luisa of Spain made twenty-five-year-old Manuel Godoy prime minister. The queen's lover had much to learn—upon taking up his duties he thought Russia and Prussia were the same country. When the saber-rattling Napoleon insisted on Spain's support against Britain, and Britain urged Spain to fight Napoleon, poor Godoy was at a loss. For years he struggled to maintain an uneasy neutrality. But, as the late-seventeenth-century philosopher Gottfried Wilhelm Leibniz said, "To be neutral is rather like someone who lives in the middle of a house and is smoked out from below and drenched with urine from above."[15] Drenched *and* smoked out, Godoy and the Spanish royal family spent several years in genteel imprisonment in France after Napoleon conquered Spain and put his brother Joseph on the throne.

More dangerous even than giving their lovers top political offices, many queens bestowed on them the highest military positions—the rank of general or field marshal—and expected them with little or no battlefield experience to lead men to war. It was a perilous custom to appoint to such a crucial position a man whose most impressive qualifications were below the waist and not above the shoulders.

When Empress Sophie of Russia fielded an army in 1687, she appointed her lover Prince Basil Golitzin the commanding general. In vain he protested that he was a diplomat and politician, not a soldier; she refused to listen. When he returned from a disastrous campaign against the Tatars, she welcomed him back to victory paeans, though some forty thousand men had been lost to fire, suffocation, or flight, and not a single battle had been fought. Undeterred, the empress sent him to war two years later in Crimea, where Golitzin lost thirty-five thousand men.

In the 1790s Manuel Godoy was proclaimed admiral general of Spain and the Indies. He strutted impressively in his naval uniform and bicorn hat with plumes; but Godoy hated boats and open water, and whenever he went onboard to inspect a ship, he tried to quell rising nausea.

If a king gave his mistress an obscenely expensive diamond necklace, all other women at court would turn pea green with envy. Naturally, such a gift was not suitable for a man; the queen's lover wanted honorary orders for distinguished service, medals edged with dazzling diamonds and colorful fluttering ribbons. Many of these men had never fought a battle in their lives, but still eagerly sought decorations for martial valor. Their goal was to stride through palace corridors with an entire galaxy of shimmering stars and clanking medals on their chests.

Catherine the Great's lover Gregory Potemkin was made a knight of the Order of St. Andrew, Russia's highest order. He was given the Black Eagle by Prussia and the White Eagle by Poland. Denmark bestowed upon him the Order of the Elephant, and Sweden the St. Seraph. Joseph II of Austria made him a prince of the Holy Roman Empire. Louis XV balked at giving the empress's lover the Order of the Holy Ghost, claiming it was only for Roman Catholics, and the prudish George III flat out refused to give him the Order of the Garter. But Potemkin's battlefield courage and political acumen made him a worthy recipient of such honors.

Many noble dinner guests of Caroline, Princess of Wales, protested at sitting down at the same table with her lover Bartolomeo Pergami, a man of humble birth. No European monarchs wanted to bestow upon him their elite orders. In 1816 the princess took ship to Malta, where she arranged for her lover to become a knight of Malta. Then she traveled to Jerusalem, where she founded a new knighthood called the Order of Saint Caroline, and appointed Pergami the master of the order. In Sicily she bought Pergami the small estate of Franchini, which rendered him a baron. The new baron Pergami della Franchini, knight of the Order of Malta, master of the Order of St. Caroline, was now sufficiently exalted under British rules of etiquette to sit down at Caroline's table, though guests still grumbled about his low birth.

In the late 1830s Queen Victoria's mother, Victoire, the

duchess of Kent, wanted to reward her lover John Conroy. But Queen Victoria, who despised her mother's lover, firmly blocked the path in Britain to any honors. The resourceful Victoire, a German princess, twisted a few arms and arranged for German principalities to give him decorations and medals. The duchess arranged for him to be called "excellency"—but only in Germany, which galled him.

The duchess further obtained an award for Conroy from Portugal, which included the signal honor that wherever he walked, guards preceding him would drum in his honor. But Conroy never made it to Portugal, even though he tried to organize several trips over the years—just to hear the drums.

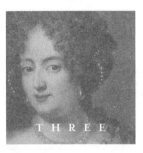

THREE

MEDIEVAL QUEENS, TUDOR VICTIMS

Uneasy lies the head that wears a crown.

—WILLIAM SHAKESPEARE

❄

HUMAN NATURE BEING WHAT IT IS, WE CAN ASSUME THAT back in the cave the mate of the powerful chief—the man who wielded a big stick to bring home mammoth meat—looked with lust upon a muscular young hunter and wondered about the size of his stick. Alas, records of Ice Age love affairs simply don't exist.

Nor are there many records that attest to medieval queens taking lovers. Expected to reflect the virtues of the Virgin Mary, most queens probably never considered adultery as an option, no matter how horrible their husbands were. And yet, having examined the emptiness of palace life and the sorrows of the marital bed, well can we understand why a queen would have been unfaithful. Looking at the earliest stories of adulterous queens, we are unsure whether to condemn their weakness or applaud their courage.

In 1109 King Alfonso VI of Castile and Leon forced his widowed daughter and heir, Princess Urraca, to marry Alfonso the Battler, king of Aragon. Feeling his end drawing near, Alfonso VI wanted his daughter to have the protection of a fierce warrior husband at her side. He died soon after the wedding and never saw Alfonso of Aragon and Urraca of Castile and Leon battling *each other* for decades. Though valiant on the battlefield, Alfonso was probably useless in bed; no one at court could comprehend his aversion to whores, mistresses, and women in general. Urraca detested her husband and soon abandoned him.

But Urraca had little need of Alfonso on the battlefield. She hopped on a horse herself and spent thirteen campaign seasons out of her seventeen years' rule waging war against unruly neighbors. Her top military commander was her lover Pedro Gonzalez, a powerful noble, whom she bore at least two illegitimate children. The queen died at the age of forty-six, giving birth to twins, some said, though no one knows. Records of the life of this intriguing woman are few and far between.

ELEANOR OF AQUITAINE,
QUEEN OF FRANCE

"I Find I Have Wed a Monk"

When eighteen-year-old Louis VII of France married the spirited fifteen-year-old Eleanor of Aquitaine in 1137, he would have gladly bedded her often, but his priests prevented it. Young as she was, she sized up her husband's band of bleating clerics at a glance and dismissed them as worthless. They sized her up, too, and were alarmed; they had wielded unlimited power over the impressionable young king. Now this power was threatened by a headstrong girl whom Louis deeply loved. The renowned abbot Bernard of Clairvaux wrote the king that he was under the "counsel of the devil," the devil being Queen Eleanor.[1]

Louis's priests often pulled the king out of his marital bed, leaving Eleanor seething with anger amongst the pillows. As a result of the priests' interventions, in a decade of marriage, Eleanor gave her husband only one child—a useless girl. "I thought to have married a king," she snarled, "but find I have wed a monk."[2]

When a penitent Louis VII vowed to go on crusade in 1146 to atone for his sins, Eleanor, bored to tears in her dark cold palace in muddy Paris, insisted on accompanying him. Various reports credited her with dressing as an Amazon in a silver breastplate as the cavalcade crossed the Hungarian plains. Once in the Holy Land, Eleanor probably had a rollicking affair with her uncle, the virile warrior Raymond of Poitiers who had claimed the kingdom of Antioch as his own. Thirty years after her visit to Antioch, the chronicler William of Tyre wrote, "Her conduct before and after this time showed her to be far from circumspect. Contrary to her royal dignity, she disregarded her marriage vows and was unfaithful to her husband."[3]

When King Louis was ready to move on to Jerusalem, Eleanor told her husband that he might do as he pleased but she would stay behind with Uncle Raymond. Stunned, Louis asked her the reason behind her eagerness to abandon him. Eleanor supposedly retorted, "Why do I renounce you? Because of your fecklessness. You are not worth a rotten pear."[4]

Weak and ineffectual, Louis didn't know what to do. But his advisers convinced the king, "It would be a lasting shame to the kingdom of the Franks if, in addition to all the other disasters, it was reported that the King had been deserted by his wife, or robbed of her."[5] Despite her probable adultery, Eleanor would be kept as queen as a matter of prestige, as well as for the rich lands she brought to France, lands which would depart with her in the event of a divorce.

When a signal was given for the French army to move out, the queen was scooped up in the middle of the night, slung over a horse, and forced to continue on crusade as a dutiful wife. She never saw her swaggering uncle again. Soon after her inglorious departure, he fell in battle against the Saracens, who plated his skull with silver and made it into a drinking cup.

In 1152 Louis gave in to Eleanor's pleas for a divorce on the grounds of consanguinity; they were fourth cousins, too closely related to a common ancestor to be legally married in the eyes of the church without a special dispensation. The real reason for a divorce, of course, was never consanguinity, which was a convenient excuse to end an unbearable marriage in a church that officially did not permit divorce. In Eleanor's case the real reason was that she had not given her husband a son.

Two months after her divorce she married the future Henry II of England, upon whom she bestowed her rich dower lands of Aquitaine as well as five sons and three daughters. Though more is known about Eleanor of Aquitaine than Urraca of Castile and Leon, much of her story was first written down decades after it occurred, often by scribes with political motivations for making her look good or evil and is, as such, suspect.

ISABELLA OF FRANCE, QUEEN OF ENGLAND

"Someone Has Come Between My Husband and Myself"

Far better records exist for Isabella of France, who in 1308 at the age of twelve married the handsome twenty-four-year-old Edward II of England. At the time of the wedding Edward had already been in love with another man, Piers Gaveston, for a decade. According to a contemporary chronicler, "As soon as the King's son saw him, he fell so much in love that he entered upon an enduring compact with him."[6]

After the nuptial celebrations in France, Edward sent all of the wedding gifts he had received from his father-in-law King Philip—gold rings and other jewels—back home to Gaveston as a present, which infuriated the French court. When the bride and groom landed in England, Edward leapt off the gangplank and ran into the arms of the waiting Gaveston. The new queen was left to clamber down the plank as best she could. At the coronation, it was Gaveston and not Isabella who seemed to be guest of honor. Edward had tapestries made for the coronation bearing not the arms of Edward and Isabella, as tradition demanded, but the arms of Edward and Gaveston, as if Edward had made Gaveston his queen.

The child-queen, unsure of herself at a foreign court, put up with the relationship but must have been relieved when four years later jealous barons, many of whom had lost their lands and castles to Gaveston, murdered him. The king became devoted to his wife and allowed her to rule England for him. But in 1320, after eight years of marital peace, Edward chose another favorite, actually two favorites, father and son, Hugh Le Despenser the Elder and Hugh Le Despenser the Younger. Though the facts are murky, it is assumed that the king was having an affair only with the son, and the father was a close political adviser exploiting the relationship to reap advantages for the family. In 1321, as the Le Despensers' star rose, Isabella's faded. The new favorites convinced the king to decrease her authority, honors, and income.

But this time Isabella was no longer a meek child. At twenty-five, she had ruled a nation for almost a decade and was not about to put up with another of her husband's lovers robbing her. On a visit to her family in France, Isabella took a powerful lover who would help her wage war against her husband. Roger Mortimer, in his early forties, had been one of Edward's successful generals against the Scots. But when the king confiscated his lands and castles, Mortimer became his deadliest enemy. Confined to the Tower of London, Mortimer arranged to have the guards drugged, rappelled down the battlements on a rope, swam the Thames, and escaped to France.

We can imagine that first night when Queen Isabella let Mortimer into her room. She had known only the smooth girlish hands of Edward upon her; in their most intimate joining her husband must have fantasized that he was actually making love to Piers Gaveston. And now this heated warrior took her, roughly at first, then tenderly. And he never, ever, imagined she was a man.

They made love at night and war during the day. Isabella began to dress as a widow and publicly proclaimed, "Someone has come between my husband and myself. . . . I protest that I will not return until this intruder has been removed but, discarding my marriage garment, I shall assume the robes of widowhood and mourning until I am avenged of this Pharisee."[7]

Armed with foreign troops, Isabella and Mortimer invaded England. Edward II and the Le Despensers fled but were soon captured. The favorites were hanged, cut down still alive, their bowels were cut out, their arms and legs hacked off, and their body parts fed to wild dogs.

It was one thing for Isabella to execute the hated Le Despensers, quite another to murder an anointed king and her husband. Shakespeare summed up the feeling when he wrote, "Not all the water in the rough rude sea can wash the balm off an anointed king." Isabella locked Edward up, forced him to abdicate, and had her fifteen-year-old son proclaimed Edward III. Because her son was young, she ruled England with Mortimer, flinging aside her widow's weeds. But Mortimer was, after all, a heterosexual version of Gaveston and the Le Despensers. Greedy, arrogant, and ambitious, he, too, confiscated estates from their rightful owners.

Public support shifted back in favor of the deposed king who, sitting in his cell, wrote self-pitying poetry. "And call me a crownless King," he opined, "a laughing stock to all."[8] Despite his wretched condition, he still posed a threat to Isabella and Mortimer, especially after two failed rescue attempts by his supporters. In 1327 Edward was murdered in his cell, supposedly by a red-hot poker being thrust up his anus inside a cow's horn, so no one would see any marks, or as one chronicler put it, "slain with a hot spit put thro the secret place posterial."[9] Isabella and Mortimer were not only detested tyrants. Now they had murdered a king.

In 1330 the eighteen-year-old Edward III eyed Mortimer's increasing arrogance with concern. The young king was worried that his mother's lover would have him murdered as well and reign in his stead, perhaps hoping to found his own dynasty with Isabella, who was still only thirty-four years old. Together with numerous barons robbed by Mortimer, Edward had him arrested. He was hanged, and the grieving Isabella remained in genteel confinement for two years before she was completely rehabilitated as Queen Mother. All her sins were thrown onto the shade of Roger Mortimer.

Perhaps to make up for the misdeeds of the past, Isabella became quite pious, frequently visiting saints' shrines. In her lavish apartments songbirds sang their sweet melodies, and minstrels played courtly tunes. For the Saint George's Day celebrations in 1358, shortly before her death at the age of sixty-two, she wore a circlet of gold on her head, belts of silk studded with silver, eighteen hundred pearls (probably seed pearls), and three hundred rubies. She was buried, oddly enough, in her wedding gown, holding the casket of her husband's heart, which she had never truly possessed while he was alive.

JUANA OF PORTUGAL, QUEEN OF CASTILE: THE GOLDEN TURKEY BASTER

While Edward II fathered four children with Isabella, another early king thought to be homosexual, Enrique IV of Castile, could not rise to the occasion with either of his two wives, no matter how hard he tried. Yet this resourceful monarch came up with a novel plan—an early form of artificial insemination.

A large shambling man, painfully shy and eternally forlorn, Enrique had gorgeous golden hair and dreamy blue-green eyes which contrasted strangely with his huge yellow horses' teeth and a flat crooked nose, broken in a childhood accident. He rarely bathed, perhaps because he had a bizarre fascination for repulsive odors.

While still heir to the throne, the fifteen-year-old Enrique was married to Princess Blanca of Navarre, daughter of King Juan of Aragon, in 1440. When the couple was put to bed, heralds stood guard at the door ready to blast their trumpets when the bloody sheets were brought out. Three notaries sat next to the bed, quills poised to record the first shriek or moan as proof of consummation. Stripped of her white nightgown, Blanca slid between the sheets. Enrique entered and slipped in beside her. The bed curtains were closed. The notaries seated themselves, leaning forward, listening intently. The candles burned down, guttering in the deadly silence of the room. The notaries shifted uneasily on the hard bench.

Outside waited crowds of courtiers, as well as Enrique's father, King Juan II. But no bloody sheet came out as proof. Nothing happened. Finally the notaries gave up and went to bed. One report related, "The Princess remained exactly as she had been born."[10]

Many hoped that with time the fifteen-year-old prince would fulfill his connubial duties; perhaps his youth and the frayed nerves of the wedding night had frightened him. But the months went by, and then the years, and no bloody sheet *ever* emerged. Some whispered that the prince was homosexual, and indeed he kept company with men known to be gay.

It was a somber event indeed when the ruler of a Spanish kingdom—Castile, Leon, Aragon, Galicia, or Valencia—died without an heir. Fractious neighboring kingdoms, all jockeying for superiority, were eager to swoop down upon his realm and claim it for themselves. When, after thirteen years of marriage, Blanca still remained a virgin, the archbishop of Toledo moved to annul the marriage on the grounds of nonconsummation.

Blanca shamefacedly took the stand and swore she was still a virgin. She underwent a physical examination by honorable matrons who declared her to be as "whole as the day she was born."[11] She was sent back to her father, who was furious with her for not being able to rouse her husband to his bedtime duties.

When doctors examined Enrique, they found that His Majesty's "penis was thin and weak at the base, but huge at the head, with the result that he could not have an erection."[12] He began to be known as "Enrique the Impotent."

But the king did not agree that he was hopelessly incapable of making love to a woman. A new wife was needed, he claimed. Clearly his penis had been bewitched with regard to Blanca, but he had hopes that he could be aroused with a different woman and could sire an heir. As soon as he became king in 1454, Enrique ordered a new bride, Princess Juana of Portugal. The sixteen-year-old princess had flashing dark eyes, long black hair, and tawny skin. She was sleek, sinuous, and flirtatious. Freshly

scrubbed and scented after her journey, she must have been revolted when she met her groom, tall and hunched and hulking,
smelling of sweat and horse.

After the wedding ceremony, the royal couple entered the
bedchamber. The king had fortified himself with the Viagra of
the time, broth of bulls' testicles mixed with powder of porcupine
quills. He refused to allow notaries in the room. No sheet showing that night, he announced. But it was all in vain because, once
more, it was reported that "the King and Queen slept in the same
bed, and the Queen remained as intact as she had arrived."[13]

Desperate for an heir, Enrique attempted a crude type of artificial insemination. The king was masturbated—by whom records don't say, perhaps by a doctor. The bit of ejaculate coaxed
out of him, which was described as "watery," was inserted by
means of a kind of golden turkey baster into the queen, who was
lying in bed with her legs in the air. It must have been horribly
humiliating for both.

In 1461 the queen was pregnant. Enrique was delighted,
thrilled; finally he had proved himself a man. The golden turkey
baster had worked, and, although it had not been accomplished
in the usual way, he was going to have a child. But courtiers
merely snickered. They knew the queen had been allowing a
handsome young courtier, Beltran de la Cueva, into her chamber. In February a little girl was born, a princess named Juana
after her mother, but whom Castilian courtiers and soon all of
Europe nicknamed "La Beltraneja" after her real father. And
indeed she was his spitting image.

The king later divorced his erring wife, who continued to get
pregnant long after Enrique had stopped trying the golden
turkey baster trick. Enrique named his younger half sister Isabel
of Castile as his heir. The two of them signed a joint document
proclaiming that Queen Juana "had not used her person cleanly
as complies with the service of the king nor her own."[14] Isabel
married Prince Ferdinand of Aragon, and together they
launched Columbus into the New World. They also launched the
inconvenient princess Juana la Beltraneja into a convent where
she could make no claims on their throne.

"She Excelled Them All"

It is ironic that the most famous queen ever executed for adultery was wholly innocent. The raven-haired Anne Boleyn, though she was vicious and vengeful and had a heart like a chunk of ice and a tongue as sharp and tearing as a meat cleaver, had always been faithful to her marriage bed. But it was never sex alone that did in a queen, even if Anne had been guilty. It was politics.

In 1526 Henry VIII, casting about court for a new mistress, fell passionately in love with Anne, the nineteen-year-old niece of the powerful Howard clan. Ambitious in a world where women held little power, Anne realized that as royal mistress she could whisper suggestions into the king's ear after lovemaking, seeds that often took root and bore fruit. But her older sister Mary, blond and soft and pretty, had been Henry VIII's mistress and was cast aside like used goods. No. Anne would never stand for that.

And then she looked at the queen, old and barren at forty-one, hobbled with arthritis, her waist thick from years of fruitless childbearing. Henry had not slept with Queen Catherine, a Spanish princess, in years. All the queen's children, except a useless girl, had died at birth. Why should Henry not divorce his barren wife and marry young fertile Anne to beget sons? Queen Anne. Ah, that would be power indeed.

At thirty-five, Henry was at his physical peak. He stood six foot one, a giant for his time. He was powerful in his physique, and though he had gained weight recently he carried it magnificently beneath his padded, broad-shouldered coats. He had short red-gold hair and a cropped beard. His ice blue eyes were small, intense, and never missed a thing.

Henry was the quintessential Renaissance man. He played the lute, the virginals (an early kind of organ), the recorder, and the harp. He wrote music, sang, and pirouetted gracefully on the dance floor. He spoke four languages fluently, composed poetry and music, and pursued astronomy and science. An avid sportsman, he rode, jousted, threw spears, bowled, and played tennis. Henry was a man of keen intellect, deep religious devotion, and outbursts of vicious cruelty. He was an utterly selfish man who could not bear to hear he would not get his way. And now he wanted his way with Anne Boleyn. And ambitious Anne wanted her way with him.

But to keep the king interested for the years it would take to unharness himself from Queen Catherine, Anne had to awaken his desires without assuaging them. And so she became his mistress in all things but sex. Vivacious Anne offered Henry friendship, entertainment, witty conversation, challenging political dialog, and theological debates. She danced, sang, played the lute, hunted with him, and organized tournaments and pageants for his amusement. Anne held out the promise of incredible sex and numerous sons to her overheated monarch, if only he would divorce his faithful queen and marry her.

Like many royal mistresses before and since, Anne was no classic beauty but made up for it with charm and personality—she made a room crackle with life by simply stepping into it. A palace servant remembered Anne "for her excellent grace and behavior." Another wrote, "Albeit in beauty she was to many inferior, but for behavior, manner, attire and tongue, she excelled them all, for she had been brought up in France."[15] Her greatest asset was her rapid-fire wit. Conversing with Anne was akin to fencing, the thrusts and retreats of sharp blades.

The Venetian ambassador wrote, "Madame Anne is not one of the handsomest women in the world; she is of middling stature, swarthy complexion, long neck, wide mouth, bosom not much raised, and in fact has nothing but the English king's great appetite and her eyes, which are black and beautiful."[16] Her unbounded self-confidence made her seem beautiful, though her skin was a bit sallow, her chest a bit flat.

Anne led the fashions at Henry's court, trading in the tight wrist-length sleeves for wide sleeves hanging down to the knee. She rejected the unattractive peaked gable headdress for the lovely crescent-shaped French cap. Anne wore rich gowns of royal purple, a color reserved for royalty, embroidered with silver and gold and studded with precious gems.

Her life as queen-in-all-but-name at the numerous Tudor royal palaces was luxurious. The magnificence of the king was manifested in his lodgings, apparel, barges, and coaches. Royal rooms were decorated with elegant tapestries in vivid colors, elaborately carved tables, and chairs upholstered in velvet. Anne sat in the queen's chair of estate at royal events and presided over great feasts. Her huge four-poster bed boasted gold fringe from Venice and gold tassels from Florence. She accompanied the king as he went on his rounds to the various royal palaces—often thirty trips a year.

The court's absence allowed the staff to clean out a residence, wash the walls of urine, sweep out the flea-ridden rushes on the floor, and allow the water supply in palace wells to build up. Henry was one of the few premodern rulers who abhorred dirt. He issued edicts prohibiting urinating in hallways and throwing food on floors. Peeing in the king's cooking hearth was strictly forbidden. Palace officials painted large red crosses on outside walls that were frequent targets of urination in the hopes that no one would want to desecrate such a holy symbol. They were often disappointed.

Henry made sure his palaces had conduit systems, a spring-fed early type of plumbing which used lead pipes to bring water to kitchens, fountains, fishponds, and gardens and had the added value of flushing out the sewers beneath the palace. The royal family, and the most important courtiers, had running water in their own rooms, though it was not usually heated. Henry VIII's bath at Hampton Court, however, had water piped in hot from a stove in the room next door. Despite Henry's momentous efforts to achieve cleanliness, he was often pestered by fleas and lice, and he usually wore a piece of fur to bed in the hopes that the critters would jump on the fur and not on the king.

But the unprecedented cleanliness and luxury of Henry's court were not enough for Anne. She had a political agenda. At Anne's goading, Henry exiled his devoted wife to a drafty castle where she would die, and he publicly proclaimed his daughter,

Princess Mary, a bastard. He then broke from the Catholic Church, putting to death all subjects who would not recognize him as head of the Church of England. He tossed monks and nuns into the streets and grabbed church properties for himself. Time-honored political alliances were shattered, new ones were forged. Like a puppeteer, this not pretty daughter of the minor nobility held the strings to the kings and queens and cardinals of Europe, the pope and the Holy Roman Emperor and, by lifting a finger, made them dance.

Only after six years, when Henry's divorce from Catherine was well under way and Anne the acknowledged fiancée, did she finally accept Henry into her bed. After so many years of waiting we can imagine the blessed release of that first night, the taste of her skin, the feel of his weight, the cries of pure delight in the dark. It was a providential coupling for England. Anne cleverly became pregnant immediately with the greatest monarch the nation would ever have. Desperate for a son, Henry wanted to make sure the prince Anne was carrying would be born within the sacred bonds of marriage, an undisputed legal heir. He secretly married Anne in January 1533.

A century after Henry VIII, the earl of Sandwich said, "He that doth get a wench with child and marries her afterward it is as if a man should shit in his hat and then clap it upon his head."[17] Very soon after his second marriage, Henry must have felt as if he had indeed clapped such a hat upon his head. Anne Boleyn stubbornly gave him a princess—the future Queen Elizabeth—instead of a prince. Nor was the new queen popular with the English people. There were so few cheers during Anne's 1533 coronation that it resembled "a funeral rather than a pageant," wrote the Spanish ambassador.[18]

After her first miscarriage in 1534, Anne knew she was in trouble. Two pregnancies and no son. Henry became impatient; his small eyes narrowed when he looked at her. She tried to revert back to the role of mistress which she had played so well—sexual, scintillating, witty, despite her worry, despite her exhaustion. Yet often she cracked under the strain, letting loose a torrent of vitriol against the very man who had moved heaven and earth to place her on the throne. She hacked away at him with her sharp cleaving tongue, something which patient Queen Catherine had never done.

Thin and worn, her eyes feverishly bright, she looked older than her age. At court her sharp desperation, nervous nastiness, and sense of impending doom contrasted unpleasantly with plump sweet young things buzzing around her. And Anne noticed the king's eye roving to *her* ladies-in-waiting. These ladies no longer hoped only to become the king's mistress; they wanted to become queen. Anne had proven that a queen could easily be replaced; in her greatest victory were the seeds of her ultimate defeat.

But it was the men, after all, who proved more dangerous. On her scramble to the top Anne had alienated powerful courtiers. Sensing Henry's growing dislike of his queen, political factions sprang into action against her. Anne was a religious reformer; there were many at court who yearned to go back to the bosom of the old church and thought that with Anne removed, the king would be so inclined. Politically, Anne was pro-French; she had been raised at the French court and hated Spain, the native land and staunch supporter of Henry's first wife, Queen Catherine. But many at court wanted to drop the French alliance and form one with Spain.

There were those who wanted to remove Anne for reasons of pure personal greed. The cunning Seymour brothers, knowing of the king's increasing interest in their plain sister Jane, saw riches and power coming their way as soon as Anne was gone. Those who had been displaced from lucrative court positions by Anne's powerful family joined the fracas.

Henry, who had waited seven years in a messy divorce from his first wife to marry Anne, was now heartily sick of her and impatient to marry Jane Seymour. He wouldn't tolerate another protracted divorce that raised questions about the legitimacy of future children. The easiest way to disencumber himself from Anne would be to charge her with a capital offense—adultery was always a good missile to sling at a queen—and have her executed. The newly minted widower could then remarry immediately.

Possibly there were more sinister forces at work than just Henry's longing for an heir combined with Anne's political enemies. Some modern scholars believe that the fetus she delivered in January 1536 was deformed, the surest sign of God's displeasure in the sixteenth century. If this was true, Henry must have felt the accusing finger of God pointing straight at him. The king refused to accept the verdict; the deformed child could not have been his. Anne must have had a lover. Moreover, such abominations were Satan's spawn. Anne must have been dabbling in witchcraft.

That theory explains why some courtiers saw Anne holding Elizabeth, a perfectly formed child, up to Henry on the day before her arrest, and arguing emotionally, perhaps trying to prove to him that she brought one well-formed child into the world and could produce another.

Accusations of adultery must always include the name of the lover, preferably a political enemy. Two Boleyn supporters controlled access to the king and would have to be neutralized immediately: Henry Norris—groom of the stool and gentleman of the privy chamber; and William Brereton—a leading gentleman of the privy chamber. While their titles sound humble, these men who handed the king his clothes or tidied up his rooms were immensely powerful. They had the royal ear and permitted or forbade entrée to the king's apartments; it was, indeed, the highest honor to obtain such a position.

George Boleyn, Viscount Rochford, Anne's influential brother, would also have to be removed at the same fell stroke. His wife, Lady Jane Rochford—perhaps revenging herself for his sexual neglect of her—helped the king's case by testifying that she had seen indications of George's sexual involvement with his sister. Two other men—the young musician Mark Smeaton and Sir Francis Weston—had good looks to recommend them as proof of the queen's lasciviousness.

But perhaps there was another reason to choose this particular group of five. If the goal was to remove the Boleyn faction, why were the leaders, her uncle and father, not charged with incest as well? They were far more powerful than any of the five accused. Some scholars think that all of the accused may have been homosexual, a sin considered worthy of death and eternal damnation, and indeed there may be evidence that Anne's brother and Mark Smeaton were involved with each other. Still in existence today is a book from the 1530s attacking the institution of marriage with the names of George Boleyn and Mark S. inscribed in the front. An expensive book, it may have been an unusual and somewhat inappropriate gift from the viscount to the musician.

On May Day 1536, the day when virgins danced around an ancient phallic symbol, decorating it with colored ribbons, when witches were thought to fly through the night sky on brooms, Anne's alleged lovers were arrested. The following day, May 2, Anne herself was arrested. After a brief trial, all five men were found guilty of adultery with the queen and condemned to die.

While most people of the time readily admitted that they were hopeless sinners, the last statements made by the accused men on the scaffold seemed to indicate sins more grievous than usual. Since they were not guilty of adultery, what sins were they referring to? At his death, George Boleyn confessed that he was a great sinner whose sins had deserved death many times over. Brereton implied his innocence of the charge of adultery with the queen but guilt for some other heinous offense. "I have deserved to die if it were a thousand deaths. But the cause whereof I die, judge not," he said.[19]

Weston said his fate was a warning to others not to count on this mortal life, for "I had thought to have lived in abomination yet this twenty or thirty years and then to have made amends."[20] Poor little Smeaton had admitted under torture that he had been the queen's lover. Nor did he deny it on the scaffold, perhaps because such a crime would have been less sinful than his homosexuality. "Masters, I pray you all pray for me for I have deserved this death," he said.[21] Norris said nothing.

Henry, trying hard to believe the allegations which would enable him to marry his sweetheart Jane Seymour in a matter of days, wallowed in self-pity. Most kings with unfaithful wives— truly unfaithful wives—went to great efforts to obtain a divorce without mention of the word *adultery*, which cast suspicion on children of the marriage a well as the king's virility. The Spanish ambassador wrote that no man ever paraded with such frequency the fact that his wife had betrayed him, and with so little sign that he minded. Henry multiplied the number of Anne's lovers until he was convinced she had had no less than a hundred of them.

At her adultery trial on May 15, the queen was accused with dates and places. Yet many are clearly impossible. Two of the dates are October 6 and 12, 1533, at Westminster Palace when Anne was still recuperating from the September birth of Princess Elizabeth. Locked in a darkened room, surrounded by clucking ladies, the queen was not permitted to leave until her "churching" ceremony later in the month. Her supposed rendezvous with Mark Smeaton at Greenwich Palace on May 13, 1535, was also untrue; the queen was then residing at Richmond Palace. Out of twenty encounters, eleven were clearly fabricated.

Oddly, none of Anne's ladies was charged along with her as accessory to her adultery. And surely Henry, in his sweeping capture of knights, pawns, and the queen on his chessboard, would have captured errant ladies-in-waiting. Yet none was ever mentioned—further proof of her innocence.

One eyewitness of the queen's trial reported, "She made so wise and discreet answers to all things laid against her, excusing herself with her words so clearly as though she had never been faulty to the same."[22]

And yet it was clear that Anne had enjoyed flirtations with handsome young courtiers; numerous witnesses attested to it. Before a tribunal of cold-faced judges, jollity of any nature sounds sinful. And particularly for a queen accused of adultery, reports of laughing, flirting, and dancing seemed damning evidence of her sins. It would have been harder to accuse a dull, plodding queen who spent most of her time in church.

Evidently Anne's vivacity was enough to condemn her. The court found, "Because thou has offended our sovereign the king's grace in committing treason against his person and here attainted of the same, the law of the realm is this, that thou hast deserved death, and thy judgment is this: that thou shalt be burned here within the Tower of London, or on the Green, else to have thy head smitten off, as the king's pleasure shall be further known of the same."[23] An odd thing happened when Anne's puppet strings were cut—the puppets remained standing; it was the puppeteer who fell down limp.

Anne was only twenty-nine when she emerged pale and dry-eyed from her long night's vigil in the Tower of London to walk to the scaffold prepared for her. Eyewitnesses reported that on that day, May 19, 1536, she was breathtakingly beautiful. Underneath her white ermine cloak, she wore a black velvet gown edged with pearls over a red quilted petticoat—colors chosen, perhaps, to conceal the blood that would soon wash over them. Anne's behavior had rarely if ever been queenly; but on this day she was truly regal.

The scaffold was three or four feet high, draped in black, surrounded by a crowd, the Lord Mayor and alderman and hundreds of ordinary Englishmen; no foreigners were permitted to see an English queen die. She was given four loyal ladies-in-waiting to accompany her to the edge of eternity.

Witnesses said that on her walk to the scaffold—a walk all too long, all too short—she kept turning around looking perhaps for a messenger to come bearing a royal pardon. She must have hoped that in the last moment, the king, who had once so loved her, would not let her die. Perhaps he would exile her to France, arrange for her to take nun's vows and become an abbess. But after she climbed the scaffold and took one last look around, there was still no messenger.

In the sixteenth century a condemned person was supposed to humbly accept God's will and show courage in the concluding scene that would define an entire life. Ranting against injustice, protesting one's innocence, or trembling with fear was considered to be in very poor taste. Knowing her part, Anne strode front and center for her address. "Good Christian people, I have not come here to preach a sermon; I have come here to die," she began. "For according to the law and by the law I am judged to die, and therefore I will speak nothing against it.

"I am come hither to accuse no man, nor to speak of that whereof I am accused and condemned to die, but I pray God save the king and send him long to reign over you, for a gentler nor a more merciful prince was there never, and to me he was ever a good, a gentle, and sovereign lord. And if any person will meddle in my cause, I require them to judge the best. And thus I take my leave of the world and of you all, and I heartily desire you all to pray for me."[24]

Anne spoke "with a goodly smiling countenance."[25] We can picture her low clear voice carrying over the crowd as the spectators bent forward to catch each word. After her speech, her ladies, weeping, removed her ermine mantle. Anne took off her headdress, showing for a moment the shining raven's wing hair that had bewitched a king, then tucked it up under a cap. This and her low neckline would avoid dulling the sharp stroke of the blade.

She bade farewell to her attendants. One of them tied a handkerchief around her eyes so she would not see the blow coming. She knelt down and repeated the words, "Jesu, receive my soul; O Lord God, have pity on my soul. To Christ I commend my soul!"[26] Suddenly, with one swift blow, it was over, her head rolling on the scaffold. The executioner held it up by the hair. The lips were still moving in prayer.

Her ladies covered the bleeding torso, the bleeding head, in white drapes that all too soon became red, a seething growing inundating red. Neither Henry nor the Tower constable had thought about a coffin for the queen, and so she was placed in a box used to ship bow-staves from the Tower Armory to Ireland. But the box was too short. Only the torso would fit, and her head was tucked underneath her arm. Indeed, it was by this story that nineteenth-century workmen identified her body when they repaved the church in which she had been buried. It was a poor resting place for a queen executed for adultery she did not commit.

"Rose without a Thorn"

After Anne Boleyn's death, the religious reform party was stymied at the advent of her successor, the Catholic Jane Seymour. Important positions at court were taken away from the disgraced Boleyn supporters and given to the Seymour family and their friends. But Jane died in childbirth barely a year after her marriage, and Henry chose as his fourth queen the Protestant Anne of Cleves. Suddenly the reformers were in power, and the Catholics in despair.

Catholics at court hoped to find a young mistress for the king whom they could use to balance the scales in their favor. Anne Boleyn's uncle, Lord Thomas Howard, duke of Norfolk, who had obtained royal permission to remain Catholic throughout the English reformation, was now itching to throw one of his numerous attractive nieces into the royal bed. He was delighted when nineteen-year-old Catherine Howard, a new maid of honor to Anne of Cleves, came to court and immediately won the king's favor. One Howard relative reported that the "King's Highness did cast a fantasy to Catherine Howard the first time that ever his Grace saw her."[27]

It would be a meteoric rise in the fortunes of a neglected girl. As a daughter of an impoverished younger son of the Howard clan, her mother dead, Catherine was sent at about the age of ten to live with the crusty old matriarch of the Howards, Agnes, dowager duchess of Norfolk. Catherine slept with other girls and servants in a dormitory on the top floor of the house. As the years passed she grew into a beautiful voluptuous teenager, but her mind remained that of a child, empty-headed, thoughtless, and impetuous.

If we are to judge by Catherine's only extant letter, she could barely write. The dowager duchess believed a girl's education consisted mainly of housekeeping, good manners, spinning, embroidery, and a little music. In 1536 the grande dame asked Henry Manox, the son of a neighbor, to instruct the girls on the lute and the virginals. Manox fell in love with the fifteen-year-old Catherine who, though not in love herself, was interested in his advances.

Knowing that Manox inhabited too low an orbit to marry, Catherine wisely refused him intercourse. But he pressured her to at least let him feel her private parts. "I am content," Catherine replied, "so as you will desire no more but that."[28] The two met in a dark and empty chapel, and so the thing was done. The dowager duchess, catching the two of them fondling each other, boxed the young man's ears and sent him on his way.

Having won this much from Catherine, Manox boasted to the other servants that he would marry her. Mary Lassells, the duchess's maid, upbraided Manox for daring to marry a Howard. But he told her to hold her peace. "I know her well enough for I have had her by the cunt, and I know it among a hundred," he affirmed. "And she loves me and I love her, and she hath said to me that I shall have her maidenhead, though it be painful to her, and not doubting but I will be good to her hereafter."[29]

But by now Catherine had a better prospect than Manox the music master. Francis Dereham, of good birth and some wealth, was a gentleman-pensioner of the duke of Norfolk and visited the duchess's household regularly. Dereham possessed the exquisite manners of a young courtier; he was extremely handsome and well-dressed. Catherine nearly toppled over with love for him at first sight.

The girls' dormitory was locked every night but the ardent swains intent upon visiting their sweethearts had several options. They could climb up the lattice to an upstairs window. Some of them could pick the lock of the dormitory door. If all else failed, one of the girls could steal the key from the duchess's chamber after she had fallen sound asleep. From 1537 to 1539 Catherine made merry with Francis Dereham in the dormitory at night. Dereham and the other visiting suitors brought with them "wine, strawberries, apples, and other things to make good cheer."[30]

It was here, then, if not before with Manox, that Catherine lost her virginity with Francis Dereham. She would later acknowledge that they had become "carnal lovers."[31] Later, one witness said that Mistress Catherine "was so far in love" with Dereham that they embraced "after a wonderful manner, for they would kiss and hang their bellies together as they were two sparrows."[32]

Catherine would draw her heavy bed curtains when Dereham came to call, yet many dormitory residents not so fortunate to have lovers complained about the noise. One of them, Alice Restwold, protested that "she was a married woman and wist what matrimony meant and what belonged to that puffing and blowing" that went on in bed.[33]

Catherine knew something of primitive means of birth control. At one point, when warned that she could get pregnant, she replied that "a woman might meddle with a man and yet conceive no child unless she would herself."[34]

Catherine and Dereham considered themselves married and, indeed, in the eyes of the Church, they could have been, if they privately exchanged vows of their intention to marry and had sexual relations. When acquaintances suggested that Dereham show less affection for Catherine in public, he retorted, "Who should hinder him from kissing his own wife?"[35] Though from a better family than Manox, even Dereham was no match for a Howard and Catherine must have known it. Dereham pushed her for marriage, and she toyed with him. But Fate had a grander marriage in store for Catherine Howard.

We can picture the Howard clan watching with eagle eyes when Henry first met his new bride, Anne of Cleves, on January 3, 1540. They must have crowed with delight at the royal bride-groom's horror of his wife's appearance. She was tall, poorly built, with pockmarked skin and no social graces whatsoever—quite a contrast to plump, petite Catherine. The king dubbed Anne his "Flanders mare." Two days before the wedding, Henry growled, "If it were not that she had come so far into my realm, and the great preparations and state that my people have made for her, and for fear of making a ruffle in the world and of driving her brother into the arms of the Emperor and the French King, I would not now marry her. But now it is too far gone, wherefore I am sorry."[36]

Henry claimed he could not consummate the marriage because "her body was disordered and indisposed to provoke or excite any lust in him." He said that he "could not overcome his loathsomeness" of her, "nor in her company be provoked or stirred to the Act." His doctor advised the king not to force himself, as this might cause an inconvenient debility of the royal private parts. Anne was delighted to find that in the divorce agreement, she was given two palaces, a generous income, several carriages, a large retinue of servants, and the right to retain her head.

The king was suddenly single once more, and the successful candidate would be much more than his mistress; she would be queen of England. Seizing on Henry's clear interest in Catherine, the duke of Norfolk dangled her in front of the king like bait. Catherine, the neglected, impoverished niece who had been sent to court with modest attire, suddenly began appearing in a tantalizing array of gowns and glittering jewels. Her large tribal family showered the court with praise for "her pure and honest condition."[37] Eager to please her family, the king began to swing his ponderous bulk away from religious reform and back in the direction of orthodoxy.

But silly Catherine was a poor candidate for queen. Like a good-natured dog, she thought only of present enjoyment or pain. Thinking of past errors or future repercussions seemed beyond her limited intellectual capacity. She enjoyed each moment to the utmost until the master's voice bellowed loud and threatening. Then she feared and, like a dog, did not understand the words but only that she would undergo imminent punishment.

Nonetheless, pushed by her ambitious relatives, flattered by the urgent suit of the king, Catherine married Henry on July 28, 1540. Almost immediately, the queen was obliged to fill her household with Howard relatives and supporters. She persuaded Henry to grant manor houses, rich estates, and revenues to her relatives and their friends. In August 1541 she was foolish enough to make Francis Dereham—her former lover and perhaps her legal husband—her private secretary.

Bitter jealousy arose at court among those who had lost their positions to the Howards. The Seymour family in particular were furious that many of them had been replaced by the queen's supporters. A more intelligent woman would have used her position as queen to make peace among the factions, strewing some appointments and favors in the enemy's direction to maintain equilibrium. But Catherine was the thoughtless tool of her relentlessly ambitious uncle and obediently fulfilled all his commands.

Only five years earlier, Catherine's first cousin, the brilliant and manipulative Anne Boleyn, had fallen to her enemies. How was the harebrained Catherine to survive in a scorpion's nest of intrigue? Sitting at the apex of Howard ambitions, Catherine was the weakest link in their faction. If the silly girl were to fall, so would they all.

Initially she was protected by Henry's extravagant demonstrations of love. Recapturing the passions of youth for the last time, the king called Catherine a "jewel of womanhood"[38] and his "rose without a thorn."[39] The French ambassador reported that he had "never seen the King in such good spirits or in so good a humor."[40] One chronicler wrote, "the King had no wife who made him spend so much money in dresses and jewels as she did, who every day had some fresh caprice."[41] For Christmas and New Year's gifts in 1540, Henry gave her a brooch "containing 27 table diamonds and 26 clusters of pearls," another brooch made of 33 diamonds and 60 rubies surrounded by pearls; and a "muffler of black velvet furred with sables containing 38 rubies and 572 pearls."[42]

Catherine, though she loved the jewels, gowns, and parties that came with her new position, was bored in her husband's presence and repulsed by him physically. At fifty, the king was often ill, cantankerous, and impatient. He had swelled to some 350 pounds. Each day a festering ulcer on his thigh had to be drained of foul-smelling liquid. When it clogged up, the king suffered painful fevers until the liquid ran free again. The French ambassador wrote home after one bout of fever, "This King's life was really thought to be in danger not from the fever but from the leg which often troubles him because he is very stout and marvelously excessive in eating and drinking."[43]

Household accounts from around this time show several bills from tailors for letting out the king's doublets. According to one courtier, "The King was so fat that three of his biggest men that could be found could get inside his doublet."[44] Even his beds had to be enlarged and given extra supports to accommodate his increasing bulk.

Let us imagine the queen's duties in the royal four-poster. The king would likely have suffocated his petite bride if he had perched on top of her. He must have required her to ride astride him, careful not to disturb the stinking wound on his thigh. She who had played with the charming Manox, who had rutted with the sexy Dereham, now had to perform loathsome sex acts on an obese and smelly old man. We can picture the happy king, perfectly sated, snoring, as his young wife lay silently beside him, her heart sinking. And the following day her bright eyes wandered to the young and handsome courtiers dancing gracefully before her as she sat on the throne next to Henry, who was too fat to dance.

It was no surprise that Catherine fell in love. Thomas Culpeper, a gentleman of the king's privy chamber and a favorite of Henry's, was in his late twenties, personable and polished. Culpeper was young while the king was old, slender and healthy while the king was fat and sick, merry while the king was sullen. Trim and athletic, the virile Culpeper offered her exquisite delights instead of the rising disgust she must have felt in bed with Henry. There was no festering sore on his muscular thigh, no mountain of fat on his tight belly.

Every queen must be aided and abetted by a loyal lady-in-waiting to hide her love affair, and Catherine was assisted by Lady Jane Rochford, who had been married to Anne Boleyn's brother. Every few weeks when the court moved to a different palace, Lady Rochford chose for the queen the rooms with an easy escape route, a secret staircase or garden door. In the only extant letter written entirely in her own hand, Catherine wrote Culpeper, "Come when my Lady Rochford is here for then I shall be best at leisure to be at your commandment."[45]

When Henry made a royal progress through northern England in the fall of 1541, Catherine and Culpeper had sex on several occasions. The obliging Lady Rochford whispered to Culpeper how and when to enter the queen's chamber. While staying at Pontefract Castle, the king knocked loudly on the queen's door while she was in bed with her lover, and only after some time did Lady Rochford open the door.

Courtiers could see that the queen was in love with Culpeper by simply looking at her when she spoke to him. Indeed, everyone seemed to know except Henry, living in a state of second youth and marital bliss. The day before he found out about Catherine's unchaste past, the king gave a public thanksgiving for his virtuous queen. As courtiers tried to keep a straight face, the king proclaimed, "I render thanks to thee, O Lord, that after so many strange accidents that have befallen my marriages, Thou hast been pleased to give me a wife so entirely conformed to my wishes as her I now have."[46]

The plotters and planners of the queen's downfall could not move too hastily. They needed time, needed evidence. Indeed, it was a servant who suddenly caused the house of cards to fall, John Lassells, whose sister Mary Lassells, chamber woman to the dowager duchess, was well aware of Catherine's loud nighttime activities in the dormitory. One day when the fiercely Protestant John Lassells was bemoaning the rise of the Catholic faction, his sister, now Mary Hall, said of the queen, "Let her alone, for if she holds on as she begins we shall hear she will be nought within a while."[47] Mary, furious that she had not been given a plum position at court by Catherine, as so many other dormitory girls had been, told how Manox had boasted that he had fondled the queen's private parts. Delighted, John Lassells informed the council in London.

In October 1541 the three ministers left in charge of London during the king's progress were informed by John Lassells that the queen had "lived most corruptly and sensually." The powerful Howard council members were traveling with the king and the three members left behind were all Howard enemies, including Jane Seymour's still influential brother Edward. They were delighted at the accusation, though no one had the courage to tell the king the news. Finally, Archbishop Thomas Cranmer wrote a delicately worded letter and handed it to the king when he returned.

Instead of becoming angry at the accusation, Henry was perplexed. He thought it was probably idle gossip sprung from jealous women, or a plot set afoot by religious reformers displeased by a Catholic queen. Nonetheless, he instructed the council to investigate the rumor. John Lassells and Mary Hall were both interviewed. Based on their testimony the music master, Henry Manox was called in and admitted that he "used to feel the secret and other parts of the Queen's body." Unwilling to remain the focus of the investigation, Manox tipped off investigators to the existence of his more successful rival, Francis Dereham. Hauled before the inquisitors, a trembling Dereham foolishly admitted that he "had known her carnally many times, both in his doublet and hose between the sheets and in naked bed."[48]

Henry met with the privy council who read him the confessions of Manox and Dereham. Black rage bubbled up in him like poison. And the sudden realization swept over him that he was old, that he was obese, that he was repulsive in every way. She had never loved him. She had pretended. *Pretended* to love him as she pocketed his jewels and costly gifts, as her ambitious family grasped at pensions and appointments.

Trembling with rage, the king called for a sword to kill the woman who had betrayed him, swearing she would never have "such delight in her incontinency as she should have torture in her death."[49] Then he collapsed into a fit of weeping. Wiping tears from his fat cheeks, the king bewailed his "ill luck in meeting such ill-conditioned wives" and blamed his council for "this last mischief."[50] By the time his tears had dried, his youth had vanished forever.

Catherine, oblivious to the danger, was dancing in her chamber with her maidens when the guards came to arrest her. The captain told her it was "no more the time to dance."[51] On November 7 the queen herself was interrogated by Archbishop Cranmer who reported, "I found her in such lamentation and heaviness as I never saw no creature, so that it would have pitied any man's heart to have looked upon her."[52] He actually feared for her sanity.

Sobbing, Catherine denied she had done anything wrong. Initially she claimed that Dereham had forced her with "violence rather than of her free consent and will."[53] Then she admitted in some confusion that Dereham had "lain with me, sometimes in his doublet and hose, and two or three times naked; but not so naked that he had nothing upon him, for he had always at least his doublet and as I do think, his hose also, but I mean naked when his hose were put down."[54]

She submitted a confession of sorts to the king, begging his forgiveness. "I your grace's most sorrowful subject and most vile wretch in the world, not worthy to make any recommendations unto your most excellent majesty, do only make my most humble submission and confession of my faults." She explained, "First at the flattering and fair persuasions of Manox, being but a young girl, [I] suffered him at sundry times to handle and touch the secret parts of my body which neither became me with honesty to permit nor him to require. Also Francis Dereham by many persuasions procured me to his vicious purpose and obtained first to lie upon my bed with his doublet and hose and after within the bed and finally he lay with me naked, and used me in such sort as a man doth his wife many and sundry times, but how often I know not. . . ."[55]

She excused herself for not telling the king during their courtship of her unchaste past because "I was so desirous to be taken unto your grace's favor and so blinded with the desire of worldly glory that I could not, nor had grace to, consider how great a fault it was to conceal my former faults from your majesty, considering that I intended ever during my life to be faithful and true unto your majesty after."[56]

The queen refuted any marriage precontract with Dereham, which would have invalidated her royal marriage and could have saved her from the wrath of Henry if he had never legally been her husband. Dereham, however, asserted that they were precontracted to each other, pleading that he was therefore innocent of debauching a maiden. But Henry was less concerned at the technicalities of a possible precontract than by the fact that Catherine had taken Dereham into her service at court. If she had been truly sorrowful about her unchaste past, why would she want her former lover there as a constant reminder? Did she take Dereham into her bed *after* marriage?

At this point Catherine's crime was—perhaps—bigamy. There was no law on the books requiring candidates for the position of queen to tell the king of all past sexual activities. Catherine must have been praying that her escapades with Culpeper would not be revealed. But it was Dereham, clapped in prison, who led investigators to her extramarital affair. In a cowardly attempt to prove he had not slept with the queen since her marriage, he pointed out that Thomas Culpeper had been the sole object of her desires.

When questioned about Culpeper, Catherine said that it was Lady Rochford who had pushed her into his arms, arranging secret meetings with him that Catherine wanted to avoid. Lady Rochford, for her part, said she was merely following the queen's orders to arrange meetings for the two. She believed "that Culpeper hath known the queen carnally considering all things that she hath heard and seen between them."[57]

Lady Rochford went mad on the third day of her imprisonment. Such information extracted from her about the queen's adultery was only available during her brief moments of lucidity. Perhaps guilt had driven her mad, guilt at sending her husband to the scaffold with a pack of lies years before. Revenge for his not wanting her, for ignoring her as she lay in bed panting with desire, while he went out to find a man. Now, with exquisite irony, she would meet the identical fate as George Boleyn. The Spanish ambassador wrote, "Lady Rochford would have been tried and sentenced at the same time, but on the third day of her imprisonment she went mad. She recovers her reason now and then, and the King . . . gets his own physicians to visit her, desiring her recovery that he may afterwards have her executed as an example."[58]

Under interrogation, Culpeper insisted that he was the innocent victim of the queen's unquenchable desire. Catherine, he said, demanded they meet, as she was "languishing and dying for love for him."[59] He finally confessed that "he intended and meant to do ill with the queen and that in like wise the queen so minded to do with him."[60] This was Catherine's death blow, for if Henry could have forgiven her for an unchaste past before she met him, he could never do so for sullying the marriage bed and taking the risk of presenting him with a spurious heir.

Howard enemies, seizing upon this good fortune, tried to implicate the entire clan in a conspiracy, hoping to topple the too-powerful duke of Norfolk. Many Howard relatives and supporters were imprisoned for weeks or months. Indeed, so many were thrown into the Tower that the constable had to move out and give his own rooms to prisoners.

The duke of Norfolk, who had placed two queens on Henry's throne, both of whom were accused of adultery, was seen stumbling about the palace wiping tears from his eyes, bewailing that his nieces had caused the king such pain. He wrote a pitiful letter to Henry begging him not to "conceive a displeasure" against him, who was "prostrate at your royal feet."[61] He called Catherine his "ungrateful niece" and loudly proclaimed that she should be burned alive.[62]

His histrionics must have worked, for everyone in the clan remotely involved in the case was tossed in prison except for the duke. Even the squawking old dowager duchess was thrown in jail, though her worst fear was that Catherine, rejected by the king, would be sent back to make trouble once more in the dormitory. She was shocked when all Howard prisoners were tried, found guilty of concealing treason, and sentenced to life imprisonment and forfeiture of goods.

Over the ensuing months, however, one by one the prisoners were quietly released and their goods restored to them. Those relatives fortunate enough to avoid prison put on their richest finery and paraded through the streets to show they did not care about Catherine's fate. The French ambassador reported to his king that such behavior was "the custom and must be done to show that they did not share the crimes of their relatives."[63]

Imprisoned for three months in Syon House outside of London, Catherine seemed not to understand what was happening. Her spirits bounced back and she spent her time "making good cheer, fatter and handsomer than ever."[64] She spent hours in front of the mirror trying on jewelry.

Dereham and Culpeper were sentenced to the full rigor of a traitor's death, but Culpeper, being a gentleman at court with influential friends, found his sentence commuted to a merciful beheading. It is ironic that the man who had slept with Catherine after her marriage was given a lesser punishment than the man who had slept with her before. On December 10, 1541, the sentences were carried out. Dereham, for having robbed the queen of her virginity, was hanged until nearly unconscious, cut down, his private parts cut off and thrown into the fire as he watched; he was then slit open and disemboweled, and finally beheaded. The heads of Dereham and Culpeper adorned Tower Bridge and slowly rotted; Dereham's arms and legs graced other buildings.

Manox seems to have disappeared from the scene after his interrogation. Detailed Tudor records mention no fine, imprisonment, or execution. Perhaps he fled England, or faded into a welcome mundane life with a woman who would never become a queen.

A new law was passed retroactively that stated if the king should "take a fancy to any woman," believing her to be "a pure and clean maid when indeed the proof may or shall after appear contrary," and should the lady "couple herself with her Sovereign Lord" without informing him of "her unchaste life," then "every such offense shall be deemed and adjudged High Treason."[65]

Most adultery trials of queens were closed, their details hidden from public view, but Henry invited all the foreign ambassadors to witness this one. Indeed, the French ambassador wrote to King François I in Paris, "Many people thought the publication of the foul details strange, but the intention is to prevent it being said afterwards that they were unjustly condemned."[66] And condemned they were. On February 11, 1542, Catherine's death warrant for high treason was signed, along with that of Lady Rochford.

After having lived a thoughtless life, Catherine gave great thought to her death. She asked that a block be brought in to the Tower so she could practice laying her head on it properly and not feel awkward the morning of her execution. Since dying well was considered even more important than living well, for it was the last impression left behind, Catherine met death with a dignity she had never possessed in life.

And so Catherine Howard was sacrificed to the vicious ambitions of the Howard clan and their jealous enemies. Just as in the sacrifice of an ox in the ancient world, she was laden with flowers and marched to an altar where, soon after, the swift flash of steel ended her life.

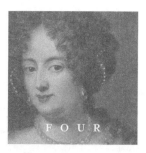

FOUR

THE SEVENTEENTH CENTURY: ESCAPE FROM THE GILDED CAGE

For glances beget ogles, ogles sighs,
Sighs wishes, wishes words, and words a letter . . .
And then, God knows what mischief may arise,
When love links two young people in one fetter,
Vile assignations, and adulterous beds,
Elopements, broken vows and hearts and heads.

—LORD BYRON

✻

SEVENTEENTH-CENTURY MONARCHS WERE SOMEWHAT LESS
brutal to their unfaithful wives than Henry VIII; though some
queen consorts indeed lost their heads over handsome men, not
a single one did so in the literal sense. Many hoped to escape
from the servitude of an unhappy marriage, though this was usually only possible in widowhood. A divorce or annulment offered
jubilant freedom spiced with disgrace. And some dreamed of
true escape, the escape of simply running away.

"This Disagreeable Frenchwoman"

The summer of 1666, the eighteen-year-old Princess Maria Francisca Isabel de Savoy arrived with her retinue in Lisbon harbor to marry King Alfonso VI of Portugal. Delighted at the prospect of being a queen, she had turned a deaf ear to rumors that her new husband was fat, impotent, and mentally retarded. Many people were just jealous, she thought. True, the king had suffered a nearly fatal fever at the age of three which left him slightly paralyzed on his right side. True, his tutors had given up in despair trying to make him sit still and learn something. True, he had once tried to shoot a comet out of the sky, and his favorite pastime was galloping through the streets with his ruffian friends, knocking down pedestrians. But most kings suffered from some debility or other, and at twenty-three, he really couldn't be all that bad.

When the satin-clad crowds rushed onto her ship to welcome their new queen, Maria Francisca looked about for her new husband in vain. King Alfonso was in the palace hiding. He did not want to get married and had only agreed to it once he realized a refusal would result in his throne going to his younger brother, Pedro. Pedro, handsome, intelligent, beloved by all. Pedro, whom the Portuguese would have preferred as their king. Alfonso would do anything to prevent Pedro from ascending the throne, even if it meant that Alfonso, hopelessly impotent, married a princess.

The king had tried to counter the reputation of his impotence by surrounding himself with the most infamous prostitutes, whom he paid generously to tell stories of his sexual exploits. He even found a little girl who resembled him and, claiming her as his illegitimate daughter, brought her out at public events. The child's mother was forced to walk along casting longing glances at the king, which he ardently returned. Only later did she swear that she had never had sex with the king, though he had tried, and the child had been fathered by her cousin.

Now despite all his efforts at pretended virility, Alfonso had been backed into a corner. If he had stayed a bachelor, his incapacity might have been rumored but never proved. Now it was only a matter of time before the whole world knew for sure.

And now, with the bride waiting, Alfonso's anxious ministers finally prevailed upon the king to row out to the ship. At first glance Maria Francisca finally understood all the rumors about her new husband. He was so terribly obese that he looked like a huge barrel set on two stubby pegs. Too lazy to leave his bed for meals, Alfonso was served his huge portions lying down. Required to hear Mass in the morning, he allowed the priests to celebrate it in his bedroom but insisted they not wake him.

Alfonso was so terrified of catching cold when he did venture forth that he wore six or seven mismatched coats, one on top of the other, and three or four hats, perched one on top of the other. When this epitome of royal grandeur was presented to his lovely bride, he made a face—a grin thought some, a grimace said others—and left. The new queen looked with shock at the ungainly bulk of her retreating husband, and then her eyes strayed to his handsome, slender brother bowing before her. It must have been a relief to her in the coming months that her repulsive husband never once touched her. The king rarely set foot in the queen's apartments, but his brother visited for several hours each day. Bereft of a real husband, Maria Francisca became close—some said too close—to her brother-in-law.

Because the marriage remained unconsummated, Prince Pedro and the queen were keenly aware of the possibility of an annulment. And if the marriage were annulled, perhaps they could receive a papal dispensation and marry each other. If Alfonso were put away for mental incompetence, they could rule Portugal. To this end they formed their own faction at court—the anti-Alfonso faction—and started winning powerful courtiers over to their side. For Alfonso was no better a king than he was a husband; his cruel favorites acted with impunity, and the country was swiftly falling into a state of anarchy. The queen's relationship with Pedro offered political advantages to the nobles who encouraged it. No outraged accusations of adultery would echo through the Portuguese court to condemn the queen.

Alfonso, fascinated by sex despite his impotence, often hired talented prostitutes to climb into his bed and stimulate him as best they could. When he had had enough, he invited his friends, who had been watching, to jump into bed and finish the business. The king received a certain satisfaction from watching others reach climax even if he could not.

The queen, unconcerned by her husband's pathetic escapades with whores, was deeply concerned that he seemed desirous of doing the same thing with her—playing with her and then calling in his favorites to finish the job so she would become pregnant. A pregnancy would solve all his problems; he would remain king, a virile potent king, and eclipse the despised Pedro forever.

Beginning in April 1667 Alfonso continually solicited Maria Francisca to visit him in his apartments late at night in the company of two of his lusty favorites. According to custom, if the king wanted to sleep with the queen at night, he went to *her* apartments, with her ladies hovering nearby, never the other way around. Suspecting what he had in mind, the queen politely refused to visit him in his apartments. His face red with rage, Alfonso put his hand on his sword and vowed that if she did not come of her own accord within twenty-four hours, he would drag her to his bed or have her carried there by four of his attendants.

Maria Francisca, never knowing when she would be carted into the king's rooms and raped, finally had enough. On November 22, 1667, she retired to a convent and sent word to Alfonso that she considered the marriage null and void due to nonconsummation after sixteen months. As soon as the king received the letter, he raced to the convent to drag her out. When the doors were not opened despite his furious knocking, Alfonso called for axes to break them down. At that point Prince Pedro arrived with a large retinue of armed men vowing to defend the queen, and the defeated monarch rode slowly home.

Alfonso's worst nightmare had come true. When he waddled

back to the palace, he was taken prisoner and admitted his impotence under questioning. The bishop of Lisbon decreed the marriage null and void.

When the queen wrote the council asking permission to return home with her dowry, the councilors presented themselves at the convent door with hats in their hands and tears in their eyes, begging her not to abandon the realm. And besides, they had already spent the dowry. Exactly as she had foreseen, they implored her to marry Pedro and stay on as their queen. Everyone admired the way she had deftly handled her idiot husband. Portugal needed such a queen. The council went to Pedro and begged him to marry Maria Francisca for the good of the nation. The prince gallantly replied that he would. But when they asked him to accept the throne as well, Pedro refused. As a matter of honor, he would not become king as long as his brother lived, but would rule for him as regent.

Alfonso was placed in genteel confinement. When the deposed monarch learned that his marriage had been annulled and his bride handed over to Pedro, he said, "Ah, well! I don't doubt that my poor brother will soon regret having been mixed up with this disagreeable Frenchwoman as much as I do."[1]

Maria Francisca had gotten the man she wanted, kept her position as Portugal's highest lady, and nine months after the wedding gave birth to a daughter. Despite her happiness, she never forgave her former husband and reveled in disparaging him. "After getting drunk according to his wont," she wrote her sister, "he fell with his head in a basin of water, where he would certainly have been drowned if someone had not promptly pulled him out; but though he lives as a brute beast, he lives, and that is sufficient to keep us always anxious and exposed to the malice of our enemies."[2] Like Maria Francisca, many Portuguese feared that if Alfonso escaped, he would round up his former favorites, punish those who had deposed him and wreak havoc in the realm.

Though poison never passed Alfonso's lips, Pedro made sure that plenty of alcohol did, in the hopes that his brother would drink himself to death. One day, however, Alfonso pledged himself to sobriety, much to the irritation of the Portuguese government. The ambassador of Savoy wrote that Alfonso's Jesuit jailer had spoken of his regained health with "evident regret."[3]

But in the end it was food, not liquor, that did him in. With nothing to do, the prisoner grew fatter than ever. He could barely rise from his bed and had difficulty fitting through a doorway. According to some reports, walking became such an ordeal that he would lie down on the floor and call for an attendant to roll him down the hallway. After fifteen years' confinement he died of a stroke in 1683 at the age of forty. Pedro and Maria Francisca became king and queen in name as well as in fact.

The Portuguese prided themselves on the fact that Alfonso had lived so many years after his abdication despite the threat he posed. "If these things had happened in Spain," a Jesuit priest cheerfully pointed out to the ambassador of Savoy, "the King of Portugal would not have lasted so long; but here we are good Christians."[4]

MARGUERITE-LOUISE OF FRANCE, GRAND DUCHESS OF TUSCANY

"You Would Never Die but by My Hand"

The one royal woman to escape her marital prison without the sudden blessing of widowhood or annulment was Marguerite-Louise d'Orléans, the first cousin of Louis XIV. In 1661, at the age of sixteen, the princess was married by proxy to Duke Cosimo de Medici, heir to the Tuscan throne of his father, Grand Duke Ferdinand II. The bride was petite, voluptuous, and boasted sparkling turquoise eyes and chestnut ringlets. When marriage negotiations had commenced three years earlier, the prospective groom was struck with wonder by her portrait, and she was suitably impressed by his.

But by the time the marriage contract was signed, Marguerite had fallen deeply in love with her cousin, Prince Charles of Lorraine. A swashbuckling soldier, the eighteen-year-old stormed Versailles with the irresistible aroma of gunpowder wafting about him. The young man, recently captured on the field of battle, could boast of having just been released from a Spanish prison. Of royal blood, Charles would have made an acceptable bridegroom for a French princess.

But Louis XIV had already signed the marriage documents with the court of Tuscany. Refusing to go back on his word and lose his royal dignity, he forced his cousin to fulfill his contractual obligations. Marguerite, however, was born with an uncontrollable temperament ill-suited to her royal position. Even as a child, she did not accept refusals meekly. Once, when she was told she could not go riding, she broke down the stable door, soundly cursing the grooms who stood by helplessly, grabbed a saddle, and threw it on the horse herself. Neither would she accept her marriage obediently. When the groom sent her an enormous diamond engagement ring, to show her disdain of her future husband, Marguerite gave it to one of her ladies-in-waiting.

En route to her new realm, the bride dawdled, insisting on staying longer in various cities than planned, intentionally upsetting the elaborate preparations made for her along the way and her grand welcome to Tuscany. When she finally met her groom, she wished that she had dawdled longer. Instead of the attractive prince depicted in the portrait, Marguerite's husband had bulging eyes, a jutting chin, thick wavy red lips, and large deformed ears that poked through his long curly hair. The unappealing head topped a thick squat body.

Worse than his physical appearance was his personality—"melancholy and somber," according to the bishop of Marseille.[5] Cosimo spent most of his time on his knees in front of an altar, praying. His new wife, however, "is all gallantry; she likes nothing more than singing, dancing and giving parties," according to the envoy of the republic of Luca. "The prince is all gravity," wrote the papal nuncio, "but the princess loves nothing more than laughing."[6] It was agreed that never were two characters so vastly different in temperament and education.

Marguerite cast a disapproving glance around the rather moldy grandeur of Florence. When asked how she liked her new land, she invariably replied that she would rather be back in France. Cosimo gave splendid balls, sumptuous feasts, ballets, and plays to entertain his bride, but nothing, she sniffed, could compare to the splendor of those held at the court of Versailles.

The princess found not only his theatrical performances lackluster, but also his sexual performance. After a full month of marriage, "The prince only rendered his marital duty to her three times," the Florentine bishop wrote to the French minister Nicolas Fouquet. "On all other evenings he sent a valet to her chambers saying he would not require her services that evening. Her French ladies-in-waiting expressed surprise at such compliments." The bride's sister explained, "This small show of eagerness made her put her back up and became the pretext for sour wrangling."[7]

Perhaps as punishment for her husband's lack of ardor, or the fact that she had been forced against her will to marry him in the first place, Marguerite lavishly spent his money. Her cook was ordered to obtain the most expensive meats; her kitchen cost more for one day's meals than the grand duke spent in ten. When a merchant showed her dozens of costly bolts of fabric, she took them all and told him to send the bill to her father-in-law. Leaving the palace empty-handed, the ecstatic merchant— suddenly rich—ran into the grand duke and thanked him profusely for his generosity.

As retribution for her wild spending and bad temper, Grand Duke Ferdinand ordered home Marguerite's retinue of French ladies. As revenge, she gave the women some of the most dazzling crown jewels of Tuscany to smuggle back to France. Only with difficulty were they retrieved.

When a royal woman wished to leave the palace, protocol demanded that she obtain permission from her husband, order the royal carriage and the entourage of cavalry to escort her, and climb in with her ladies-in-waiting. But Marguerite took to coming and going as she pleased, simply walking out of the palace alone and disappearing for hours. Her father-in-law put bolts on all her apartment doors, even those leading to the gardens, and set spies among her staff. She was allowed to emerge from her prison for two purposes—promenades along country paths just outside Florence and court events.

Marguerite used court events as opportunities to insult her husband, stating loudly that he not only made a terrible prince, he would make a terrible stable boy, and that she would rather roast in hell without him than luxuriate in paradise with him. As chastisement, the grand duke sent her to a lonely hunting lodge in the swamps, with forty soldiers and six horsemen to follow her wherever she went to make sure she did not run away. But Marguerite ran so fast, so far, for so many hours, that upon their return to the palace the soldiers were seen gasping for breath and clutching their sides in pain.

When Marguerite caught malaria, she claimed the royal family of Tuscany was trying to murder her, but that she would, in fact, rather die than return to her husband. Louis XIV asked the pope to threaten excommunication if Marguerite persisted, and the pontiff sent her a harsh letter. She didn't fear hell, she replied. She was already living in it.

It is, perhaps, a miracle that in nine years Marguerite gave birth to three children. Furious each time she learned that she was pregnant, she tried to induce a miscarriage by vigorous riding. When she was forbidden access to the stables, she insisted on exhausting walks for hours in the gardens. When these, too, were prohibited, she tried to starve herself to death, but her hunger proved greater than her resolve.

Much to Duke Cosimo's dismay, Charles of Lorraine visited Florence frequently. Over the years the duchess took lowborn lovers and was even thought to have invited strapping Gypsy youths into her bed. Duke Cosimo averted his eyes to men of negligible rank; but when he found a steamy love letter from Charles of Lorraine, he was aghast at her betrayal with a worthy rival.

In 1670 Grand Duke Ferdinand died. Cosimo was now grand duke and Marguerite grand duchess. But despite all the glory of her new position, by 1672 Marguerite had had enough. While visiting a Tuscan town, she wrote her husband that she would never return to him. She informed Louis XIV that there was no point in continuing the marriage—both she and her husband had committed adultery at least fifty times. Abandoning her three children, she wanted permission to return to Paris where she could have fun. But Louis XIV did not want her back in France as solid proof of a humiliating French failure at the Tuscan court. And the Tuscans *did* want her in Tuscany as their grand duchess, not a Tuscan failure at the French court. Louis informed her that if a French princess left her husband to return to France, her new home would be the Bastille.

By sheer strength of will, the indomitable Marguerite finally got her way. Exhausted by her wrangling, in 1675 Louis XIV and Grand Duke Cosimo III decided she could return to France if she lived quietly in a Paris convent away from court. But Marguerite was not the kind of woman to live quietly in a convent. She left the convent at will, attending parties at court and ridiculing her husband and the entire Tuscan nation to the delighted laughter of French courtiers. She ran up huge bills which her husband was expected to pay. And she took her pick of lovers from among servants, stable boys, and the wandering fortune-tellers who visited her.

"No hour of the day passes when I do not desire your death and wish that you were hanged . . . ," she informed Cosimo in what must be one of the nastiest letters ever written. "What aggravates me most of all is that we shall both go to the devil and then I shall have the torment of seeing you even there. . . . I swear by what I loathe above all else, that is yourself, that I shall make a pact with the devil to enrage you and to escape your madness. Enough is enough, I shall engage in any extravagance I so wish in order to bring you unhappiness. . . . If you think you can get me to come back to you, this will never happen, and if I came back to you, beware! Because you would never die but by my hand."[8]

When a strict new prioress at the convent prevented her from coming and going at will, Marguerite set fire to the building as an excuse to move out. Servants reported one day seeing the grand duchess of Tuscany chase the prioress around the convent with an axe in one hand and a pistol in the other, swearing that she would kill her. An exasperated Louis XIV finally forbade her coming to court. Marguerite continued spewing her venom at the Medici family and the Tuscan people until her death at the age of seventy-six in 1721. She was one of the few princesses ever to break free from the slavery of an unhappy marriage, and she had done so only through a fearless toxic nastiness that verged on the psychotic.

Princesses better natured than Marguerite had a harder time breaking their chains. Most never tried at all and attempted to find joy in their children and peace in prayer. Those who did seek escape often paid a heavy penalty.

SOPHIA DOROTHEA OF CELLE, HEREDITARY PRINCESS OF HANOVER: THE PRISONER OF AHLDEN

As Shakespeare wrote, "The fittest time to corrupt a man's wife is when she's fallen out with her husband."

After six miserable years of marriage, Hereditary Princess Sophia Dorothea of Hanover had definitely fallen out with her husband, Hereditary Prince George Louis, and was ripe for corruption.

On March 1, 1688, the twenty-six-year-old Swedish mercenary Philip Christoph, count of Königsmark, charged into a ballroom at the Leine Palace and commandeered her heart. A swaggering man of military bearing, he swept her a low bow, flashed a winning smile, and asked if she recalled that many years earlier they had briefly played together at her father's little court of Celle.

Königsmark's father had brought him to Celle to receive military training at the age of sixteen. He had flirted with the pretty little princess, pulled her sled over the snow, and traced with her their names on steamy palace windows with the words *Forget me not*. But soon he had been called to new training at other courts. In the intervening years he had launched a successful career as rakehell adventurer, fearless soldier, and irresistible seducer of women, bouncing around the courts and battlefields of Europe.

Standing before him once again, her Serene Highness didn't answer. Perhaps, remembering those happy carefree days before her terrible marriage, a sob rose in her throat and tears welled in her eyes, and it was all she could do to force them back down.

The threads of Sophia Dorothea's unhappy fate were woven years before her birth. Her father, George William, next in line to become duke of Hanover, had been appalled at the royal bride selected for him. Princess Sophia, daughter of the Palatine king of Bohemia, was a humorless intellectual who steeped herself in daily doses of philosophy. Her handsome mannish face and loud critical voice absolutely terrified George William.

Hemmed in on all sides, in 1658 the unfortunate groom decided to cede his inheritance to his younger brother, Ernst August, if only he would take the unpalatable bride along with it. His ambitious brother was delighted, as long as George William signed a document promising he would never marry and sire rival heirs. On the surface, at least, Princess Sophia accepted philosophically the fact that she had been handed over like an unwanted bundle of clothes from one bridegroom to the next. But hell hath no fury like a woman scorned, and the spurned princess, who had been deeply in love with George William, felt herself very scorned indeed.

Accepting the tiny duchy of Celle as his kingdom in return for the large domain of Hanover, at first George William contented himself with patronizing prostitutes on his yearly visits to Carnival in Venice. But in 1665 George William fell violently in love with a penniless but dazzling Huguenot refugee, Eleonore d'Olbreuse, a woman of dark bouncing curls, pretty pink ribbons, and soft smiles, the exact opposite of the frightening Sophia. To keep his promise to his brother, George William married her morganatically, a union which was sanctioned by the church but did not bestow legitimacy or inheritance rights on the children.

Duchess Sophia, looking down her long regal nose, detested Eleonore, the woman George William had preferred to her, and

sneeringly called her "the little clot of dirt."[9] After Sophia
Dorothea was born in 1666, Eleonore worried about the girl's
future and began agitating for an official marriage and the
child's legitimization. In 1676 Ernst August and Sophia, now secure in their position at Hanover and boasting several strapping
sons, agreed that one puny girl would be no threat. They permitted George William to officially marry Eleonore and legitimize
their daughter, thereby making Sophia Dorothea the richest
heiress in Germany.

But just to be sure, they placed a high-level spy at George
William's court to report back to them his every move. Count
Andreas Gottlieb von Bernstorff, prime minister of Celle, became George William's most trusted adviser. Clever, smooth,
and deceitful, he convinced the duke of Celle to follow his advice
even as he pocketed large bribes from Hanover.

Sophia Dorothea grew into a flirtatious beauty, with thick
dark hair, large velvety dark eyes, and a flawless porcelain complexion. Proud of her tiny hands and feet, she had an exquisite
figure and moved with exceptional grace. She was an avid reader
and talented embroiderer, played the harpsichord beautifully,
and loved to sing and dance. An only child, she was spoiled and
admired, and gave free rein to her spirited emotions.

There was talk of a marriage between Sophia Dorothea and
the future king of Denmark but Duchess Sophia, her blue blood
curdling at the thought of seeing her enemy's daughter a queen,
persuaded her friend the reigning queen of Denmark to break it
off. "Fancy a king's son for that bit of a bastard!" she cried.[10] But
neither did Ernst August approve of the girl's engagement to the
heir of his rival, the duke of Wolfenbüttel. Ernst August became
apoplectic at the thought of so much property going out of the
family, property which would remain in the family if Sophia
Dorothea were to marry his son, her first cousin, George Louis.

The day the Wolfenbüttel engagement was to be announced at
a large feast, Duchess Sophia, somewhat against her will, was dis-
patched galloping to Celle to convince George William of the
advantages offered by a marriage to her son. Sophia Dorothea,
she pointed out, would eventually reign, not over the tiny state

of Wolfenbüttel-Celle but over the huge domain of Hanover-Osnabrück-Celle. In addition, she might even one day become queen of England, as Duchess Sophia was the granddaughter of King James I and the English succession was uncertain. George William, intrigued by the advantages in both property and prestige, agreed.

The new groom who trailed such mouthwatering possibilities in his wake was a dolt, unprepossessing in appearance, intelligence, and character. Six years older than Sophia Dorothea, George Louis was known as "the pig snout" in Hanover. His own mother didn't like him and finally gave up trying to teach him literature and refinements. A poor student, he lived only for hunting and war. His parents had sent him to the court of Louis XIV to polish him up, but he returned to Germany just as tarnished as ever. He was sullen and slow, and behind his cold exterior lurked a relentless vindictiveness.

Duchess Sophia found the marriage demeaning but realized the financial benefits. "One hundred thousand thalers a year is a goodly sum to pocket," she wrote her niece Elizabeth Charlotte, duchesse d'Orléans, of the annual sum paid by the bride's dowry, "without speaking of a pretty wife, who will find a match in my son George Louis, the most pigheaded, stubborn boy who ever lived, and who has round his brains such a thick crust that I defy any man or woman ever to discover what is in them. He does not care much for the match itself, but one hundred thousand thalers a year have tempted him as they would have tempted anybody else."[11]

Upon hearing the sudden news that her bridegroom would not be the lovable admirer of Wolfenbüttel but her repulsive cousin, Sophia Dorothea screamed, took the diamond-framed miniature of George Louis that Duchess Sophia had brought for her, and threw it against the wall. "I will not marry the pig snout!" she cried.[12] But her father angrily insisted, and her mother, though trembling at the thought of her daughter's future with such a husband and such a mother-in-law, was forced to acquiesce. Taken downstairs to kiss the hand of her future mother-in-law, Sophia Dorothea fainted dead away in her mother's arms.

A few days later when, with a pale and tearstained face, she was presented to George Louis, she fainted again. Nor was George Louis pleased with the betrothal; he believed that Sophia Dorothea was a bastard and her mother little short of a prostitute. Indeed, the only thing the bride and groom had in common was their disgust at the marriage, both having been raised to detest each other. The wedding was held on November 21, 1682, in the chapel of Celle Castle as a torrential downpour beat against the stained-glass windows. Pale and trembling, the sixteen-year-old bride looked as if she were walking to her execution. Distant and cold, George Louis looked as if he were her executioner. The mother of the bride sobbed loudly, and the mother of the groom was philosophically resigned. Only the two fathers were beaming, happy at the thought of the property settlement.

Carting her dolls in a coffer behind her, Sophia Dorothea and her twenty-six-year-old maid of honor, Eleonore de Knesebeck, lumbered down the road to Hanover. Though her new home was only thirty miles away, Sophia Dorothea immediately found that Hanover was in fact a world away from her carefree childhood at Celle.

The court of Hanover was a tawdry imitation of Versailles. Like Versailles, the Leine Palace boasted gilded rooms with tall mirrors and crystal chandeliers, carved marble hearths, and gleaming parquet floors, but on a lesser scale. Aping their French counterparts with a bit less aplomb, Hanoverian courtiers shone in silks and satins, sparkled in diamond buttons and shoe buckles. And like Versailles, Hanover prized horses far above cleanliness, which is evidenced by an inventory showing some six hundred carriage horses but only two washerwomen for the entire court.

Sophia Dorothea's mother-in-law scolded her frequently for her lack of etiquette. Her own husband was coldly formal to her; sometimes she saw him looking at her as if he were repulsed. He may have become more concerned about his marriage when a famous French fortune-teller predicted that if he were in any way responsible for his wife's death, he himself would die within the year.

Sophia Dorothea's bright spirit faded in this gloomy environment of cold ceremony and constant criticism. Sometimes it revived over dinner when she would wax gay and witty, slicing and dicing her dull, plodding husband with her sharp repartee. George Louis, highly sensitive to criticism, started to resent his quicker-witted wife. He placed spies among her servants who reported back to him her every utterance, and the two began to indulge in loud and bitter arguments.

After Sophia Dorothea had a son she named George in 1683, she sheathed her rapier wit and made efforts to please the father and grandparents of her child. Dressed beautifully for court events, smiling and ingratiating to all, she eventually found favor with George Louis who, even if he did not love her, was polite and sexually faithful. In 1686 she had a daughter named after her.

Perhaps things would have gone well had it not been for Duke Ernst August's mistress, Countess Clara Elizabeth Platen. The daughter of Count Philip von Meysenbug, a penniless adventurer, as a girl Clara Elizabeth had been taken by her father to various courts in Europe to see if she could find a profitable place as royal mistress. She first stormed Versailles, but Louis XIV's mistress Athénaïs de Montespan climbed the battlements and defended her position valiantly, hounding her retreating enemy from the field. Next she went to England to besiege Charles II, but his mistress Louise de Kéroualle spotted her advance and used all the weapons in her well-stocked arsenal to vanquish the intruder. Luckless in capturing the big guns, the raven-haired beauty lowered her expectations and decided to invade the court of Ernst August, which offered less competition and a great preponderance of gentlemen. And here she gathered the laurels of victory at last.

The flirtatious young Clara Elizabeth soon married Herr Franz Ernst von Platen, a minor court official. But the woman who had set her sights on Louis XIV and Charles II was not satisfied with such mediocre status. Her husband's position at court served as an avenue to insinuate her way into the good graces of the ducal family. Within a short time Madame Platen took on twin responsibilities—lady-in-waiting to Duchess Sophia, and mistress to Duke Ernst August. If the duke ruled Hanover, the stormy Madame Platen ruled the duke, who named her compliant husband a baron, a count, and eventually prime minister. To win the gentlemen at court to her side—including George Louis—in the evenings she turned her home into a tavern, gambling den, and bawdy house where even in the midst of prostitutes she could shine unrivaled as the only noble lady present.

After a life of hard living, by the age of thirty-four Countess Platen maintained her position as the handsomest woman at court with increasing difficulty. What she lost in looks she made up for in raiment—she hid her increasing plumpness under exquisite gold-embroidered brocades, gleaming silks, and the richest velvets, all adorned with snowy white lace. She wore so many fine large diamonds that she blazed like a galaxy—diamond pins in her hair; a diamond brooch on her breast; diamond earrings, rings, bracelets, and shoe buckles. Her toilette became more complex. She piled quantities of shining false curls on her head, spritzed herself with cloying French perfume, and painted on an astonishingly thick mask of makeup. And so when the sixteen-year-old Sophia Dorothea arrived at court—fresh, unsullied, and luminously beautiful—Countess Platen cast her a lingering venomous glance.

Determined to vanquish her young rival, the countess set about finding George Louis a mistress and settled on the beautiful blond Melusina von Schulenburg, a poor girl of noble birth. The countess threw the two of them together constantly and coached Melusina on how to win over the prince. Though too slender to appeal to most men of the time, and nearly a head taller than George Louis, Melusina soon became the prince's mistress. He was seen riding and hunting with his new love and appeared publicly at the theater with her. At the same time he pointedly neglected his wife. Countess Platen's arrow had hit its mark.

Indignant to hear that her husband had a mistress, Sophia Dorothea complained to his parents and hers. Her mother was sympathetic to her plight. But Count Bernstorff, her father's prime minister, now firmly in the pay of Countess Platen, had been feeding George William stories of Sophia Dorothea's pride and temper, her sharp tongue and wifely disobedience. Impatient at her protests, the duke of Celle advised his daughter harshly to ignore her husband's infidelity, as such things were beneath the notice of a hereditary princess; furthermore, the situation was entirely due to her own bad temper. He suggested she imitate the noble example of her mother-in-law, Duchess Sophia, who was too great a lady to bother about her husband's affair with Countess Platen.

The betrayed wife found more sympathy with her in-laws, who feared that a disruption of the marriage might stop the payment of Sophia Dorothea's dowry of one hundred thousand thalers a year. But when they asked George Louis to become more circumspect with his mistress, he became enraged and went out of his way to treat his wife brutally. She, in turn, went out of hers to publicly mock her husband and his mistress, ridiculing the disparity in their height, which particularly galled him.

Trapped in her palace like an animal in a cage, Sophia Dorothea led a miserable life until that night when Count Philip von Königsmark strutted into the ballroom and playfully greeted her. It was as if the clouds parted, the fog lifted, and a glorious ray of sunshine warmed her chilled soul. Her heart beat a little harder, her breathing came a little faster. The boring little court was suddenly alive with the sparkling Swede.

It was not only Sophia Dorothea who welcomed the visitor; Duke Ernst August clapped him on the back and made him a colonel of the guard. George Louis's younger brothers adored the count and often brought him to Sophia Dorothea's little salon in the evening to cheer her up. Not surprisingly, the princess found she had much more in common with the sophisticated count than with her cold bumbling husband. Both were emotional and flirtatious; they loved music and dancing, literature and art, all things French and refined. Their conversations became the high point of her every day. Before she knew it, the hereditary princess was falling in love.

One evening at a costume ball, George Louis danced the first minuet with Countess Platen, who at forty labored under heavy brocades, heavy diamonds, and heavy makeup. For the second minuet, Sophia Dorothea got up and looked about for a partner. A sharp contrast to the blowsy charms of the countess, at twenty-two Sophia Dorothea was dressed as Flora in a white gown with flowers in her hair. For her partner she selected Königsmark, who was magnificently dressed in rose and silver brocade. Everyone noticed how well suited the couple seemed, how beautifully they danced. Everyone, including the spiteful Countess Platen, who had her own designs on Königsmark and vowed to get him into her bed.

Königsmark was a true gentleman of the seventeenth century, boasting the talent to drink, gamble, ride, fight, and make love with great gusto. Possessed of exquisite courtly manners, he sported a flowing dark wig and sumptuous clothing. Sensual, hot-blooded, an urgent need for sex always throbbing painfully in his breeches, he could rarely turn down a woman's offer. And when the opulent Countess Platen whispered in his ear an invitation to visit her that night, he eagerly accepted. Exhausted by her feverish embraces, he stumbled back to his rooms as the sun rose.

Though Königsmark enjoyed the voluptuous favors of Countess Platen by night, by day he found himself more and more bewitched by the princess. His military career as a mercenary called him to new battlefields, yet he could not tear himself away from Hanover. So he stayed on, serving the duke for a small salary, spending his inheritance with reckless abandon, and making love to the vile Countess Platen while pretending it was the princess he held in his arms. Hemorrhaging money, he and his sister Aurora lived in a grand house across the Leine Palace garden from the apartments of Sophia Dorothea, where they kept fifty-two horses and twenty-nine servants.

Finally, after two years in Hanover, in a futile effort to forget his hopeless love, he volunteered for a military expedition to the Peloponnesus in 1690. It was a disastrous expedition, and of eleven thousand men who went, only one hundred thirty returned. One of them was Königsmark, and he returned a changed man. Far away amidst the screams of men and horses, the smell of blood and gunpowder, he had realized his overpowering love for Sophia Dorothea, the unattainable hereditary princess.

Countess Platen welcomed her lover home from the wars with open arms, arms which remained open as he walked coldly past her to Sophia Dorothea. Smoldering with hatred, the rejected woman waged all-out war against the princess. She placed spies all over town and in the palace to report the princess's every move. Displaying her malice as ostentatiously as she did her diamonds, Countess Platen upstaged and insulted Sophia Dorothea at every opportunity, and always succeeded in outdressing her. She schemed with Melusina von Schulenburg on how to keep George Louis utterly enthralled, to the disadvantage of his wife.

Meanwhile Königsmark's visits to the princess, though platonic, became more intense. Seated together in a corner of her salon, he whispered to her as she bent her head over her embroidery so the ladies-in-waiting at the other end of the room couldn't see her blush. For a while the sheer intoxication of being in the same room together was enough, as the sparks danced between them. Then the two began secretly sending love letters.

By examining the letters of Königsmark to Sophia Dorothea, we can tell with some certainty when their relationship was physically consummated. His correspondence which began in July 1690 and lasted through April 1691, though filled with frilly romantic verses, had a respectful tone and ended with "Your faithful servant." But on April 30, he was more intimate, ending with "Farewell my beloved brunette, I embrace your knees."[13]

With the invaluable aid of Eleonore de Knesebeck, Königsmark had slipped into the princess's bed. "Knesebeck lives in the small room near mine," Sophia Dorothea wrote her lover. "You can come in by a rear door and you can stay for twenty-four hours if you wish without the least risk."[14] By this she meant that the tiny bedroom of Eleonore de Knesebeck was visited by neither courtiers nor servants. No one would find Königsmark hiding there.

Sometimes the lovers met in the palace garden at night when Sophia Dorothea and her maid went out for air. "As for me, every evening Knesebeck and I walk together under the trees near the house," the princess wrote. "We will wait for you from 10 o'clock to midnight. You know the usual signal. You must make yourself known by it. The gate in the fence is always open. Don't forget that you must give the signal and that I shall wait for you under the trees."[15] The signal was whistling a popular tune called "The Spanish Follies."

During these night strolls, Sophia Dorothea and Eleonore would leave the palace gardens and dart into Königsmark's house. It was a good ruse, because if they were detected they could say they had been visiting Aurora von Königsmark.

Consumed with anticipation of a sexual rendezvous, Königsmark wrote, "I hope . . . that you will give me permission to come and see you in your apartments this evening. If you don't agree to that, come and visit me tonight at my house. Let me know one way or the other. If you decide to come to me you will find that everyone in my household has retired. The door will be open. Come in boldly without being afraid of anything. I am dying with impatience to see you. Answer quickly so that I may know what to expect."[16]

Sometimes trysts went awry, either through misunderstanding or the unexpected appearance of Sophia Dorothea's husband or in-laws. Early one morning, having waited in vain to be let into the palace, Königsmark reproached his mistress bitterly: "Thursday, 2:00 in the morning: Your behavior is scarcely kind. You make an appointment and then leave people to freeze to death waiting for the signal. You should know that I was waiting in the streets from 11:30 to 1:00."[17]

To prevent their letters from being read by spies, they wrote in code, but the code of children which could easily be deciphered. Numbers referred to places and people. Königsmark was 120, Sophia Dorothea 201, Celle was 305. They had code names for individuals. George Louis was the Reformer, Eleonore de Knesebeck was La Confidante, and Countess Platen was the Fat One.

At court events, sometimes Knesebeck would give Königsmark a sign and place a letter in his hat or gloves. One day he got
the sign but found no letter. In great uneasiness he wrote Sophia
Dorothea, "I swear to you that I looked in my hat, and, as to my
gloves, I put them on, but there was nothing in them. I was angry
at La Confidante, for she had given me the signal, and yet I
found nothing."[18]

Königsmark followed the princess on her rounds of visits to
various palaces. After a rendezvous at the palace of Brockhausen,
the count wrote, "I cannot forget those delectable moments at
Brockhausen. What pleasure! What transports! What ardor!
What rapture we tasted together! And with what grief we parted!
Oh that I could live those moments over again! Would that I had
died then, drinking deep of your sweetness, your exquisite ten-
derness! What transports of passion were ours! . . . I will always
be your true lover, absent or present, wherever you may be, and
whatever may befall."[19]

"What wouldn't I give to hear midnight strike!" he wrote, eagerly anticipating a tryst. "Be sure to have smelling salts ready
lest my excess of joy cause me to faint. Tonight I shall embrace
the most agreeable person in the world and I shall kiss her
charming lips. . . . I shall embrace your knees; my tears will be
allowed to run down your incomparable cheeks; my arms will
have the satisfaction of embracing the most beautiful body in the
world."[20]

In public, the lovers signaled their passion by eye contact,
simmering glances redolent of hot embraces in the dark. "Our
restraint has its charms," wrote Königsmark, "for though the last
few days I have seen you only in places where even the language of
the eyes is scarcely possible, I have had many happy moments.
What a delight, *ma petite,* for us to be able to communicate with
impunity in the presence of thousands of people!"[21] But of
course the lovers did not communicate with impunity; everyone
noticed.

In 1692 the Holy Roman Emperor Leopold I immeasurably
raised the status of the duke of Hanover to that of electoral
prince. The title "elector" went back to the twelfth century when

German princes elected the Holy Roman Emperor by casting votes for various princely contenders. But the title of emperor, which carried an imposing cachet and little else, had remained firmly in the grasping hands of the Hapsburgs for centuries, and elections were social events where Hapsburg envoys dispensed bribes to electors.

Nonetheless, the freshly minted Elector Ernst August was bursting with pride in his honor. Watched closely by jealous rival kingdoms, he would not stand for scandal in his immediate family and took greater efforts to curb the love affair he had been observing for some time. It is likely that the love letters were intercepted beginning in 1692 and easily deciphered. We can imagine the elector's frown as he read Königsmark's gush of joy after having made love to the princess. "When I remember all our exquisite transports, all our sweet violence, I forget my grief. What ardor, what fire, what love have we not tasted together!"[22] And the especially damning "If I could kiss that little place which has given me so much pleasure. . . ."[23]

The elector, having discovered that Sophia Dorothea's love letters went through Aurora von Königsmark's hands, politely requested that Aurora leave his kingdom. His earlier fondness of the count became marked coldness. He ordered Königsmark to fight with the Hanoverian army against Louis XIV, sending him far away from the hereditary princess. Exiled from court, Königsmark had greater difficulty sending and receiving letters. He would address the missive to Knesebeck and give it to a soldier or traveler returning to Hanover. Similarly, Knesebeck would give Sophia Dorothea's letters to travelers heading out to the field. But many of these letters were misplaced or stolen, and both feared that they had lost their lover to someone else.

The princess grew pale and thin, weeping frequently. "Am I destined to sorrow all my life?" she lamented. "Shall I never be able to taste quietly the joys of loving and being loved?"[24]

While Sophia Dorothea sank into depression, her lover's thoughts strayed in the direction of violence. "I have a consolation here close to me," he wrote from camp. "Not a pretty girl, but a bear, which I feed. If you should fail me I will bare my chest and let him tear my heart out."[25] Some of his missives he signed with his own blood.

Königsmark composed a tribute to his own jealous writhing:

> *Alas! I love my own destruction,*
> *And nurse a fire within my breast*
> *Which will soon consume me.*
> *I am well aware of my own perdition,*
> *Because I have dared to love*
> *What I should have only worshipped.*[26]

While other soldiers were routinely given leave to visit Hanover, Königsmark was not. It had become official court policy to separate him from the electoral princess. On several occasions he feigned illness, pitifully moaning and begging for sick leave, which was firmly denied. Exasperated to the point of madness, one night he deserted his post and rode wildly for six days to arrive in Hanover covered in mud and sweat. Without bathing or changing his clothes, he secretly visited Sophia Dorothea.

The next day he called on Field Marshal Heinrich von Podewils who served Ernst August as president of the council of war, confessed his breach of duty, and begged for leave to stay awhile in Hanover. Taking pity on the distraught man, the field marshal, sighing, agreed. But he beseeched Königsmark to end the affair or leave the country. So many factions at court were aware of it that both he and the princess were in great danger. "My dear friend, may God guard thee," the field marshal said, "but take this advice from me, do not let thy love ever hinder thee from thinking of thy fortune."[27]

Podewils also warned Königsmark that he was being watched by spies employed by a certain lady of the court. And indeed Countess Platen had never forgiven Sophia Dorothea her youth and beauty, though she would perhaps have limited her revenge to merely destroying the princess's marriage had not both women fallen in love with the same man. Her hatred of Königsmark was far more deadly, however; he had left her crumbling altar to worship at the pure shrine of Sophia Dorothea.

Hearing of Podewils's remarks, Sophia Dorothea grew agitated. "I fear we are betrayed," she wrote. "I am trembling on the edge of a precipice, but my own danger is the least of my anxieties. I scarcely think of the misfortunes, inevitable and unavoidable, which surely await me if discovered; you, only, occupy my thoughts."[28]

"I pray always that my passion may not become fatal to me," Königsmark wrote.[29] "We are treading on dangerous ground, but when people love as we love they do not consider trifles, and if one holds the loved one, what matters the cost? Were I to see the scaffold before my eyes I would not swerve."[30]

He began having nightmares about getting caught in flagrante delicto. He wrote, "I hope that what I dreamt last night will not happen, for I had my head cut off because I was surprised with you. . . . My greatest worry was what had become of you. . . . On waking up I was bathed in sweat and my valet told me that I had shouted with a sobbing voice, 'Where is she? Where is she?' I did not fear death, but my greatest suffering was being deprived of news of you and not being able any longer to find out what had become of you. This sort of thing makes one realize how much one loves people."[31]

In a last-ditch effort to connect herself to Königsmark, Countess Platen offered him her daughter in marriage. It was not a bad offer, considering the influence, rank, and property of the girl's parents, and Sophia Charlotte Platen, though short and dumpy, had a sparkling wit and vivacious personality. But Königsmark, who had bedded the mother, was disgusted at the thought of wedding the daughter and didn't bother disguising his feelings.

Furious at being spurned again, the countess convinced the elector to exile the count from Hanover. Politely Ernst August told Königsmark his decision, and politely Königsmark departed. He rode straight to Dresden to take part in the coronation ceremonies of his good friend Augustus who had just become the elector of Saxony. The new elector gave his friend a post as major general in the Saxon army.

One evening in Dresden, at an officers' mess party to honor Königsmark, the count drank too much and began entertaining the guests with intimate descriptions of women at the court of Hanover. He told ribald tales of Countess Platen ruling through her lover, the weak elector. He titillated his audience with details of her raucous parties which inevitably became drunken orgies. They roared with laughter to hear of the milk baths she took to aid her wrinkled skin, after which she doled out the milk to the poor as townspeople commended her Christian charity. The soldiers slapped him on his back and sent him drinks when he described the fat ugly daughter Countess Platen had tried to foist on him. And then, to the sound of loud guffaws, he talked of George Louis's bony mistress Melusina von Schulenburg who towered over her royal lover. Unfortunately for Königsmark, someone in the group that night—a laughing soldier, perhaps, or a bustling servant—was a spy in the pay of Countess Platen.

Outraged at Königsmark's public insults, Countess Platen tried to rouse the lethargic Ernst August to action but he impatiently waved her away. She then informed Melusina of her international humiliation.

Melusina was a gentle soul whose only major fault was rapacity. No plotting and planning for Melusina, no upstaging her lover's wife; she quietly had sex with George Louis at night and pocketed the price the next day. But with the sound of laughter at the Dresden officers' mess echoing in her ears, Melusina picked up her heavy skirts and flew to George Louis. Weeping from shame, she upbraided her lover about his wife's affair with Königsmark and the humiliating stories the count was spreading across Europe.

Furious that his gentle mistress should be so insulted, George Louis burst into Sophia Dorothea's rooms and bitterly criticized her for her love affair. The enraged princess replied that George Louis's affair with Melusina was the real scandal and suggested that they divorce. George Louis heatedly agreed, and the quarrel escalated until the prince threw himself on his wife and began tearing out her hair. His hands circled her neck and squeezed. Her attendants in the antechamber, hearing her screams, rushed in to save her. George Louis, seeing her rescuers, threw his wife on the floor and swore he would never look at her again. He never did.

Her mother was horrified to learn of the attack. Her father, however, suggested she had earned the purple finger marks on her neck by her outrageous behavior. Her in-laws, fearing scandal and a possible divorce that would rob them of Sophia Dorothea's money, sent George Louis away to visit his sister in Berlin until tempers calmed down.

Sophia Dorothea, sick of her life in Hanover, knowing her father would never offer her a respectable haven at Celle, was ready to flee her gilded cage and live the life of a soldier's woman with Königsmark. If she escaped Hanover, her husband would divorce her for desertion. She could then marry Königsmark and live with him in some sunny foreign land. She would willingly surrender the coronet and gowns, the jewels, state carriages, and pompous ceremonies. She, of all people, knew how empty they were.

The only problem was money. Königsmark had spent his entire inheritance and was wallowing in debt. After more than a decade of marriage, Sophia Dorothea first looked into her own financial affairs. "Yesterday I read my marriage contract," she wrote Königsmark sadly, "which could not be more disadvantageous to me than it is. The Prince is the absolute master of everything and nothing belongs to me. Even the allowance he ought to give me is so badly explained that they can easily quibble over it. I was very much surprised by all this because I did not expect it at all. It hurt me so much that I had tears in my eyes."[32]

Sophia Dorothea owned a few pieces of fine jewelry and some small change. Where would they flee with so little money? Certainly they could not afford a long journey. And the longer the journey, the greater the risk they would be captured by Hanoverian agents. A sensible destination was the nearby duchy of Anton Ulrich von Wolfenbüttel, the man whose son had been Sophia Dorothea's fiancé a dozen years earlier, and the enemy of the elector of Hanover. He would protect her and be glad to embarrass Ernst August.

At the end of June 1694 Königsmark deserted his post at Dresden and rode posthaste to dislodge his royal mistress from the iron grip of the House of Hanover. Forbidden to cross the border, he disguised himself and slipped into his house with the aid of a few faithful servants. But Countess Platen's spies recognized him entering the city. Like a malevolent spider she sat silent and still, watching her prey become entangled in the unforgiving fibers of her web.

On July 1 Sophia Dorothea sent Königsmark a note asking him to visit her in her apartments that evening between eleven o'clock and midnight. The door would be opened when he whistled "The Spanish Follies." But Countess Platen had intercepted the note before passing it on and was well aware of the rendezvous. She was informed as soon as Königsmark arrived in the princess's chamber, disguised in a pair of shabby summer trousers, a worn white jacket, and brown cloak and carrying a short sword.

Countess Platen, the epitome of scandalized female virtue, raced to the elector and told him breathlessly that at that very moment the count was making love to the electoral princess. Ernst August, sick to death of Königsmark, wanted to go to his daughter-in-law's apartments to confront the guilty pair, arrest the count and exile him once and for all.

But Countess Platen had other plans. She convinced her lover that it would be beneath his dignity as elector to involve himself personally in the scandal; he should sign an order for the guards to arrest Königsmark. Armed with the order, she took four guards into the great hall through which the count would have to retrace his steps and plied them with liquor until they became violently drunk. Perhaps, as she stewed in her bitter misery, Countess Platen pictured her lover, the only man she had ever truly wanted, so desperately wanted, making love to the woman she despised more than anyone else in the world.

The princess, having smoothed down her skirts, and the count, having pulled up his breeches, set to work packing trunks for her escape the following evening. They laughed to think of the reaction of George Louis, his parents, and Countess Platen when word got out that the two had run off together. In the depths of the night Königsmark bid his royal mistress farewell and went down the corridor humming a tune. He found that the door through which he had come had been bolted, the door which he had purposely left unbolted. Someone had locked it. But who? He stopped humming. Now he would have to go through the great hall to exit. Wary of a trap, he drew his sword.

As he passed the huge fireplace, the soldiers leapt out, one of them hitting him on the head with the flat of his sword. After wounding two soldiers, the count's sword snapped. Defenseless now, he was run through the body by saber thrusts and gashed in the head by a battle-axe. As he bled on the floor, his last words were, "Spare the Princess; save the innocent Princess!"[33] Upon hearing this, Countess Platen, with the pointed brocade toe of her diamond-buckled shoe, kicked the dying man hard in the mouth.

In her jealous fury, she had plotted his death. But now, seeing him lying there, his scarlet blood staining the floorboards, she was sorry. Certainly she was afraid. First she called for a cordial, which she tried to force down his throat. Then for bandages to stanch the grievous wounds. Vanquished, she realized her lover was dead, and that she had killed him as surely as if she had run him through herself.

She raced to the elector's rooms. Panting, she told him that Königsmark had resisted arrest so violently that the guards, defending themselves, had accidentally killed him. The elector was horrified. The count had been a nobleman of Sweden, well known to its king, and Königsmark's best friend was the elector of Saxony. The bon vivant of Europe, he had highly placed connections in France, England, and Denmark. Important people would come looking for him. How to explain this arrest gone wrong, this murder in the dead of night of one man by so many armed soldiers? It was best, the elector and countess decided, to do away with the body and feign innocence of his whereabouts. After all, he had been a rakehell adventurer rolling about Europe in search of booty, battles, and women. Anything could have happened to him. No one knew that he had been murdered by the elector's guards except the guards themselves, and the elector made them swear to silence on pain of death.

But what to do with the mangled body? If they carried it outside, surely someone would see them struggling with their burden, and a fresh grave could easily be discovered. And so with the help of the guilty guards, the elector and his mistress pried loose some floorboards of the great hall and tossed the body into the darkness below. Quicklime was thrown on it to eat away the flesh and neutralize the smell. The floorboards were hurriedly nailed back on. This is how Countess Platen buried her greatest passion, her deadliest mistake, her only love. The bloodstains were scoured from the floor. But it is hard to wash away blood. Many spots do not agree to be bleached clean; they cling as mute witnesses to the life that was, to the violence done.

Sophia Dorothea had written Königsmark years earlier, "I belong so truly to you that death alone can part us."[34] And now, as she cheerfully burned papers and packed bags, she was unaware of the parting. At one point Knesebeck alerted her mistress to noises in the great hall but the princess didn't think twice about it. She thought only of the morrow, a day of freedom and joy. In the morning she would wait for Königsmark's note indicating where she and Knesebeck should find the waiting coach.

By noon she had not heard from him. Then Knesebeck told her that Königsmark had not returned home the night before and his servants were looking for him. They were worried because they had heard reports from palace servants of a commotion in the great hall during the night and had found traces of blood on the floor.

Sophia Dorothea waited patiently in her rooms. Surely some word must come. But that evening her children did not come by to wish her good night as usual. When she tried to leave her rooms to visit the elector, she was stopped. Electress Sophia coldly informed her that both she and her maid were confined to their rooms.

Königsmark's rooms were searched by the elector's agents. The count had sent many years' worth of the princess's precious letters to his sister Aurora for safekeeping but had kept those of the last six months with him. These were especially damning, not only revealing personal details of their sexual affair, but also their intended flight into enemy territory and the princess's hatred of her father.

Her love affair, which had been known for years, had been a mere irritant, a potential for scandal. When Electress Sophia's own daughter, the electress of Brandenburg, enjoyed love affairs with courtiers, her family pretended politely not to notice. A far more serious crime on the part of the princess was her plan to flee to Wolfenbüttel, which would cast Hanover into years of legal wrangling over her dowry and inheritance. This, not her adultery, was the unforgivable crime.

Count Platen, the prime minister of Hanover, met with the duke of Celle and showed him Sophia Dorothea's letters. Predictably, her father was furious, especially at her frequent descriptions of him as a brutal tyrant. He washed his hands of her, then and there, and when his wife begged him to have pity on his daughter, the duke angrily replied that he no longer remembered having a daughter.

As for Electress Sophia, she was delighted at no longer having a daughter-in-law. Though the family would smell faintly of scandal, with one fell swoop she could revenge herself on "that little clot of dirt" Eleonore of Celle, the impoverished nobody whom George William had preferred to Sophia's blue-blooded majesty. With her only child divorced and imprisoned, Eleonore would be miserable forever. And best of all, as long as Sophia Dorothea's father did not intervene, the elector of Hanover could imprison her and keep all of her money and lands.

By the evening after the murder, the princess knew that all was lost. Two weeks later Count Platen was sent to question her. He expected to find an abject woman begging for mercy, but instead encountered a haughty princess demanding to know why she was being treated in a manner so inconsistent with her station. Platen informed her, "The Elector has been aware of your relationship with Count von Königsmark."

"Where is Königsmark?" Sophia asked, suddenly frightened for her lover. "Has he been locked up too?"

"I regret to announce to Your Highness that Count von Königsmark died two weeks ago."

And so, she realized, after he had left her chamber that night, humming a little tune, her caresses and kisses still warm on his skin, he had been mercilessly cut down. The noises from the hall. The blood on the floor. Sophia Dorothea fainted dead away. The count looked on her coldly until she came to.

"Murderers; they have murdered him!" she sobbed, trying to rise. "A family of murderers . . . ! Have pity and let me go! I can't stay here any longer. . . ."[35] She howled and wept piteously, all of which Count Platen recorded to use as evidence against her.

Her wish was granted; she was taken back to Celle, not to the palace because her father refused to see her, but to the castle of Ahlden some thirty miles away, home of the local magistrate. But "castle" is a kindly word to describe the building; it was nothing more than an incredibly ugly brick house with two wings projecting off the back.

During her interrogations Sophia Dorothea swore that she had never had sexual intercourse with Königsmark. Questioned separately, Eleonore de Knesebeck swore that her mistress's liaison with Königsmark, while admittedly romantic, had never been sexual. Threatened with lifelong imprisonment and torture, Eleonore never swerved in her statements.

As punishment for her fidelity, Eleonore de Knesebeck was made the scapegoat for all her mistress's sins. *She* had turned the princess's heart against her husband. Foreign courts received an official explanation that stated Sophia Dorothea was separating from her husband "with whom she was no longer on good terms."[36] "The Princess at first displayed only some coldness towards her husband," the statement continued, "but Fräulein von

Knesebeck by degrees inspired her with such dislike to him that she begged from her father permission to return to her parents' home. Her father was displeased, and warned the Princess to place confidence in her husband. But her dislike of her husband was so intensified by the machinations of Fräulein von Knesebeck. . . . Her corrupter, Fräulein von Knesebeck, was arrested at the wish of the Duke George William."[37]

For three very good reasons there was to be no mention made of adultery with Königsmark. First, the scandal would taint the illustrious family name. Second, any mention of adultery, even if the act occurred years after the birth of legitimate children, would cast aspersions on their paternity, thereby threatening the line. And last, Königsmark had been brutally murdered and lay moldering under the floorboards of the great hall in the palace.

And indeed, in the months after the murder, Königsmark's disappearance proved increasingly nettlesome. Ernst August staged magnificent balls and entertaining plays to distract his citizens from the mysterious disappearance of the flamboyant count. But soon foreign embassies were putting pressure on the elector to find Königsmark or explain his sudden disappearance. The mystery was the talk of every court in Europe—even the majestic Louis XIV deigned to express interest. The faint odor of scandal tainting the Hanoverian royal family was quickly rising to a stench. In an about-face, Ernst August decided to offer Sophia Dorothea one last chance. If she would dutifully return to her husband and deny any knowledge of Königsmark's fate, she would be spared imprisonment and divorce.

But Sophia Dorothea proudly declared, "If I am guilty of what I am accused of, I am not worthy of the Prince, and if I am innocent, it is he who is not worthy of me."[38]

Never, ever, would George Louis touch her again, she vowed, shuddering in disgust at the thought. "We still adhere to our oft-repeated resolution never to cohabit matrimonially with our husband," the princess affirmed in her divorce petition, "and that we desire nothing so much as that separation of marriage requested by our husband may take place."[39]

The divorce decree of December 28, 1694, stated that Sophia

Dorothea would lose her title of electoral princess of Hanover. Her name was removed from church prayers and erased from official documents and, indeed, no one at the court of Hanover was permitted to speak it. It was as if Sophia Dorothea had never existed and George Louis's two children had sprung from the air. The document also decreed that the former princess would remain safely locked up in the prison of Ahlden, her money in the hands of her in-laws.

Now there was only the murder of Königsmark to fret about. Hearing of her brother's disappearance, Aurora von Königsmark came flapping back to Hanover, making every effort to locate him, and found herself once again banished by Ernst August. She then traveled to Dresden to inform personally the powerful elector Augustus of Saxony of her brother's disappearance. Overcome with passion for her, the elector took the black-eyed beauty as his mistress and vowed to find her brother dead or alive. He icily wrote Ernst August that Königsmark, his personal friend and a major general in the Saxon army, had last been seen alive going into the elector's palace but no one had seen him coming out. Elector Augustus demanded an explanation.

In response, the Hanoverian government coolly pointed out that Königsmark had just received his pay before he had gone missing and was "a debauched rambling sparke who kept irregular hours, and consequently it is next to an impossibility to give an account what may become of him."[40]

The Saxon elector pressed so hard that the guilty brothers of Hanover and Celle appealed to the Holy Roman Emperor in Austria, vowing they would remove their troops in the emperor's war with France if Saxony did not quiet down about Königsmark. The court of Vienna reproached the Saxon monarch for making such noise about a ne'er-do-well soldier when the more urgent obligations of war and international treaties were at stake. And so, with time, the efforts to locate Königsmark died, just as surely as he was dead himself. For nothing they did could bring him back to life, and the thick white blanket of quicklime was doing its job on the body lying in its dark bed beneath the floorboards.

Adulterous harem women in the sultan's court at Istanbul

were sewn into sacks and thrown into the Bosporus, disappearing under the waves. Baroque Europe was only slightly more civilized; Sophia Dorothea was sewn into the sack of Ahlden and disappeared from sight. At twenty-eight her life had shrunk to the limits of two large rooms in the old gray fortress; her tiny retinue included a governor, a gentleman-in-waiting, and two or three ladies-in-waiting, all spies paid by Countess Platen. They reported back to their employer every movement of the prisoner, every word she uttered. Perhaps to assuage his conscience, Sophia Dorothea's father permitted her a respectable allowance and the right to inherit the property which, over the years, he had put in her mother's name.

She was allowed no visitors and no correspondence with the outside world, not even with her mother for the first few years. Her keepers told her that if she behaved well and made no trouble she would, at some point, be released. And she believed them. One day when a fire broke out, the obedient prisoner stood like a statue in the corridor, holding her jewel box; as the flames crept nearer, she declared she could not move without an order from the governor.

Treated as the most dangerous prisoner in the world, Sophia Dorothea was permitted carriage rides only six miles from the fortress while soldiers waving unsheathed swords rode beside her. The first year of her imprisonment she was not even allowed to walk outside. When doctors advised fresh air and exercise to improve her failing health, George Louis remembered the prediction made years earlier by the fortune-teller—that he would follow his wife to the grave within months—and commanded that she be permitted walks.

Sophia Dorothea adapted herself to prison life by keeping busy. She oversaw the details of the kitchen, paid bills, and made contracts out of her substantial allowance. She was active in charities in the village of Ahlden, repaired the cottages of the poor, and paid for a village schoolteacher. She donated an organ, silver candlesticks, an altar cloth, and a pulpit cushion to the village church. When the village burned down, she paid for new buildings and wider streets.

After four years, she was allowed to receive visits and letters from her mother. But she was not permitted to see her children, although she wrote often to the elector begging for the privilege. He never replied. Toward the end of his life her father, his conscience pricking him, often spoke of going to visit her to alleviate the conditions of her imprisonment, but Prime Minister Bernstorff, still in the pay of Countess Platen, always dissuaded him from the idea. One day in 1705 the duke decided resolutely that he would visit her the following day. But oddly enough, that night he suddenly died. At the death of the duke of Celle, all his property went to George Louis.

With a generous allowance to buy what she wanted, Sophia Dorothea dressed beautifully, as if waiting for Königsmark to make an unexpected visit. Her spies reported that she lived in front of her mirror, trying on gowns, dressing her hair. Adorned in diamonds and brocade, she sat at table beneath a great stuffed bear, a reminder of the one Königsmark had taken as a pet. Her lover had written her once, "One favor I ask of the gods, that I may be with you always, in life and in death."[41] Was he still with her, silent and invisible yet ardently loving her in her dreary rooms? Or was he irrevocably gone, her rooms empty except for her own sad memories?

During the eternal prison days and endless prison nights, the aging captive must have remembered her own prescient words to Königsmark years before: "Without you life would be intolerable and four high walls would give me more pleasure than to remain in the world."[42] And Königsmark's clairvoyant reply: "My lot is that of the butterfly burned by the candle; I cannot avoid my destiny."[43]

The years passed; the princess grew stout and dyed her gray hair black. Realizing she would never be liberated for good behavior, she undertook a secret correspondence with her daughter, who had married the king of Prussia, begging her for help to escape. But Sophia Dorothea the younger had married a man even more brutal than her mother had. Frederick William of Prussia carried a large stick with a knot on the end to beat his family until they bled, as well as servants and ministers who displeased him. Knowing her husband wanted nothing to do with her mother, the queen of Prussia never tried to rescue her. She did her mother one favor, however, employing Eleonore de Knesebeck as her lady-in-waiting.

After her interrogation, Eleonore had been imprisoned in solitary confinement in the fortress of Schwarzfels where she would probably have remained until her death if she had not escaped. After four years, a friend of hers disguised as a roofer made a hole in her ceiling, threw her a rope, and hoisted her up. She then had to slide 180 feet down the castle wall to freedom. As she could no longer serve Sophia Dorothea, she was happy to serve her daughter. For her part, the younger Sophia Dorothea must have been eager to learn about her mother from her faithful maid.

Neither had Sophia Dorothea's son, George, forgotten her. One day in his teens, George went out hunting and galloped away from his retinue. His companions followed in hot pursuit and found him racing up to the fortress of Ahlden, his mother waving to him from a window. The governor of Ahlden refused the boy entrance, and when he returned home his father punished him severely.

After Königsmark's murder, Countess Platen lost much of her influence with the elector, who never forgave her for the mess she had gotten him in. Most of the court, aware that she had loved Königsmark and was bitterly jealous of the princess, knew that she had played a role in their disappearances. The dashing Königsmark and pretty princess had been popular, and now both were gone because of Platen. Few went to her parties after that, even fewer invited her to their own. In Celle she was absolutely detested. And how hard it must have been for her to cross the great hall, knowing what lay moldering beneath. How many times, after that night of blood and murder, did she look at her hands and shudder at the memories? As Lady Macbeth said, "Here's the smell of the blood still; all the perfumes of Arabia will not sweeten this little hand."

Four years after Königsmark's murder, Elector Ernst August died, and the new elector, George Louis, commanded Countess

Platen to retire from court. Utterly defeated, she became ill with a disease that rendered her blind and hideous to behold. Perhaps it was the last stages of syphilis.

On her deathbed, in bone-shattering pain, she cried out that her blind eyes saw Königsmark's ghost rise before her. Begging for divine forgiveness, she confessed her crime to a minister who spoke of it in her funeral oration. There were other deathbed confessions from the guards who had cut Königsmark down. And finally the world learned what had happened to the vanished lover of Sophia Dorothea.

In 1714, when Queen Anne of Great Britain died childless, George Louis became King George I. The British parliament had skipped over fifty-seven other possible heirs rendered unfit by their Catholicism. But George's Protestant religion was his only recommendation to his new realm. He was an unpopular king who never learned to speak a word of English, forcing his courtiers and ministers to communicate in German or French. He cared little about his new kingdom and showed far greater interest in the British treasury, which he repeatedly raided, carrying bags of English gold to Hanover every few years.

Instead of bringing his new subjects a beautiful queen, George flaunted his two ugly mistresses, the good-natured Melusina von Schulenburg, whose youthful beauty had by now entirely disappeared, and Countess Platen's daughter Sophia Charlotte von Kielsmansegge, the one she had tried to unload on Königsmark, who was as fat as Melusina was thin. Given his father's affair with Countess Platen, it is possible that George was sleeping with his half sister. Hearing nothing of a wife, many Englishmen assumed their new king was a widower. Some, upon learning that he had locked up his wife in a castle for twenty years, assumed that she had gone stark raving mad.

George had a terrible relationship with his son and heir, the future George II, who never forgave his father's treatment of his mother. For his part, whenever George looked at his son, he saw his detested wife—her dark eyes and hair, her shining complexion, her passion and pride. An English wit quipped, "George I could not have been such a bad man, for he never hated but three people: his mother, his wife and his son."[44]

And so Sophia Dorothea would have been queen of Great Britain, had she not divorced her husband. She might, technically, *have been* the queen of Great Britain, since the validity of her hurried and secretive divorce was unclear. King George, terrified that she might escape, sail to England, and proclaim herself queen, had her watched more closely than ever.

In 1722 Sophia Dorothea's mother and only friend, Eleonore of Celle, died at the age of eighty-two. And now the prisoner was alone. She inherited her mother's property but found herself without a link to the outside world and, worse, with no one to love her. She lived on for four more years and then, after an imprisonment of thirty-two years, she died November 13, 1726, at the age of sixty. Her last days were painful ones, her bright spirit burning away in fever. Screaming in agony, she called out for divine vengeance against her husband, her torturer, her executioner. Before she died, she asked for quill and paper and wrote one last terrible letter.

When George heard the news of Sophia Dorothea's death, he immediately made plans to attend a performance that evening given by a troop of Italian comedians. The court of Hanover went into mourning for their former princess, but word came from London that the king forbade anyone to wear black. He tore up her will in which she left all her possessions to her children, claiming them instead for himself. He then issued orders to remove everything from Ahlden that had belonged to her and burn it. He wanted nothing left to prove she had ever been there, wanted no relics of his martyred wife to prolong the story of her unjust imprisonment. He even neglected to bury her body.

For two months her coffin lay in a room of the castle of Ahlden. Only at the persistent urgings of the superstitious Melusina, who saw the dead woman's angry spirit circling the palace in the form of a crow, did George command her body to be tossed into the family crypt below the church of Celle, with no religious service. But as hard as the king tried, he could not forget the description of Sophia Dorothea's deathbed, where in her last agony she screamed the most terrifying curses at him. As the months passed, he slept poorly and became nervous. He decided that he needed a rejuvenating visit to his native Hanover.

George arrived at the German border on June 19, 1727. After a large dinner and a short rest, he ordered his departure for three A.M. Stepping into his carriage to set out for Osnabrück, the king was handed a letter by a stranger who stepped forward and begged to present it to His Majesty personally. Used to receiving petitions from his subjects, George took it into the coach. A couple of hours later, as the summer sun rose over green fields, he opened the letter. It was from his dead wife, cursing him for his cruelty. She promised to meet him before the tribunal of God a year and a day after her death. For decades he had tried so hard to repress the shrill voice that had called to him of his guilt. Yet as the coach lumbered forward, that voice came clearly now, rending the early morning air with a clarion cry of vengeance from beyond the grave.

The king dropped the letter and began to shake violently. His tongue hung out of his mouth. "I'm finished," he panted to his chamberlain. When the coach arrived at the town of Linden, the king was bled, but insisted on continuing the journey. "To Osnabrück!" he cried over the rising chorus of protest. *"Nach Osnabrück!"* When the coach arrived there, his servants opened the door and thought he had fallen asleep. But he had suffered a stroke and was near death. They brought him into the palace to die in the very bed in which he had been born. And the fortune-teller's prophecy, given forty years before—that if he were in any way responsible for his wife's death, he would follow her within the year—had proved correct.

Britain did not grieve for its unloved king. The only one who truly mourned was Melusina von Schulenburg, now the wealthy duchess of Kendal. For four decades she had loved him and was perhaps the only person ever to have loved him. The good-hearted Melusina was comforted by frequent visits of her dead lover in the form of a little bird who flew into her rooms regularly and fed from her hands.

Certainly the king's son did not grieve. George II, knowing that his father had burned his mother's will, now in turn burned his father's will and claimed all *his* property. One morning, shortly after George I's death, Lady Suffolk visited the royal chambers and saw two portraits of a beautiful woman wearing the royal robes of a generation earlier—portraits of Sophia Dorothea which the new king had kept hidden from the wrath of his father. If Sophia Dorothea had survived George I, her son would have released her from prison instantly and installed her as queen dowager of Great Britain.

George II, eager to solve the mysteries of his parents' divorce more than thirty years earlier, commanded that he be shown the secret Hanoverian records and, after reading them, set them on fire, watching the evidence of his mother's adultery burn to cold ash. But neither Sophia Dorothea's husband nor her son had burned all the evidence of her love for Königsmark. His sister Aurora, safely out of Hanover, had taken with her some two hundred of their love letters—1,399 pages in all—which she passed down in her family as cherished possessions. Today they are preserved at the University of Lund, Sweden.

In 1754 another packet of sixty-four letters mysteriously came into the possession of Frederick the Great of Prussia. These "not very honorable souvenirs" of his grandmother, as he called them, are also at Lund.[45] None of the letters of the last six months of the love affair—those confiscated by Elector Ernst August and used as evidence against the princess—has ever been found.

It is possible that Königsmark, who had energetically bounced around the courts of Europe, resurfaced even after death. Decades after his murder, workmen repairing the floor of the great hall in the Leine Palace reportedly found a nearly decomposed skeleton, covered in quicklime. The rumor quickly spread that the corpse had a ring bearing the Königsmark coat of arms. The Leine Palace, that place of secret lovemaking and sudden death, was destroyed by Allied bombs in World War II.

The castle of Ahlden, the cage in which Sophia Dorothea sighed and remembered for thirty-two years, is now an antiques auction house. Her remains lie in the crypt of St. Mary's Church at Celle. The visitor enters through a trapdoor next to the altar. It is a small, low space, with thick walls and the smell of mildew. Lead coffins are pushed together three rows deep, imposing coffins set atop wide legs, ornamented with engravings of angels and coats of arms upon their lids. On the side, away from the great ones, is a low, narrow coffin, very plain and utterly alone. In it is all that is left of Sophia Dorothea. Even in death she was punished; her coffin had to be lower than those of her exalted relatives.

And yet, it is the only one on which visitors place fresh flowers daily; the glorious caskets of her relatives remain eternally unadorned. All their palaces, built to sing their praises forever, were reduced to rubble by the firebombing of 1943. But the unhappy tale of a miserable girl still moves us. We make pilgrimage to her crypt to lay flowers on her small, mean coffin.

Perhaps her spirit had her day at the tribunal of God with George Louis, and a loving reunion with her Königsmark. As he had written her so many years earlier, "It is better to die than to live without being loved."[46]

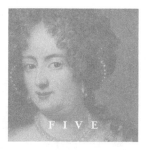

FIVE

EIGHTEENTH-CENTURY RUSSIA: THE UNCHASTE EMPRESSES

Hard-hearted you are, you gods! You unrivaled lords of jealousy—scandalized when goddesses sleep with mortal.

—HOMER, *THE ODYSSEY*

MYSTERIOUS AND PERPLEXING, RUSSIA HAS ALWAYS BEEN A nation of exaggerated contradictions. A land of gentle kindness and vindictive cruelty, of medieval piety and reckless debauchery, of opulent splendor and wretched filth. Forests glitter with snow; precious gems sleep deep beneath black earth, and rolling plains stretch endlessly toward the horizon. Tempestuous and scintillating, the Russian soul is easily angered and quick to forgive. It is the greatest of nations, the worst of nations, encompassing the unexpected, the vast, and the priceless.

In the late seventeenth century Russia remained secluded in a heavy pall of Orientalism. Men wore long robes and long beards; women were sequestered in a *terem,* a Russian version of the harem, and prevented from contact with unrelated men.

Russian Orthodox superstition ruled every aspect of life, and foreigners—those frightening non-Russian, non-Orthodox heathens—were kept securely in their own area just outside of Moscow, lest they infect God-fearing natives with their devilish ways.

For some thirty years before his death in 1725, Peter the Great single-handedly wrenched Russia's gaze from east to west, a Herculean task well suited to a giant six feet eight inches tall in a world where the average man measured five foot four. This arduous effort was continued for another thirty-four years, starting in 1762, by Catherine the Great, the most extraordinary Russian monarch ever, who was, in fact, German. And so a gloss of Western civilization was daubed thinly over the rude barbarism of medieval Russia, a Russia with raging passions little calmed by the strains of the minuet. "It is as if there were two peoples," wrote the chevalier de Courbon, a French diplomat at the court of Catherine the Great, "two different nations on the same soil. You are in the 14th century and the 18th century at the same time."[1]

It was a land of unlimited opportunity. Unlike in France and England, with their rigid social structure, in Russia the most humble souls could soar unhindered to greatness. The fabulously wealthy Alexander Menshikov, governor-general of St. Petersburg and commander of the armed forces, started life as a pie seller. Empress Catherine I, wife of Peter the Great, had been a laundry wench and prostitute. His Serene Highness the duke of Courland and regent of Russia, Ernest Biron, launched his brilliant career by shoveling horse manure.

Foreign visitors, offended by the barbaric brutality and horrendous table manners of Russian nobles, were most perplexed at their bizarre hygiene. Emerging from an Oriental past, Russia kept the Eastern tradition of bathing daily and, though the most backward nation in Christendom, boasted the cleanest people. Russian nobles flaunted the largest, most dazzling emeralds and diamonds in Europe; visitors from golden Versailles routinely expressed their astonishment at stones the size of hens' eggs glittering obscenely on men and women who seemed unaware of their value. Perhaps foreign visitors would have been equally astonished to find that fully half of these courtiers who shone like the sun did not know how to write, and a third did not know how to read.

In this land of unnerving contradictions, perhaps the greatest was this, that only a few years after blasting free of the *terem,* women ruled the most chauvinistic, testosterone-rich European nation for seven decades. On the other hand, France, which had for centuries recognized the political brilliance of the fair sex, had a law that prevented a woman from inheriting the throne in her own right.

The rule of women in eighteenth-century Russia gave rise to the flowering of the male favorite. The kings of western Europe had their silken mistresses, but the empresses of Russia had their muscular young studs. Some of these lovers wanted power, others just riches, and a few desired only the love of the monarch. As only men could command armies—even a feisty Russian empress would not gallop with her soldiers into battle—imperial lovers often served as generals. Others, less attracted to the smell of gunpowder and screams of men, served the empress in a political role. But of all their duties, those reserved for the night were by far the most pressing.

Catherine I

"There Is a Fire Burns in My Breast"

Peter the Great liked to boast that he spent less on whores than any king in Europe. However, the paltry sums expended were the result not of sexual moderation but of negotiating skills. The czar's drunken orgies with prostitutes were legendary across the continent. True to the double standard of the time, Peter expected his wife to remain scrupulously faithful.

Having thrown his critical, aristocratic first wife, Eudoxia, into a remote convent, Peter fell in love with the illiterate daughter of a Livonian gravedigger. Martha Skavronskaya had been captured as war booty and worked as a laundress for the

Russian army. The soldiers passed her around until the czar claimed her for himself and eventually married her. Martha—who took the name Catherine upon converting to Russian Orthodoxy—was cheerful, plump, and jolly, the perfect companion for a ruler whose eccentricities swung from visionary genius to sadistic insanity. Had the czar selected a fine-boned French princess for his bride, she might very well have packed her bags and galloped home.

Peter never mastered the Western fashion of eating with knife and fork. The czar ate with his fingers and wiped his mouth on his sleeve. The refined Polish ambassador Manteuffel, terrified of dining with this monster of bad manners, heaved a sigh of relief after his meal, praising the czar who "neither belched nor farted nor picked his teeth—at least I neither saw nor heard him do so."[2]

For all his bad manners, Peter was resolved to pull his backward nation out of the muck and mire of the Dark Ages. Though monarchs rarely traveled outside their realms in the eighteenth century, Peter often visited western Europe to learn technology and customs, as well as to make foreign alliances.

Uncomfortable in the limelight and detesting royal receptions, he went incognito for large portions of his journeys to London, Paris, Hanover, Berlin, and Frankfurt. Peter once stayed several months in the Netherlands to become a master shipwright; with this firsthand knowledge he built the first Russian navy. Living in a hut under an assumed name, Peter was furious when Dutch subjects recognized him as the czar—the only loping Russian giant with a wart on his cheek that they had ever heard of. When a stranger on the street cheerfully called the czar by name, he was often rewarded with a bruising blow to the head.

Having enjoyed the customs of western Europe, Peter returned to Russia and cast a critical eye on his own backward traditions. He ordered the upper classes to attend "assemblies" dressed in Western fashion where they would dance the minuet and play cards and chess. Guests were commanded by imperial decree to cultivate small talk with members of the opposite sex.

Men were forbidden to get drunk before nine p.m.; ladies were not permitted to show signs of any inebriation whatsoever. At these assemblies the czar stood sentinel with a cudgel, ready to spring on anyone spitting on the floor, picking his nose, or talking with his mouth full, and beat him senseless.

In the West a smooth clean-shaven face was a sign of culture and a long ratty beard a sign of barbarity. When Peter returned to Russia, he immediately began grabbing his courtiers by their beards and cutting them off. He once gave a banquet where a clown attacked all the beards in the room with a giant pair of scissors. Though the czar wept with laughter, his subjects wept with shame; beards were the sign of a good Orthodox Christian. Some men safeguarded their shorn beards, instructing relatives to place them in their coffins so they could meet God as one of his faithful flock. Not content with beards, Peter stalked the streets wielding a pair of hedge clippers, ready to cut off the long Oriental sleeves he saw, reminders of an ancient superstitious past.

For all Peter's love of Western fashions, he never developed the profound respect for wigs so noticeable at the French and German courts. In the early eighteenth century the best wigs, made of real human hair, stood several inches above the top of the head and tumbled in ringlets down to below the shoulders. A wig was often the single most expensive item of personal adornment, washed, powdered, and curled with great reverence. Peter, however, used his wig as a hat, slapping it on his head when he went outdoors. In the palace, whenever he, wigless, felt cold, he would grab a wig from a servant's head and plop it on his own. Sometimes when he grew warm, he would snatch the wig off his head and stuff it in his pocket. Whenever he became angry with someone, he would pluck off the offender's wig and toss it across the room.

In Paris, Peter received a gift from the king of France—a long ornate wig from the finest court wigmaker, the cost of which could have purchased a small estate. But the czar liked to wear short chin-length wigs, with his own dark straight hair hanging below the white curls. To the horror of his French hosts, the czar attacked his gift with a pair of scissors, cut off the bottom half, and smacked it on his head with a satisfied grin.

One Western institution Peter did not like was the Roman Catholic Church. Upon his return to Russia he founded the Synod of Fools and Jesters to make fun of the Vatican and appointed his former tutor, a notorious drunk, as the Prince Pope. The Prince Pope was given a palace, a generous salary, and twelve stuttering servants. During his "official" ceremonies the Prince Pope wore a miter of tin, carried a tin scepter, and babbled an incoherent mixture of blessings and obscenities. Tucking his white robes up over his bowed legs, he danced, made obscene gestures, burped and farted. When blessing the faithful, he smacked them on the head with a pig's bladder. As an icon to kiss, he presented a statue of Bacchus with an enormous erection.

Initiates into the cult of the Prince Pope were asked not "Do you believe?" but "Do you drink?" After giving an answer in the affirmative, they held their mouths open while vodka was poured down their throats. In the Prince Pope's processions, the czar, dressed as a Dutch sailor, led the way, beating a drum, while the Prince Pope, with playing cards sewn to his gown, rode astride a barrel pulled by twelve bald men. "Cardinals" waving vodka bottles rode in sleighs pulled by oxen, while "dignitaries" sat on carts pulled by bears, pigs, and dogs. In other processions Peter had a seven-foot-six-inch giant, dressed like a baby, seated in a sleigh pulled by twelve midgets.

Peter's diplomatic gatherings were no better than his papal ceremonies. A Hanoverian diplomat, invited to the palace for a reception, found himself locked in a room for three days with two large barrels set before him; one contained the alcohol he would have to drink before he was permitted to go home, and the other was to hold bodily wastes. On another occasion Peter ordered all his dead-drunk diplomatic guests to go into the forest and cut down trees. The ambassadors swung wildly and fell down amid gales of laughter; by some miracle no one was hurt. Many diplomats urgently wrote their governments begging to be recalled from Russia and sent to a country less deleterious to their health.

Foreign diplomats and native Russians alike were panic-stricken when Peter learned the art of tooth pulling. With a pair of pliers always in his pocket, the czar requested those he encountered to open their mouths for inspection, and if he found a rotten tooth he would immediately yank it out. Proud of this accomplishment, he kept the teeth he pulled in a little leather pouch, which is now in the Hermitage Museum of St. Petersburg. It was just a short step to learn the executioner's art, and Peter executed at least five condemned men himself, proud of how cleanly he sliced through bone and sinew.

This, then, was Catherine's husband. Surely no other woman in the world could have lasted as long or kept Peter as happy. Cheerful, helpful Catherine never once complained about his sexual escapades or violent temper tantrums. Putting aside every desire of her own, she devoted herself to calming her mad giant. After a decade together, he married her in 1712, their two daughters aged five and two skipping along as bridesmaids. The very proper English envoy was speechless when Peter told him that the marriage was "guaranteed to be fruitful," since he already had five children by his bride.[3]

In 1716 Peter had his detested son and heir, Alexis, Eudoxia's child, tortured to death in prison. Seven years later his young sons with Catherine were all dead, and his once large brood of children had dwindled down to their two daughters. To protect their future he decided to crown his wife as his successor and empress in her own right. Peter had to threaten his subjects with death if they uttered "foolish and drunken rumors" about Catherine.[4] But he could not threaten foreign courts, which had a good hearty laugh at a former laundress and camp follower ascending the double-eagled throne of imperial Russia.

For her coronation the empress wore a purple mantle embroidered with golden eagles costing four thousand rubles, and her crown was made of four pounds of precious stones. Peter crowned her himself as she wept and babbled in a most undignified manner, throwing her arms around her husband's knees. He raised her up and placed in her hands the orb, symbol of sovereignty. But she wasn't getting her hands on his scepter, symbol of power. That he kept for himself.

At the age of forty Catherine was exhausted from spending twenty years of her life pacifying her volatile, sadistic husband. Though she pasted a professional smile on her face whenever she heard of Peter's orgies, she must have been deeply hurt. She had grown corpulent from bearing ten children and taking out her unexpressed frustrations at the table. Life as empress of all the Russias was, perhaps, not as good as life as a laundress.

And then William Mons began to flirt with her. Peter's handsome chamberlain Mons was blond, elegant, and foppish, a complete contrast to his master. He sent her romantic verses confiding his deep love for her. Some reported that Catherine's passion for William was "so violent that everyone perceived it."[5] Everyone except Peter, who was eventually informed by an anonymous letter. In November 1724 the czar found the two in a rendezvous in a palace garden and angrily told Mons to leave. No sooner was Mons back in his room lighting a pipe than the secret police came. Enraged that the servant girl he had raised to empress was unfaithful, Peter had several courtiers interrogated and tortured, and their letters seized.

Catherine's female accomplice had been, as tradition decreed, her lady-in-waiting. Matriona Balk, the sister of William Mons, had arranged the secret meetings and taken letters back and forth. But most of the other ladies-in-waiting had either been involved or at least known about the affair.

William Mons was condemned to be beheaded, but not for having sex with the empress. It was a gentlemen's agreement that he would suffer his penalty under the name of another crime, stealing from state coffers. It would preserve Peter's pride. Mons spent his last hours writing romantic verses:

> It is love which brings about my downfall
> There is a fire burns in my breast
> From which I know that I must die.
> I know the reason for my downfall:
> That I have loved
> Where I should only honor.[6]

On November 16 the handsome William Mons climbed up the scaffold, heard his sentence read out, bowed, took off his cloak and jacket, and asking the headsman to be quick, placed his head on the block. He was quick. Mons's head was placed on a stake, his body tied to a wheel. Matriona Balk and the other guilty ladies-in-waiting were whipped on their bare backs, also allegedly for corruption. Matriona was exiled to Siberia.

Throughout all this, Catherine showed a calm serenity, knowing that any sign of agitation would inflame Peter, who might send her to the scaffold as well. The day of her lover's execution, the empress calmly attended her daughters' dancing lesson. The French envoy reported, "Although the Empress hides her grief as much as possible, it is painted on her face, so that everyone is wondering what may happen to her."[7] The next day Peter issued orders that no one was to obey any command given by the empress. Catherine was immediately cut off from all funds and had to borrow money from those ladies-in-waiting who had not been whipped and exiled. Perhaps she wondered if she would be sent to a convent like his first wife, Eudoxia, or murdered in prison like his son, Alexis.

The day after Mons's execution, Peter drove her in an open sleigh to see the grisly remains of her lover. She betrayed no emotion, not even when the edge of her gown rubbed against a black and stiffened leg projecting from the wheel. After they returned to the palace Peter stomped up carrying a priceless Venetian vase. "Do you see this?" he asked. "It's made from the simplest materials. Artistry has made it fit to decorate a palace, but I can return it to its former valueless condition." He smashed it on the floor.

"Of course you can," she replied with characteristic practicality, "but do you think that you made the palace any more beautiful by breaking that vase?"[8]

Peter, furious that Catherine showed no emotion despite his threats, decided the situation called for something more. That evening when Catherine returned to her room she found William Mons's gaping head staring at her in a bottle of alcohol on her table. She ignored it. After several days, realizing he would get no reaction from her, Peter had the head removed.

The Saxon envoy wrote his master, "They almost never talk to each other. They no longer eat together, they no longer sleep together."[9] Peter muttered ominously about Henry VIII's effective manner of dealing with Anne Boleyn. But in the meantime, he was angling to marry his two daughters to Western rulers, and slicing off their mother's head for adultery would not help his case. He already was encountering problems disposing of the girls because they were illegitimate, born to the czar's washerwoman mistress before he had married her.

In December 1724 Peter was stricken with a urinary tract infection which became rapidly worse. By January he was suffering from kidney stones and a relapse of the venereal disease he had picked up in his youth. A physician perforated his swollen bladder and removed four pounds of urine. But the bladder was already gangrenous.

When Peter died on January 28, 1725, Catherine was proclaimed empress. Dazed, she blindly signed documents placed before her, wandered around Peter's workrooms, and handled his beloved tools. She never gripped the reins of power but handed them to her numerous lovers.

A mere figurehead, Catherine loved pomp and ceremony, especially banquets where she overate and drank herself senseless. She took different men into her bed every night and ordered new carriages and daring gowns. But it made no difference. For nothing could fill the huge gap where Peter had stood, all six feet eight inches of him. He had so completely dominated her life that when he was torn out of it, the space would remain forever vacant. She tried to pack the emptiness full with food and drink and sex, with games and pageants and midnight wanderings. But still the void remained.

Worn out by excess, Catherine died in 1727 after two years as empress. She was forty-four years old.

Elizabeth, daughter of Peter the Great and Empress Catherine I, did not succeed directly to the imperial throne. At her mother's death the nobles proclaimed as czar Peter II, the thirteen-year-old son of her murdered half brother, Alexis. When the sickly boy died after three years, Elizabeth's waspish cousin Anna was chosen as empress by nobles who hoped to find the disappointed, neglected woman putty in their hands. Widowed six weeks after her marriage at the age of seventeen, she had not been permitted to remarry and had lived in lonely exile for two decades. Surely she would be grateful to those who put her on the throne. They were mistaken.

Tart, sour, and yellow-faced as a lemon, Anna set about wreaking revenge on those who had wronged her. And Elizabeth, by virtue of her impudent youth and blond beauty, wronged the empress on a daily basis. Elizabeth had inherited her commanding height from her father and stood taller than most men. She had a ravishing figure, a dazzling complexion, and gorgeous wide blue eyes. When New Year's fireworks ushering in the year 1737 shattered a window, cutting Elizabeth's face, Anna was delighted. She was less pleased when the wounds healed perfectly, leaving no trace of a scar.

Worse than the sin of her beauty was the fact that Elizabeth was politically inconvenient. Many discontented factions at court hoped that the statuesque daughter of Peter the Great would stage a coup and proclaim herself empress. Anna, well aware of these hopes, debated whether she should imprison the girl, murder her, or send her to a convent.

Elizabeth's behavior proclaimed that she lived for love, not for politics. Reckless and extravagant, she took into her bed pages, peasants, ambassadors, doctors, and soldiers. The duque de Liria, who served as Spain's ambassador to St. Petersburg, reported, "The behavior of the Princess Elizabeth gets worse and worse each day. She does things without shame, things that would make even the humble blush."[10]

She was described as "content only when she was in love," and refused to hide her passions under a veil of false modesty.[11] Her lack of restraint possibly kept her alive, for the ruling powers saw her as a person of no political significance, a woman who lived for sex and dancing.

Yet Elizabeth's flighty persona was a concoction to help her survive in a scorpions' nest. While vaunting her numerous love affairs, she carefully concealed her political acumen. The British envoy's wife reported, "In public she has an unaffected gaiety, and a certain air of giddiness that seems entirely to possess her whole mind. . . . In private I have heard her talk with such a strain of good sense and steady reasoning that I am persuaded the other behavior is a feint."[12]

Sensing the cold hand of death upon her, Empress Anna arranged for her niece's son, the infant Ivan, to succeed her. This would serve the twin purpose of disinheriting Elizabeth and allowing Anna's lover of thirty years, Ernest Biron, to rule as regent. But in 1741, after only a year, Biron was chased out of power by an opposing faction and Anna Leopoldovna, Ivan's mother, became regent.

Anna Leopoldovna was not a very good regent. Though married to a German prince, she spent most of her time rolling in bed with her lover, the Saxon ambassador. To the great amusement of courtiers, the regent's husband was often seen banging angrily on her bedroom door.

Numerous powerful families tried to persuade Elizabeth to stage a coup and proclaim herself empress. Afraid of bloodshed, Elizabeth hesitated until she heard rumors that Anna Leopoldovna was planning on claiming the imperial crown for herself and having her inconvenient cousin shut up in a convent. Elizabeth shuddered at the thought of religious life because, as one contemporary wrote, there was "not an ounce of nun's flesh about her."[13]

On November 25, 1741, hours before she was to be arrested, Elizabeth rallied loyal troops and invaded the palace. The coup was ridiculously easy; the people wanted the daughter of Peter the Great to rule. Anna was imprisoned in one fortress and her infant son in another. Elizabeth was gentle with her former enemies who now swarmed to proclaim their loyalty. She swore never to sentence anyone to death for political crimes. She outlawed the torture of children under seventeen and the cutting off of women's noses. Even the humblest subjects were encouraged to hand Elizabeth petitions for redressing injustice.

Unlike her three female predecessors—her mother, Catherine I; Empress Anna; and the regent Anna Leopoldovna—Elizabeth took her governmental responsibilities quite seriously, working most of the day, reading reports, presiding over meetings, forcing rival ministers to make peace. Mercurial and temperamental, Elizabeth had an arsenal of tactics to get her way—flashing a brilliant smile, stamping her foot in impatience, swearing like a fishwife, complimenting and cajoling.

Not only had Russian politics declined in recent years, so had Russian court manners. Forty years earlier Elizabeth's father had beaten French courtesy into his unruly courtiers. Now Elizabeth was forced to issue an edict that courtiers were to appear in "good and not in verminous dress."[14]

When Elizabeth mounted the throne, her lover of several years was Alexei Razumovsky, a Cossack village shepherd whose exquisite singing voice had procured him a job in the royal chapel. His voice, clear and achingly sweet, pierced the smoke of incense and burning tapers, danced about the glinting icons, and rose into the vaulted arches. Curious to see the owner of this voice, Elizabeth prowled around the church until she found a tall, dark, and muscular young man with flashing black eyes. Elizabeth was smitten and began the greatest love affair of her life.

As the lover of the empress, Razumovsky became a patron of Russian drama and opera and made Russia a leading European center for the study and performance of music. Unlike Elizabeth, who was convinced that too much reading could prove fatal, Razumovsky loved books and encouraged literature.

The new empress made no secret of her love affair; she openly held hands with Razumovsky and kissed him in public. Razumovsky served the empress every night with such devotion that court wags called him the "Night Emperor."[15] The church bleated its disapproval, suggesting the empress make the union a moral one. And Elizabeth, superstitious almost to paranoia, most likely married the singing shepherd secretly in 1742. That year she made him a count and appointed him court chamberlain. She bestowed on him a palace in Moscow and another in St. Petersburg.

Unlike most royal lovers, Razumovsky loved his imperial mistress deeply and remained unspoiled by the wealth and honors heaped on him. In a court of vicious self-seekers, it seemed that Razumovsky alone was gentle and kind. He made no efforts to hide his humble origins and invited his family to court. His terrified mother was plucked off her dirt farm and dolled up in a white wig and satin gown to meet the empress. When she caught a glimpse of a splendid-looking female in a full-length mirror, she assumed it was Empress Elizabeth herself who stood before her and curtsied deeply.

Having decided never to marry officially and bear legitimate children, Elizabeth summoned the fourteen-year-old German son of her dead older sister to Russia to be her heir. Elizabeth, who liked swaggering red-blooded men, tried to hide her disappointment when she met this narrow-shouldered, twitching boy with an annoying high-pitched voice.

When Elizabeth set about choosing a bride for the unpromising Grand Duke Peter in 1744, she wanted a princess who was attractive but would not eclipse her own beauty at court. As she entered her late thirties she found herself in the position of Empress Anna fifteen years earlier, who had looked on the radiant youth of Elizabeth with thinly veiled hostility. She covered her graying hair with yellow tint, rouged her sagging cheeks, and wore increasingly elaborate gowns to hide her heavy hips. She alone was permitted to wear the largest hoopskirts at court and changed her gown six times a day.

Having studied portraits of all suitable brides, Elizabeth chose for her sixteen-year-old nephew the humble fourteen-year-old Princess Sophie of Anhalt-Zerbst, a tiny German principality. The empress was pleased with her choice; the bride's impoverished family would not demand privileges or treaties from Russia. Though the girl was attractive, she was no raving beauty. Slim as a twig, her figure would not rival the baroque curves of the empress.

The princess's features were too strong to be considered beautiful; her blue eyes were heavily hooded and her chin jutted out to a stubborn point. Her mouth, a narrow line when at rest, could flash a winning smile. But Catherine—the name she took upon converting to Russian Orthodoxy—boasted rich chestnut hair and a fresh prettiness. Though only five foot three, the girl had such excellent posture that she was often thought to be much taller.

In her memoirs, Catherine recalled her introduction to the empress. "No one could see Elizabeth for the first time without being overwhelmed by her beauty and her majesty," she wrote. "She was very tall and very stout, without it being in the least bit disfiguring or in any way impeding the grace of her movements. Her hooped dress was of glittering cloth of silver trimmed with gold. Her unpowdered hair glistened with diamonds and one black feather curled against her rosy cheek."[16]

It occurred to Elizabeth that her tall, heavy frame would look better in men's clothing. Her thick muscular legs looked handsome in white silk stockings and knee breeches. Her expanding abdomen and hips were covered by a flaring coat. The empress began to hold "metamorphosis" balls, in which all the men were required to come dressed as women, and the women as men. Generals and ministers alike were required to wear corsets and hoopskirts and put powder and patches over a five o'clock shadow. Holding dainty fans in clumsy hairy fingers, the men stumbled about awkwardly on high heels. At one such ball, a fat major general tripped on his hoopskirt and fell on top of Grand Duchess Catherine, nearly breaking her arm. But on the whole, Catherine and the other women were delighted to find themselves liberated from corsets, hoops, and high heels, and they had a wonderful time romping about the ball dressed as men.

But Elizabeth's mounting distress at aging was not limited to metamorphosis balls. Once she dyed her hair black and, displeased with the result, found she could not get the dye out. She had to shave her head and as a matter of course made all the ladies at court do the same. They cried pitifully as their long coveted locks were shaved. As her father, Peter the Great, had taken shears to the beards of his courtiers, so did Elizabeth stalk palace corridors wielding a large pair of scissors to despoil the tresses of pretty young women, crying that she did not like their hairstyles. Catherine wrote, "These young ladies claimed that Her Majesty had taken off a little of their skin along with their hair."[7]

Despite the advancing hand of time, the daughter of Peter the Great did not need such stratagems. Age and weight gain did not rob her of her magnificent height, blazing energy, beguiling smile, and firm stride. Nor did she have any problem finding lovers. Unburdened by fidelity to Razumovsky, Elizabeth would often call another favorite to make love to her after her ladies had retired. She still cooked for Razumovsky, and babied him when he was sick, and gave him splendid diamond buttons and shoe buckles and epaulettes glittering with gems. Grateful for the attention, gentle Razumovsky did not mind the competition from other men. In 1749 she took a new lover, her gentleman of the bedchamber, Ivan Shuvalov, and moved him into an adjoining apartment. Handsome Shuvalov was in his early twenties when Elizabeth was about to celebrate her fortieth birthday.

Like Razumovsky, Shuvalov became the patron of theater, music, literature, and the arts. He established the Academy of Fine Arts and Russia's first university. He brought French plays to the Russian stage. At one of these plays Elizabeth fell in love with the young man in the lead role, a cadet named Nikita Beketov, whom she promoted to colonel and invited to live in the palace.

But Beketov was no actor. Her chancellor Alexei Bestuzhev had resented the influence of her lover Shuvalov and decided to replace him with a man of his own. He handpicked Beketov as a youth likely to appeal to the empress's prurient interest and arranged for him to take the lead role in the play. Bestuzhev then dressed the young man in a way that would attract the empress—

dripping with lace, diamond shoe buckles glinting in the footlights, diamond rings sparkling on his fingers.

But though Elizabeth took Beketov into her bed, she did not oust Shuvalov. And Razumovsky remained always gracefully lingering in the background. She took a fourth lover, a young man named Kachenevski, whose beautiful voice had hypnotized her when she heard him in a church choir. For a while she had four acknowledged lovers at once.

Behind each handsome face were roiling political factions and greedy family ambitions. The Shuvalov family, well aware that Beketov was the pawn of their enemy Bestuzhev, spread rumors around court of his disgusting homosexual orgies. They delivered to the vain boy a jar of cosmetic ointment which, when he applied it to his delicate skin, made him break out in a rash that looked just like smallpox. Or perhaps, it was whispered, his rash was the result of some venereal disease caught only from homosexual activity. Their ploy paid off; he was ejected from the palace immediately.

By 1751 Elizabeth began having painful digestive problems and convulsions. Sometimes she was in such pain she would lie motionless for days, looking up at the cupids on the ceiling, ever young, ever in love, ever mocking her age and illness and loss of beauty. Reviving, she would spend hours dressing for a ball, then look in the mirror and, saddened by the sight, decide not to go.

For years it was confidently believed that Elizabeth was a dying woman. But after the most awful attacks of fainting and paralysis, she would defy the odds and recover completely. Finally, on Christmas Day 1761 Elizabeth died at the age of fifty-two, having suffered from fever and vomiting for nearly two weeks. In her last illness she turned from her more recent favorites back to her greatest love and probable husband, Alexei Razumovsky. In her last agony, her only comfort was listening to Razumovsky's exquisite voice, the one she had first heard thirty years before in the palace chapel, singing old Ukrainian lullabies to her. As soon as she breathed her last, her nephew Peter was proclaimed czar, and Razumovsky locked himself in his rooms and sobbed.

The death of Empress Elizabeth meant that Grand Duchess Catherine was now empress consort. But as consort she possessed no power in her own right; power rested in the twitching hands of her imbecile husband, Czar Peter III. And Peter wanted nothing so much as to kill his annoying wife.

Peter had been poised to inherit the German duchy of Holstein and the kingdom of Sweden. He had a mania for all things German, particularly his hero Frederick the Great, and was a devout Protestant. But fate in the form of Aunt Elizabeth, empress of Russia, decreed that he must give up Germany and Sweden and everything dear to him and embrace a strange language, religion, and customs. The change unbalanced the sensitive child who was dragged kicking and screaming to his new domain, and whose mental health seemed to decline with each passing year.

When Catherine first met Peter, he was tiny for his age but good-looking in a vapid blond way. Within the year he caught smallpox; the fever unhinged what was left of his mind, the lesions gouged out his skin as if they had been acid. The groom was now a disfigured giggling idiot; his nose was red and swollen, his eyes watering, his skin scabbed and mutilated. When Elizabeth announced the date of the wedding, Catherine recoiled. "I had a very great repugnance to hear the day named," she wrote, "and it did not please me at all to hear it spoken of."[18]

The elaborate church wedding was followed by a long banquet and a dance. But Empress Elizabeth, intent on getting herself an heir from this ill-matched pair, was in a hurry to get them to bed. Peter, she realized, would never be able to rule Russia. A child must be born soon to lead Russia into the future.

Ceremoniously placed in the bridal bed, Catherine waited for her groom. "Everyone had gone and I remained alone for over two hours," she recalled, "not knowing what I had to do, whether to get up or remain in bed." Finally, Peter came, climbed into bed, and guffawed. "How it would amuse my servants to see us here in bed together!"[19] Then he fell asleep. Peter had been informed of the sex act only a few days before the wedding and seemed not to understand it. Catherine, who had only been told the night before of her marital duties, must have been both relieved and humiliated by her husband's lack of interest.

At sixteen Catherine was ready and willing to have sex. Even as a child she gave a hint of her future intense sexuality; she would ride her pillows astride, as if they were a horse, a form of masturbation, we can assume, until she finally fell off in exhaustion. "I was never caught in the act, nor did anyone ever know that I traveled post-haste in my bed on my pillows," she confessed in her memoirs.[20]

Peter often did keep his wife up all night, but instead of making love he took his toy soldiers to bed, playing until dawn, having mock battles on the covers. Sometimes he made Catherine drill for hours at night with a heavy musket over her shoulder. Peter trained a pack of hounds to drill, and when he wasn't beating them, he kept them locked up in Catherine's closet where they urinated all over her clothes. "It was amid this stench," Catherine reported, "that we slept."[21]

The empress surrounded Catherine with strict chaperones to ensure the future heir would be Peter's, a prince of Romanov blood. But after seven years, Catherine still remained a virgin. Like Louis XVI of France, Peter suffered from phimosis, a condition in which a long flap of foreskin prevented intercourse. Circumcision was the only remedy, but Peter refused.

The disgruntled empress, realizing any heir would be better than no heir at all, relaxed her vigilance and encouraged Catherine to take a lover, the darkly dashing Sergei Saltikov. The twenty-six-year-old was a born seducer, vain and sleek, the kind of man who, reeking of cheap cologne, sneaked up back staircases. Debonair and well-built, Saltikov was everything Catherine's skinny, pale, obnoxious husband was not. When encouraged to relieve the twenty-three-year-old grand duchess of her unwanted virginity, Sergei accepted the mission with alacrity.

When Catherine became pregnant, Empress Elizabeth ordered

Peter's friends to get him drunk and hold him down as the doctor, who had been waiting in the wings, was brought in to perform a circumcision. When the czarevitch had healed, Catherine was forced to swallow her revulsion and seduce him. Much to Elizabeth's chagrin, Catherine had two miscarriages in quick succession before becoming pregnant a third time with the future Czar Paul I, who was born in 1754.

As Empress Elizabeth cooed over the cradle, a court lady coolly remarked how dark the child's complexion was, compared with Peter's paleness. "Hold your tongue, you bitch," the empress roared. "I know what you mean. You want to insinuate he is a bastard but if he is, he is not the first one that has been in my family."[22]

After the birth Saltikov was sent on diplomatic missions to various European courts, and word got back to Catherine that he talked of her as a triumph, even as he seduced other court ladies. Not only had she been casually tossed aside by her first lover, but Catherine had no contact with her infant son, who was being raised by Elizabeth.

Worst of all, she knew that her husband's mind was becoming completely unglued. One night he came late to their room and attacked her with a sword. Thinking fast, Catherine gamely suggested that he give her a sword, too, so they could duel. He walked away and she slumped against the wall, thinking how close she had come to being killed.

Lonely and sexually frustrated, Catherine cast about for a new lover. He was provided by the British ambassador, Sir Charles Hanbury-Williams, who had in his suite a handsome young Polish count. At twenty-three, Stanislaus Poniatowski was thoughtful and sensitive and offered the startling advantage of having attended the major salons of Paris.

Hoping to further relations between Russia and England, Sir Charles brought the blond, hazel-eyed Poniatowski to Russia with the sole intention of landing him either in the bed of Empress Elizabeth or Grand Duchess Catherine. Eager to advance the fallen fortunes of his family in Poland, Poniatowski allowed himself to become a sexual pawn in the hands of Sir Charles.

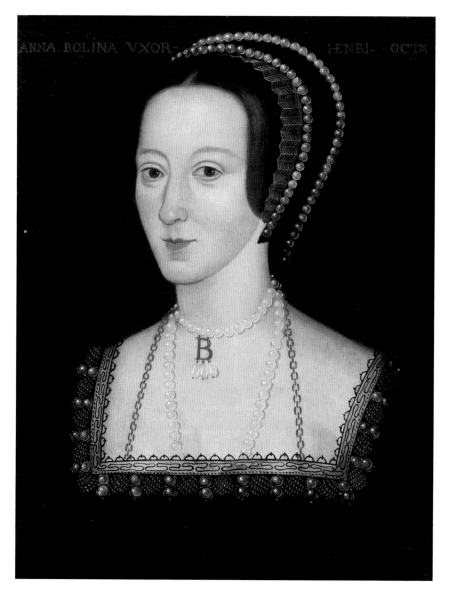

ANNE BOLEYN, QUEEN OF ENGLAND
NATIONAL PORTRAIT GALLERY, LONDON

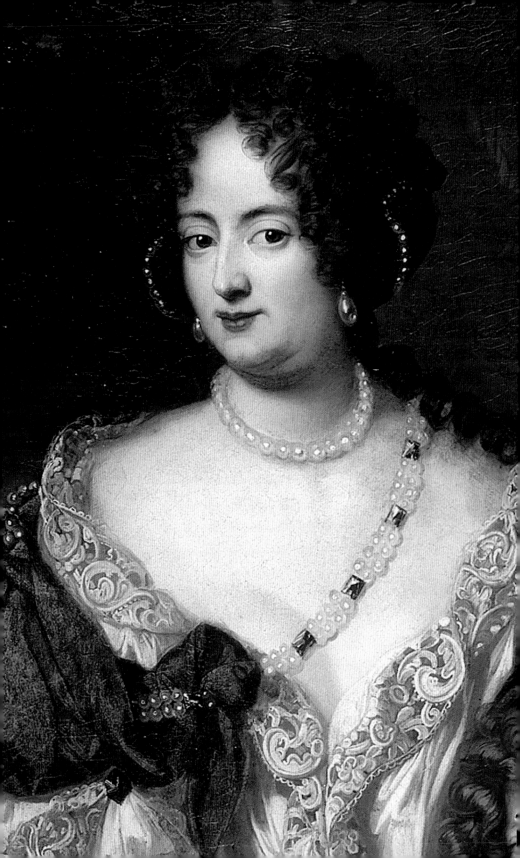

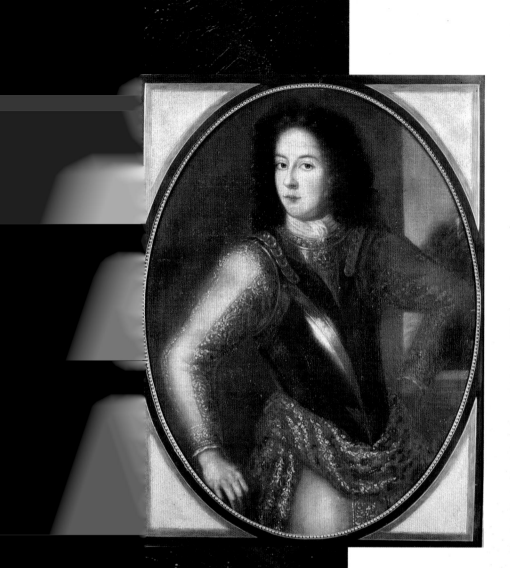

(*Left*) Count Philip von Königsmark,
lover of Sophia Dorothea
Historisches Museum, Hannover

(*opposite*) Sophia Dorothea,
crown princess of Hanover
Bomann-Museum, Celle

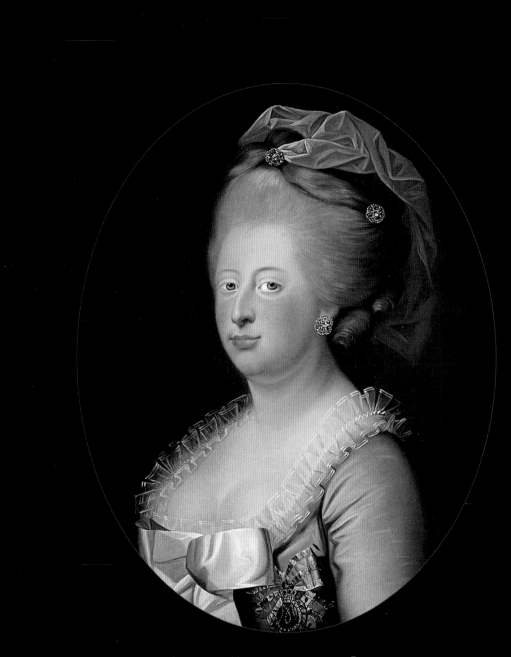

CAROLINE MATILDA, QUEEN OF DENMARK
BOMANN-MUSEUM, CELLE

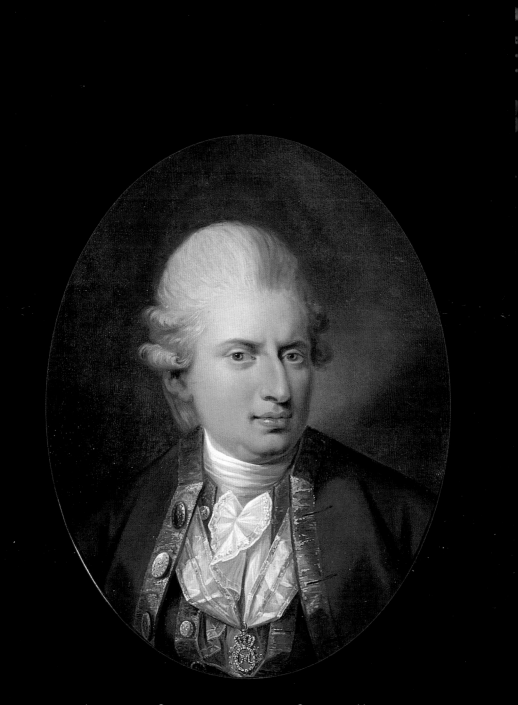

JOHANN VON STRUENSEE, LOVER OF CAROLINE MATILDA
BOMANN-MUSEUM, CELLE

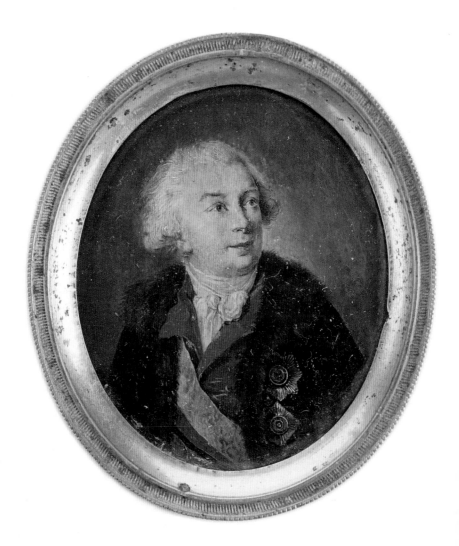

IVAN SHUVALOV
Portrait by Elisabeth Vigée-Lebrun
© RMN/Musée National des Châteaux de Versailles et
de Trianon/Vertrieb: bpk, Berlin

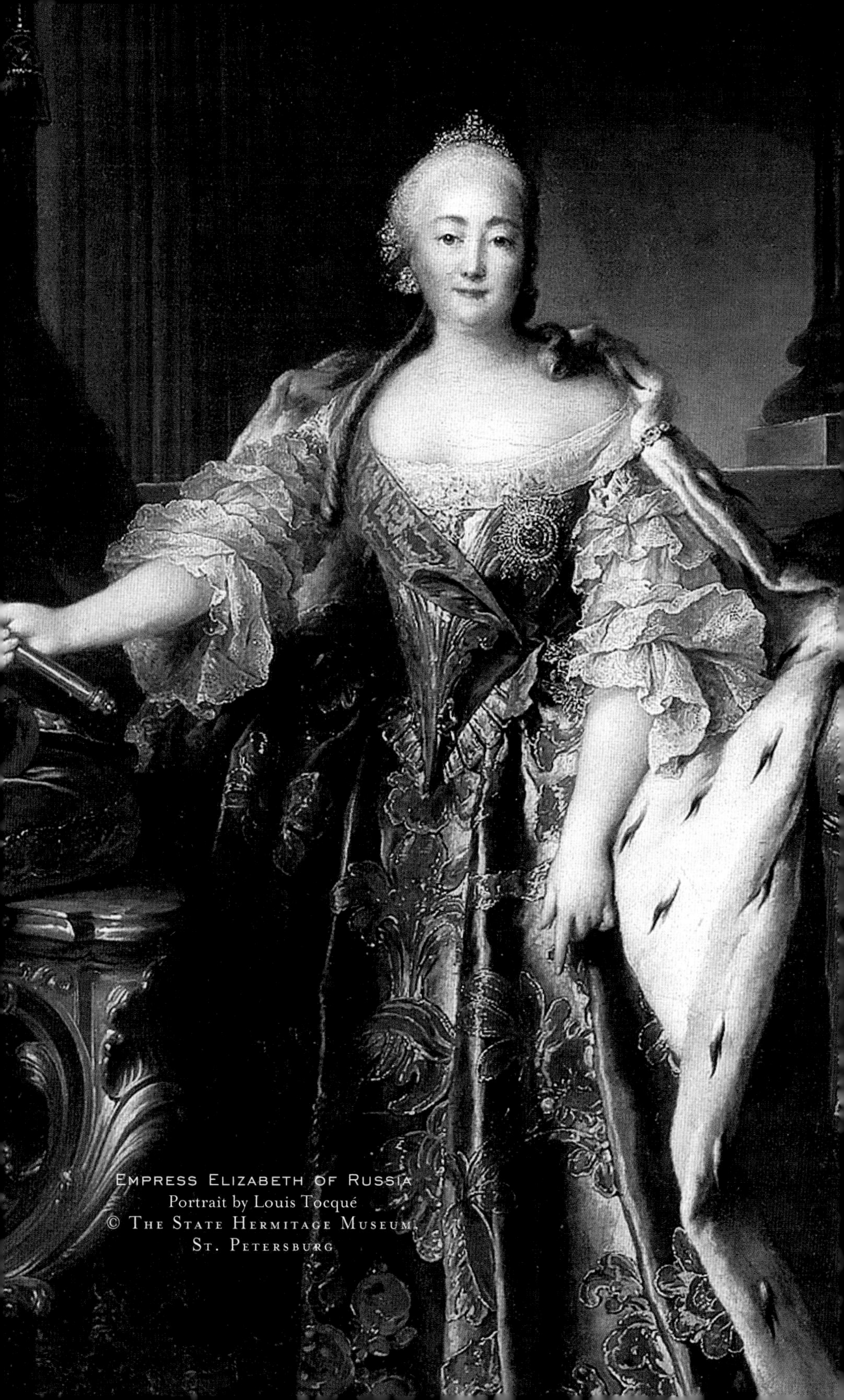

EMPRESS ELIZABETH OF RUSSIA
Portrait by Louis Tocqué
© THE STATE HERMITAGE MUSEUM,
ST. PETERSBURG

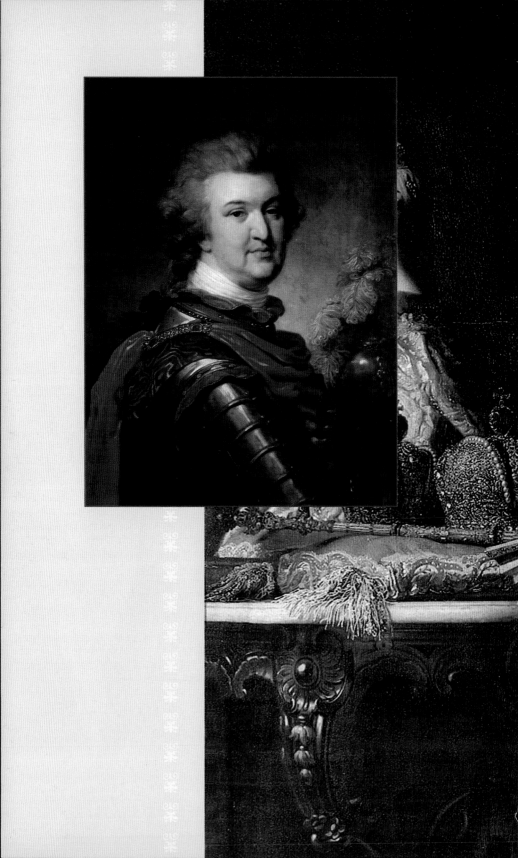

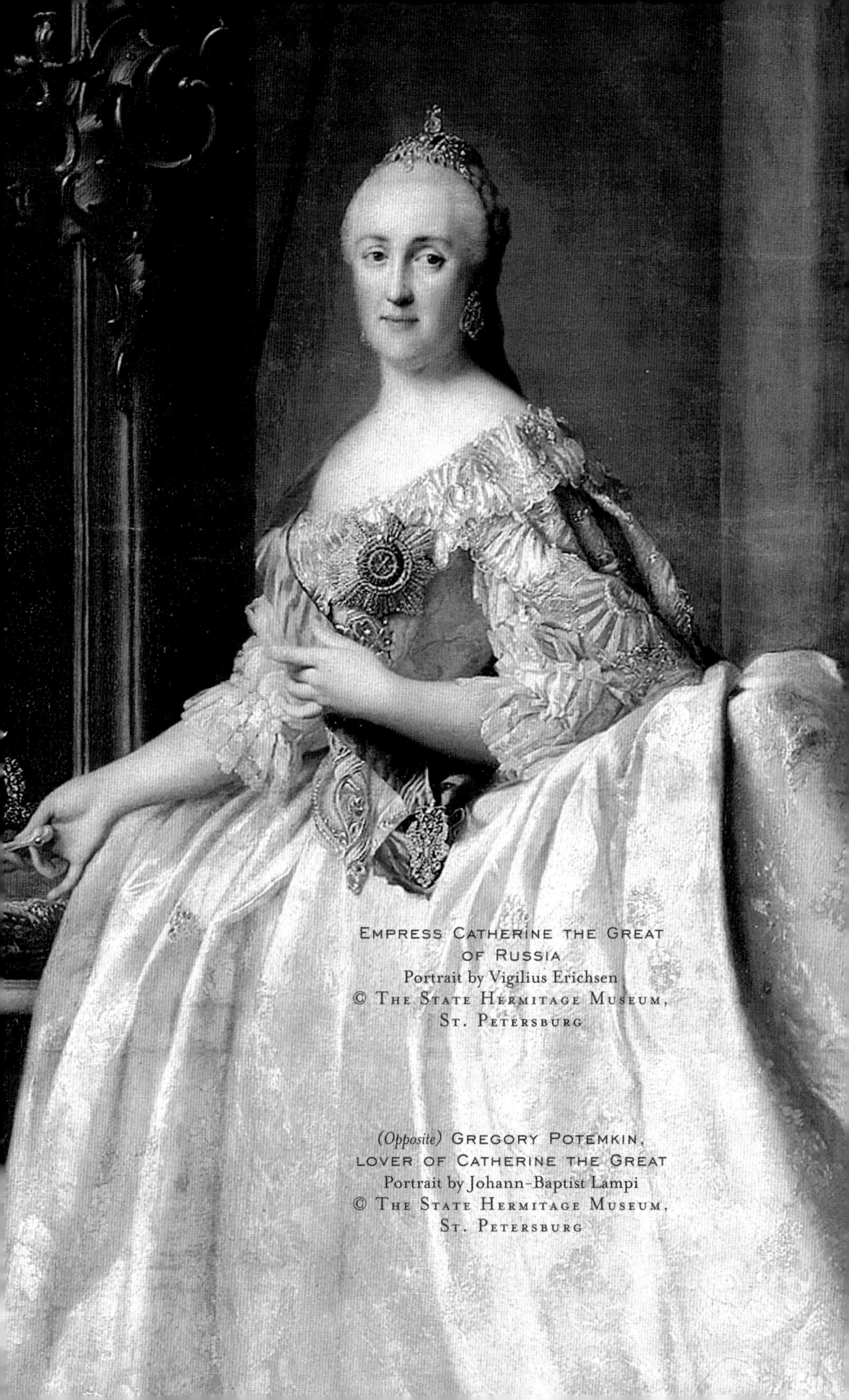

EMPRESS CATHERINE THE GREAT
OF RUSSIA
Portrait by Vigilius Erichsen
© THE STATE HERMITAGE MUSEUM,
ST. PETERSBURG

(*Opposite*) GREGORY POTEMKIN,
LOVER OF CATHERINE THE GREAT
Portrait by Johann-Baptist Lampi
© THE STATE HERMITAGE MUSEUM,
ST. PETERSBURG

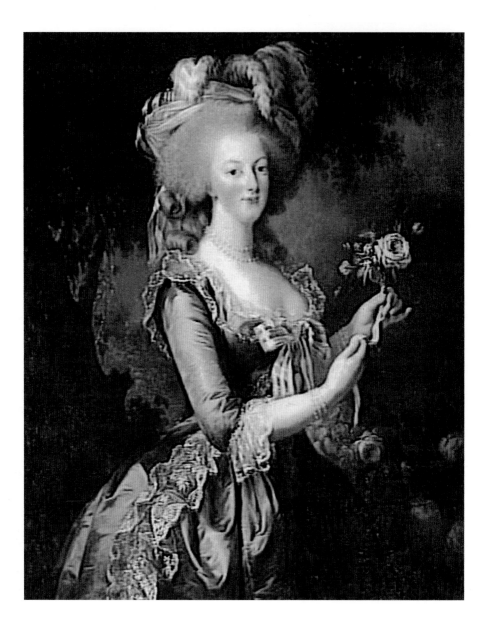

QUEEN MARIE ANTOINETTE OF FRANCE
Portrait by Elisabeth Vigée-Lebrun
© RMN/Musée National des Chateâux de Versailles et de
Trianon/Vertrieb: bpk, Berlin

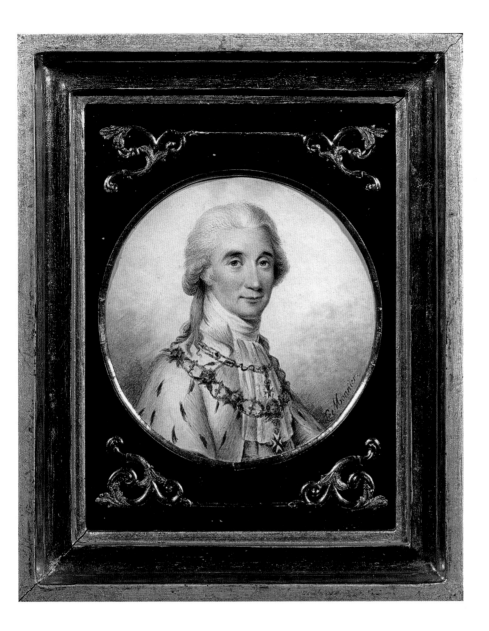

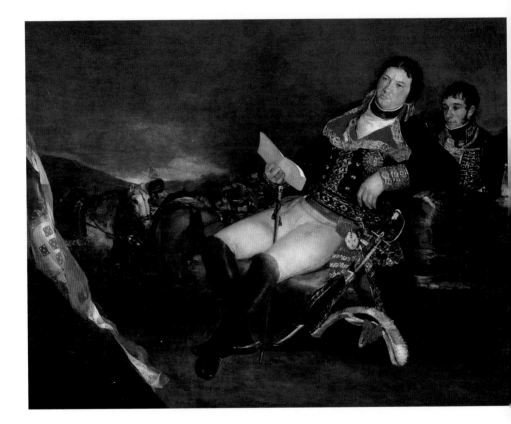

MANUEL GODOY, LOVER OF QUEEN MARIA LUISA OF SPAIN
Portrait by Francisco de Goya
MUSEUM OF THE ROYAL ACADEMY OF FINE ARTS OF SAN FERNANDO,
MADRID

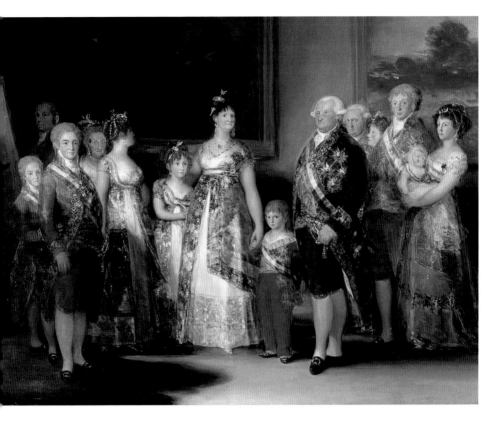

QUEEN MARIA LUISA OF SPAIN,
HER HUSBAND, KING CARLOS IV, AND THEIR FAMILY
Portrait by Francisco de Goya
© MUSEO NACIONAL DEL PRADO, MADRID

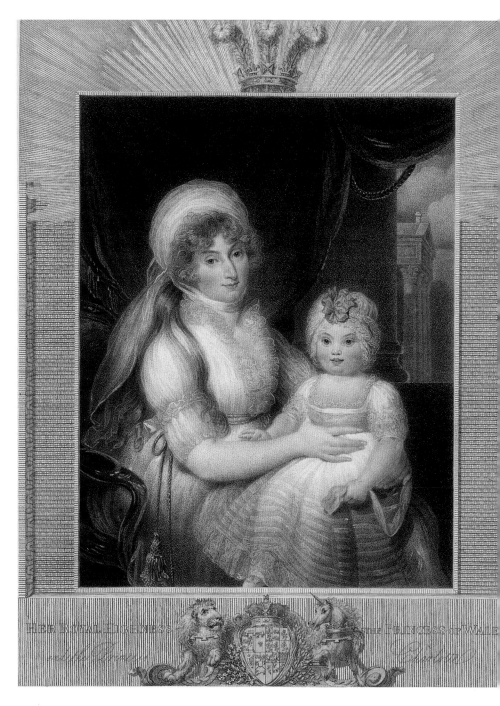

CAROLINE, PRINCESS OF WALES, AND HER DAUGHTER
Portrait by Collyer
THE TRUSTEES OF THE BRITISH MUSEUM, LONDON

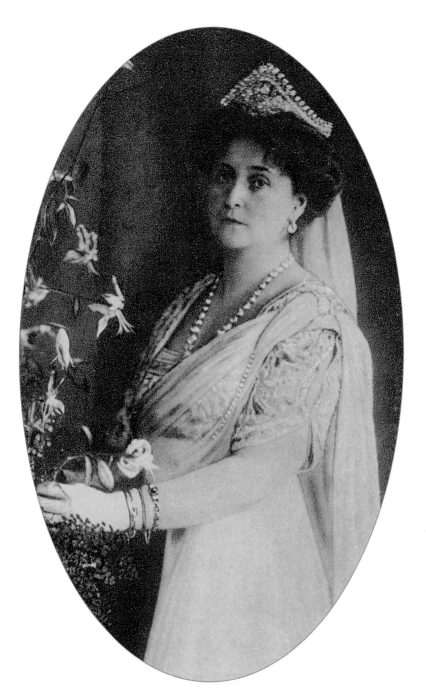

EMPRESS ALEXANDRA OF RUSSIA
© DAVID KING COLLECTION, LONDON

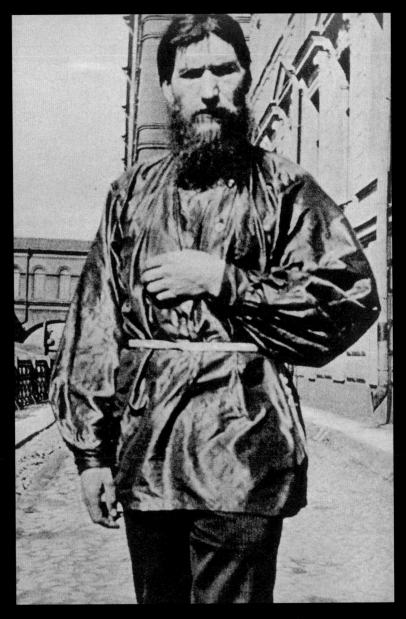

GREGORY RASPUTIN, REPUTED LOVER OF ALEXANDRA
© DAVID KING COLLECTION, LONDON

When Sir Charles introduced the young Pole to Catherine, he noticed how she never took her eyes off him. One observer said the grand duchess had the look "of a wild beast tracking down its prey."[23]

The English ambassador worked assiduously to get the two into bed together. Though Poniatowski enjoyed flirting with the grand duchess, whom he found achingly attractive, he was terrified that an affair would send him to Siberia. Catherine had to seduce a professed virgin and, after a while, began to despair. How to get this fearful young man into bed? A good friend of hers came to the rescue and one night brought Poniatowski to the entrance of her private apartments. As Poniatowski wrote in his memoirs years later, he found the door half open, and inside Catherine was waiting for him in "a simple white gown trimmed with lace and pink ribbons, and looking so enticing as to make one forget the very existence of Siberia."[24]

One day when Poniatowski and several courtiers made a formal visit to Catherine, her little dog gave the love affair away. The dog, who detested strangers, came prancing up to Poniatowski, tail wagging, then turned to the others and barked ferociously. The courtiers eyed each other meaningfully and tried not to laugh. The Swedish ambassador pulled Poniatowski aside and said, "My friend, there can be nothing more treacherous than a small dog; the first thing I used to do with a woman I loved was to be sure and give her one, and it was through them that I learnt if someone was more favored than myself. It is an infallible test. As you see, the dog wanted to eat me up, as he did not know me, but he went mad with joy on seeing *you* again, for it is clear that this is not the first time you have met."[25]

Catherine was not alone in her infidelity. Liberated from his impotence, Peter had taken a mistress, who, if possible, was even uglier than himself. Elizabeth Vorontsova was fat and hunchbacked with disfiguring smallpox scars on her face. Worse, she was slatternly and fearless, insulting people with a gusto that made Peter whinny with laughter. Peter and his mistress would insist that Catherine and Poniatowski join them for dinner. Catherine always played the role of good sport; but the gentlemanly Pole hated the forced dinners with his mistress, her husband, and his mistress.

Catherine gave birth to Poniatowski's daughter in 1757, a sickly child who lived less than a year. Peter, though an idiot, was no fool. He went around in public commenting cheerfully, "I have no idea how my wife becomes pregnant, but I suppose I shall have to accept the child as my own."[26]

In 1758 French and Austrian factions at court, fearing Poniatowski's pro-English sentiments, arranged with Empress Elizabeth to have him ordered back to Poland. Tired of the intrigues at court and the embarrassing dinners with his mistress's drooling husband, he was not sorry to go. Moreover, Catherine's sexual demands were becoming deleterious to his health. In one of his more lucid moments, Peter described his wife as a woman "who would squeeze all the juice out of a lemon and then throw it away."[27] Poniatowski had not been thrown away, but he didn't have a drop of juice left when he took the road to Poland. Catherine cried as long and bitterly as she ever would in her life. "I sensed he was bored," she wrote, "and it nearly broke my heart."[28]

Over the years, Catherine suffered from the capricious moods of Empress Elizabeth, which swung from loving generosity to vicious cruelty. But the last two years of her life, sensing that Catherine, not Peter, would lead her beloved Russia into the future, Elizabeth made peace with the grand duchess. "She is a paragon of truth and justice, she is a woman of great intelligence," the empress remarked, "but my nephew is a monster."[29]

Looking about court for her next lover, Catherine realized her choice must fall on a Russian as foreign lovers ruffled the feathers of squawking rival diplomats. One day in the summer of 1759 the bored, frustrated grand duchess looked out of her window and saw in the courtyard below a guardsman with the face of Adonis and the body of Hercules. It was love at first sight, and she sent for him immediately.

At thirty-four the magnificent Gregory Orlov was a man of action, of energy, of deeds. A few years earlier in a battle against the Prussians, Orlov, bleeding copiously from three serious wounds, had led a cavalry charge and vanquished the enemy.

Towering head and shoulders over other men, this colossus reportedly boasted a penis of tremendous size. He was one of five exceptional soldier brothers renowned for courage, physical strength, whoring, drunkenness, and gambling.

Unlike the smoothly seductive Saltikov or the sweetly ardent Poniatowski, Orlov was like a thundering flood, submerging everything in his path with his crashing brute force. Physically intimidating, he rolled into Catherine's life and into her bed, and completely possessed her, body and soul. Catherine had, perhaps, always longed for a man to take her, rape her. In Orlov she finally found that.

Catherine's choice of Orlov as her lover may not have been solely determined by his lovemaking skills. Peter disliked his wife more and more each passing day and openly expressed his hatred of her. When he became czar, he would kill her unless she moved first. Orlov and his four burly brothers were highly regarded by their regiments and could, when the time came, assist Catherine in climbing onto the throne. The grand duchess kept her love affair secret, smuggling Orlov into her rooms at night for sex and plotting.

In December 1761 Empress Elizabeth lay dying. For years Catherine had planned for this moment, knowing that either her husband would destroy her or she would destroy him. It was one or the other. But now, as that moment approached, Catherine was in no position to act. She was six months pregnant with Orlov's child, ample reason for Peter to divorce her, imprison her, and murder her.

On Christmas Day Empress Elizabeth died, and Peter was proclaimed Czar Peter III. He hated Russia and now, as its leader, would do all in his power to humiliate the country he ruled and the wife who reigned beside him.

Catherine, her pregnancy hidden in a loose and fashionable sack gown, was the first to swear allegiance to the new czar, prostrating herself on the floor before him. She sat vigil with Elizabeth's corpse in the church, day and night, while Peter publicly insulted the memory of his aunt by not saying a single prayer at her bier, joking with her ladies-in-waiting and emitting his own shrill raucous cackles over the corpse. He seemed to think the funeral procession was a colossal joke, and instead of keeping pace behind the coffin as chief mourner, lagged behind and then rushed to catch up, throwing the whole procession into disorder. Russians were scandalized at the behavior of their new emperor and contrasted Peter's behavior with the respectful decorum of Empress Catherine.

Worse than his behavior at the funeral, Peter immediately concluded the Seven Years' War against his hero, Frederick the Great of Prussia, who had been beaten into a corner by valiant Russian soldiers. Peter returned to an astonished Frederick all the territories Russia had won with the blood of its fighting men. He wore a huge ring with a portrait of Frederick, whom he called "the king, my master."[30] Peter ordered the elite Preobrazhensky regiment to wear new uniforms modeled on those of King Frederick's guards. Russian soldiers were aghast to find that their new emperor was a skinny heel-clicking weakling wearing an enemy uniform and barking drill orders in German.

Equally threatening to Russians were Peter's edicts to seize church properties, rid the churches of all icons except those representing Christ and the Virgin, and force Orthodox priests to dress like Lutheran ministers. Within weeks of his accession, he had alienated the army and the church, which together formed the keystone of support crucial to any reign.

Peter treated his mistress Elizabeth Vorontsova as the reigning empress and went out of his way to publicly humiliate Catherine. Vorontsova's behavior had become even more shocking now that her lover was emperor. A German visitor reported, "She swore like a trooper, had a squint, stank, and spat when she talked."[31] Catherine scathingly referred to her as "Madame de Pompadour," advertising the difference between the coarse slattern of Peter III and the graceful mistress of Louis XV. When Peter became drunk, he boasted that he would divorce Catherine, marry and crown his mistress, and declare Catherine's son Paul a bastard. With Orlov's help, Catherine made sure that these boasts were repeated in every barracks in St. Petersburg.

But Catherine's primary concern was how to give birth secretly while living a few rooms down the hall from her husband. One of her devoted servants, Vasily Skourin, knowing that Peter loved to watch buildings burn, set fire to his own house as Catherine went into labor. Peter raced across town to see the fire and for hours stared as if hypnotized by the golden orange flames licking the walls, the black smoke curling to the sky. He listened intently to the crackle and sizzle of burning wood and shrieked with joy when the beams crashed down.

While the emperor was indulging his passion for pyromania, the empress gave birth to her lover's son. A trusted lady-in-waiting smuggled the baby out of the palace wrapped in a beaver skin, which resulted in the surname given him—Bobrinsky—a derivation of the Russian word for beaver. Peter, living in his hazy world of Prussian drill maneuvers and pyromania, never knew that his wife had even been pregnant.

In an effort to support his master, the king of Prussia, Peter decided to join his attack on Denmark. Russian troops were furious to learn that they would be fighting for their sworn enemy Frederick the Great. Moreover, the emperor, whose idea of military valor was beating helpless animals and trembling servants, decided he would lead his men personally, dressed in a Prussian uniform. Peter's antics played directly into the hands of the Orlov brothers, who were winning over followers in their regiments eager to proclaim Catherine empress.

To prepare for his journey to Denmark, Peter set out for the palace of Oranienbaum several miles outside of St. Petersburg, which he transformed into an army camp. He ordered Catherine to move to the nearby palace of Peterhof, where he planned to join her to celebrate his name day on June 29, the Feast of St. Peter. But Catherine heard that the emperor was setting her up to have her arrested the evening after the celebration.

Catherine, who kept up a friendly correspondence with Poniatowski in Poland, wrote him, "It was six o'clock in the morning of June 28, and I was fast asleep when Alexis Orlov came into my room and woke me up by telling me in the calmest manner that I must get dressed and come with him to St. Petersburg, where the army was ready to proclaim me their empress."[32]

Soldiers quickly swarmed her carriage as regiments raced to support her. By nine o'clock in the morning, she was kneeling at the high altar of Kazan Cathedral, receiving the archbishop's blessing as Catherine II, autocrat of all the Russias. She would not rule as regent for her eight-year-old son Paul—a reign that would have ended when he turned sixteen—but as empress in her own right until her death.

After receiving the church's blessing, Catherine quickly changed into the green uniform of a colonel of the guards, a flaring coat, knee breeches, high black boots, and a fur-trimmed tricorn hat. She rode at the head of her troops to review the fourteen thousand men at arms who had proclaimed their loyalty. The new ruler looked like an ancient Greek goddess of victory, bold, confident, triumph shining in her eyes, her long dark hair tumbling in waves down to her waist.

Suddenly a twenty-two-year-old subaltern of the horse guards rode boldly out to her and, remarking that her uniform was lacking a sword knot, he gallantly gave her his own. His superior officers disapproved of his audacity, but the empress, pleased at his chivalric gesture and handsome appearance, accepted his gift with a smile. She asked his name. It was Gregory Potemkin.

For the next twelve years he would dream of a proud young empress in a green uniform, astride a white horse, a glorious future reflected in her smile. After the tumults of that day, the young soldier went to his room and wrote her a love poem: "As soon as I beheld you, I thought of you alone. Your lovely eyes captivated me, yet I trembled to say I loved. O Heavens! The torture to love one to whom I dare not declare it. One who can never be mine! Cruel Gods!"[33] But the gods were not as cruel as he thought. Potemkin would have his chance with her, but not yet.

Meanwhile, Peter and his companions arrived at Peterhof to find the palace almost empty and Catherine nowhere in sight. Upon learning of the coup, Peter's advisers urged him to flee the country to save his life, to return to the town of Kiel, which he possessed as duke of Holstein. Peter, however, petulantly insisted that he return to negotiate with his wife. He should have fled; the Orlov brothers took Peter prisoner and forced him to sign an act of abdication. A disappointed Frederick the Great dryly remarked that Peter III "let himself be driven from the throne as a child is sent to bed."[34]

Unlike many of her contemporaries, Catherine was not vindictive. She would have preferred to send poor stammering Peter back to his duchy of Holstein. "This young man, frankly speaking, deserved pity rather than censure," she wrote in her memoirs.[35] But she knew that as long as he lived, her husband would always be a focus of discontent and rebellion, and her throne would sit on a shaky foundation. Catherine was, above all, a practical woman. Within a week, Peter was dead.

Gregory Orlov's brother Alexis had killed him, claiming in a letter to Catherine that it had occurred accidentally during a drunken brawl. For the public viewing, the corpse wore a high collar to cover the black finger marks on its neck and a huge hat to shade the face black and swollen from asphyxiation. Doctors declared the emperor had died of a "hemorrhoidal colic" with brain complications. Few Russians were upset at Peter's murder. Even the great philosopher Voltaire, a friendly correspondent of Catherine's, shrugged off the matter. "I know that she is reproached with some trifles about her husband," he wrote, "but these are family affairs with which I do not meddle."[36]

Upon taking the throne she found an empty treasury, two hundred thousand peasants on strike, a restless army unpaid for eight months, rebellion across the empire, unfathomable corruption in the legal system, and a near paralysis of commerce. Working fourteen hours a day, Catherine undertook reorganization of almost every aspect of Russian government with traditional German efficiency, presiding personally over council and senate meetings, peppering officials with probing questions they could not answer, and prolonging their working hours. Catherine worked her ministers harder than any man could have. Indeed, she considered herself a male soul wrapped in a female body, and though delighting in that body, she considered other women weak, whining, and utterly useless.

Within a year of taking the throne she had founded an

orphanage, a school for midwives, an organization for public health, and a school for the daughters of the nobility. An avid student of French philosophy, at the outset of her reign Catherine hoped to create a just and equitable society. Out of a population of some nineteen million Russians, almost eight million were serfs, slaves owned either by individual families or the state itself. Russian wealth was usually measured in serfs—or "souls," as they were called—rather than money or land. Catherine, who had hoped to free the serfs, soon found that this lofty goal was all but impossible in her turbulent realm. Threatened by the loss of their most prized possessions, the nobles who had supported her would have toppled her. "You philosophers are lucky men," she wrote to Denis Diderot. "You write on paper and paper is patient. Unfortunate Empress that I am, I write on the susceptible skins of living beings."[37]

She invited to Russia doctors, dentists, engineers, craftsmen, architects, gardeners, artists, and, of course, her favorite philosophers. Her offers were not always accepted. The philosopher Jean d'Alembert, obviously referring to Peter's death, sent his regrets. "I am too subject to hemorrhoids," he explained. "They are too serious in that country and I want to have my rear end hurt in complete safety."[38]

At the outset of her reign, no one thought she would survive more than a few months. One French visitor called Russia "an absolute monarchy tempered by assassination."[39] And indeed Catherine started, horrified, whenever there was a sudden noise, as if expecting a knife or bullet to rip into her back. Suffering from intense stress, she put on weight and aged rapidly in the months after her accession.

To secure more firmly her shaky grip on the throne, Catherine generously rewarded her supporters. All five Orlov brothers were made counts and given large amounts of cash. Gregory Potemkin, whom she had not forgotten, was promoted two ranks and given ten thousand rubles, an ample reward for a sword knot.

Never one to hold a grudge, Catherine gave her dead husband's obnoxious mistress, Elizabeth Vorontsova, a house in

Moscow and arranged for her to marry a senator. Sergei Saltikov was appointed envoy to France, given twenty thousand rubles for his journey and two years later loaned twenty thousand more to clear his considerable debts. His reputation as a scoundrel wafted around him like a bad odor; the ladies avoided him as much as the politicians he was supposed to court. Jaded, faded Saltikov, his jowl sagging a bit more with each passing year, must have kicked himself for having so unceremoniously dumped the insignificant little grand duchess. He soon dropped out of the foreign service, living in obscurity until his death in 1813.

Stanislaus Poniatowski, who had always remained on good terms with Catherine, received the greatest reward of all, a crown. In 1763 Catherine signed a treaty with Frederick the Great of Prussia in which Frederick would not protest Poniatowski's election as king of Poland. The Polish crown was part reward for his former services in bed, part political strategy; Catherine knew that Poniatowski's gentle nature would render him a mere puppet of Russia. At first, he refused the crown. "Don't make me king, but bring me back to your side," he implored, still deeply in love with her.[40] But having enjoyed Orlov's animalistic rutting, she shuddered at the thought of Poniatowski's pale slender hands upon her.

He finally relented and once seated on the Polish throne tried his best to be a good king. Catherine quickly dispelled any illusions he might have had of his own power, however. She sent thousands of troops to Warsaw to keep the peace, as she said, but in reality to force her puppet king to dance to a Russian tune.

As empress in her own right, Catherine no longer had reason to hide her love affair with Gregory Orlov. Indeed, she flaunted him, taking his arm proudly; in palace ballrooms this brilliant pair parted the crowds as Moses had parted the Red Sea. Orlov was such a splendid specimen of manhood that even those at court who detested him were forced to admit his overwhelming physical magnificence. For all his brute strength, he had the features of a classical statue and moved with an elegant animal grace. A stranger arriving at court could pick out the empress's lover at a glance—the tallest, handsomest man in the room, wearing the finest gold-embroidered suit with diamond buttons, and a large miniature of Catherine hanging from his breast, set in a frame of huge diamonds. Orlov was a tremendous asset to the court for his decorative value alone.

Catherine's lover was often seen reclining on a couch in the empress's bedroom, wearing only a bathrobe. Lazy and in love with the trappings of royalty, he had few political ambitions. The French envoy reported that Orlov was "very handsome, but very stupid."[41]

Many at court hated the increasing arrogance and power of the Orlovs. All petitions and favors passed through their hands. Gregory Orlov held a morning reception as if he were royal himself, and all favor seekers were expected to show up and pay their respects. Princes of noble lineage were forced to trot next to his carriage as mounted escorts when he sat inside.

Over the first decade of her reign, Catherine remained faithful to her lover, putting up patiently with his increasing moodiness, rude treatment, and flagrant infidelities. The French envoy wrote, "He is emperor in all but name and takes liberties with his sovereign such as no mistress in polite society would tolerate from her lover."[42] Catherine loved him passionately, but her love was tempered by fear. The Orlov brothers had brought her to the throne and had murdered an emperor for her. She had rewarded all five with key government positions. Boasting thousands of devoted supporters in the army and government, the kingmakers could, perhaps, unmake an empress.

When Orlov pressed her to marry him, Catherine must have seriously considered his proposal. She sent an emissary to Alexei Razumovsky, the late Empress Elizabeth's lover and reputed husband, seeking a precedent for a Russian empress to marry secretly. When questioned, Razumovsky opened a chest, took out a parchment scroll tied with a faded pink ribbon, and tossed it into the fire. "No," he said softly. "There is no proof. Say that to our gracious sovereign."[43]

Catherine, a student of history, found herself in the uneasy position of Mary Queen of Scots two centuries earlier. Though not directly involved in the murder of her idiot husband, Henry

Darnley, soon thereafter Mary married his murderer, James Hepburn, earl of Bothwell—who some said had been her lover—and the resulting uproar lost her the throne. Taking her cue from history, Catherine refused to marry Orlov.

One evening at a dinner party at the Hermitage Palace, Gregory Potemkin appeared. Catherine recognized him instantly. She had been secretly watching over his career for years since that exhilarating day when he had presented her with the sword knot. Though tall, vain, and authoritative like Orlov, Potemkin had less regular features. His wide slanting eyes and full sensual lips gave him a slightly Asian look. Hearing of Potemkin's talent for mimicry, she asked him to imitate someone, and he mimicked her own guttural German accent. The guests were appalled at his boldness, but Catherine laughed heartily. In talking to him she discovered that he was highly educated, deeply religious, and politically brilliant. She enjoyed his conversation so much that the Orlovs became jealous. Potemkin disappeared.

Though Gregory Orlov still reigned supreme, gradually Catherine became aware that he was tiring of her as a woman. His lovemaking was no longer a pleasure but a boring duty with a woman grown heavy and middle-aged. His forceful taking of her had made her feel fresh and young again every night. But now the ardor had vanished, the ravishing had become mechanical groping in the dark.

The truth was that Orlov had fallen deeply in love with his young cousin. At forty-three, for the first time, Catherine felt she was growing old. Youth was slipping through her fingers like water, and even with the power of the empress of all the Russias, she could not hold on to it. All her wealth and majesty, her dazzling intellect and steamy sexual passion could not compare with the soft budding charms of a fourteen-year-old.

Catherine was not one to scold and reproach. When peace talks with Turkey were required in the summer of 1772, she sent Orlov as her representative in a coat embroidered with a million rubles' worth of diamonds. Glinting in the sunshine, he left.

"I cannot live one day without love," she wrote.[44] And now, with Orlov gone, she cast about court for a replacement. Her glance fell on Alexander Vasilchikov, a good-looking twenty-eight-year-old with excellent manners. He was sweet and modest, with beautiful black eyes and a sensual mouth. Sensing the empress's interest in the young man, Orlov's enemies took advantage of his absence to push Vasilchikov into the imperial bed.

Soon the young man was showered with valuable presents. By August he had been made gentleman-in-waiting. By September he was aide-de-camp and had moved into Orlov's former rooms adjoining those of the empress. Courtiers were amazed that this quiet mouse of a man had replaced the magnificent Orlov. Most thought that the moment Orlov returned from his mission, the "nonentity," as he was called, would disappear in an hour.

When Gregory Orlov heard that his enemies had placed another man in the empress's bed, he came thundering back to St. Petersburg in a black rage. But Catherine, rather than taking back the man who had tormented her with his infidelities, bribed him to go away. She gave him one hundred thousand rubles outright and an annual pension of one hundred fifty thousand; the Marble Palace, which was under construction; the use of all palaces outside St. Petersburg until his own was completed; and ten thousand serfs from the crown. In addition, she gave him all the furniture and paintings from his apartments in the Winter Palace, the Sèvres dinner service for one hundred guests that she had ordered from France the year before, and another dinner service in heavy silver.

As all expected, Vasilchikov did not last long. His performance in bed was evidently satisfactory, yet his intellect was limited and his conversation dull. One contemporary described him as having his "head stuffed with hay."[45] Catherine was sophisticated, cultured, and witty and needed a lover with whom she could discuss politics, art, and theology. Poor Vasilchikov seemed to have no opinions at all on these subjects. He grew peevish, felt himself outmatched, and claimed to be ill. "I'm just a little whore," he sniffed, clutching at imaginary pains in his chest.[46]

In 1773 Catherine recalled Orlov to court but refused to take him back into her bed. Frederick the Great, never one to mince words, reported that Gregory Orlov had returned to all his former offices "except that of fucking. It is a terrible business when the prick and the cunt decide the interests of Europe."[47]

By late 1773 the empress had admitted that Vasilchikov "bores me to tears."[48] She couldn't stop thinking of the fearless Potemkin, now a general fighting on the Danube. There had always been a sizzling chemistry between them, but the time had never been right to call him to her bed. On his periodic visits to St. Petersburg, upon encountering Catherine, Potemkin would drop to his knees, ardently kiss her hands, and openly declare his passion for her. The empress chuckled at these displays; courtiers hated him for his galling presumption.

Potemkin was, perhaps, the only man in the world who was Catherine's equal physically and intellectually. Well over six feet tall, he had a broad chest and powerful shoulders. His thick, unkempt tawny hair gave him a leonine appearance. Fearless, flamboyant, and easily bored, Potemkin had a brash genius, a primitive brilliance.

But he was no longer the handsome lithe soldier who had presented the brand-new empress with a sword knot. An infection had rendered his left eye clouded and blind and, though he was sensitive about it, he never bothered to wear a patch. Still powerfully built, there was a little too much swash in his buckle. Yet neither the disfigurement of his face nor the swelling of his physique diminished the man's attractions. Potemkin was a raw force of nature against which it was futile to fight. His magnetism engulfed the most crowded ballroom. Women threw themselves into his burly arms. He was the man every woman wanted to sleep with. He was the man other men wanted to be, or to kill, or both.

But if his looks had deteriorated in the intervening decade, so had those of the empress. She looked older than her forty-four years, her waist had thickened, and her hair had turned gray. But like Potemkin, she was a force to be reckoned with and not only because she wore a crown. Her sparkling wit had, over the years, increased its luster. Her self-confidence was equal to if not surpassing his. Her physical passions would forever remain untouched by time, as would his. And like him, she had the face of a handsome middle-aged man.

Now, at the age of thirty-four, Potemkin received a letter from the empress, ordering him back to St. Petersburg "for the purpose of the confirmation of my feelings for you."[49] He had been waiting eleven years for this letter. But when Potemkin arrived in St. Petersburg eager to take up the appointment of empress's lover, he was furious to find Vasilchikov still sulking in the official paramour's apartments. The truth was, Catherine hesitated to install Potemkin as her favorite with all the perquisites of wealth and power. Perhaps she instinctively felt that Potemkin would be unstoppable once unleashed. A towering tidal wave, roaring toward shore, cannot be persuaded to turn back to sea. A thundering volcano, heaving burning ash and molten lava down the mountainside, does not reconsider and pull back. Nor would there be any half measures with that other oversized natural wonder, Gregory Potemkin.

The Orlovs, in particular, felt threatened by Potemkin as they never had by Vasilchikov. Potemkin, once rooted in the palace, would never permit himself to be dislodged. The tempestuous general threatened to upend the entire existing power structure at court.

One day Gregory Orlov was descending a staircase in the palace when he chanced to meet Potemkin coming up. Gaily, Potemkin asked Orlov whether there was any news at court. Orlov replied, "Nothing very much, except that you are coming up and I am going down."[50]

Potemkin, whose many virtues did not include patience, stormed and raged for Catherine to dismiss the mediocre Vasilchikov. Potemkin finally ran off to a monastery, vowing never to return until the young man was banished from the palace. The empress yielded and Potemkin returned. Buckling under the weight of valuable presents, pensions, and honors, Vasilchikov retired grudgingly to his new mansion and whined about his dismissal for decades to anyone who would listen.

With Vasilchikov gone, the empress could now focus exclusively on Potemkin. Grisha, she called him, a nickname for Gregory. She wrote him little notes throughout the day, some political, others sexual: "There is not a cell in my whole body that does not yearn for you, oh infidel!" "I thank you for yesterday's feast. My little Grisha fed me and quenched my thirst, but not with wine. . . ." "My head is like that of a cat in heat. . . ." "I will be a 'woman of fire' for you, as you so often say. But I shall try to hide my flames." "Beloved, I will do as you order, should I come to your room, or will you come to mine?"[51]

"Oh, Monsieur Potemkin!" she gushed. "By what sorcery have you managed to turn a head which is generally regarded as one of the best in Europe." She cooed, "We remain together for hours on end without a shadow of boredom, and it is always with reluctance that I leave you. I forget the whole world when I am with you. There is something extraordinary that words cannot express, for the alphabet is too short and the letters are too few." She called him "my little pigeon, my golden pheasant, my kitten, my little father, my dear little heart."[52]

Catherine's unbounded excitement may have had something to do with the size of Potemkin's penis, which was reported to be enormous. Many years after Catherine's death when the Hermitage Palace had been turned into a museum, the curator reported that Catherine had had a porcelain cast of Potemkin's penis in her private collection. He removed this object from its silk-lined wooden box and showed it to several visitors who admired "the glorious weapon" of Potemkin.[53] Alas, it is not listed on the current Hermitage inventory and no one has seen it in years.

The lovers often met in the sauna at night, Potemkin insisting on meals being served there. Many at court noticed the lights in the bathhouse and the servants scurrying in and out with dishes. Here they bathed, ate, drank, made love, and ran the empire.

In his dispatch to London, British ambassador Sir Robert Gunning remarked, "Nowhere have favorites risen so rapidly as in this country. But there is no instance even here of so rapid a progress as that of the present one."[54] And indeed Potemkin's ascent was nothing short of meteoric.

His rewards far outstripped those of Catherine's other lovers. Upon landing in the imperial bed, Potemkin was given 150,000 rubles in cash; an army officer lived well on 300 rubles a year. He received a salary of 12,000 rubles a month. His meals and wine, amounting to some 100,000 rubles a year, were paid for by the imperial budget, and Catherine personally covered his substantial gambling losses. Every feast day, of which the court celebrated many, he received another 100,000 rubles as a present.

Catherine gave him a diamond-hilted sword and a portrait of herself set in diamonds to dangle above his heart, just like the one she had bestowed on Orlov. He was given his own lavish palace as well as apartments leading directly to hers in all the imperial palaces. She named him a count and later a prince and appointed him member of the secret council and vice president of the council of war, with the rank of general-in-chief.

Many scholars believe that Catherine and Potemkin were secretly married in 1774, and indeed the rumor reached the courts of Europe soon thereafter. Her correspondence supports the theory as she began to call him "my dearest husband" and "my tender spouse," signing herself "your devoted wife."[55]

Potemkin, who loved to amuse, shock, impress, and terrorize by turns, flaunted his relationship with the empress. He appeared at her official morning receptions barefoot, wearing a dirty dressing gown with his chest hair poking out, and a pink bandana wrapped carelessly around his head. He wanted to make it clear that he had just popped out of bed on the other side of the door. The elegant speeches of the empress and courtiers were punctuated by the loud crunches of Potemkin nibbling on a radish. Not wishing to single him out for rude behavior, Catherine initiated a new rule in the Hermitage Palace—courtiers would no longer be permitted to blow their noses on the curtains.

Innocent of underpants, Potemkin often received official visitors with his private parts dangling out of his half-open dressing gown. Though he could dress himself as ornately as any

French courtier at Versailles, he wanted to show the world that he didn't have to. That sort of thing was for lesser men.

Unlike any of her other lovers, Potemkin was a born statesman and a brilliant general. He became her viceroy, her political partner, her right hand. Potemkin and Catherine were the Antony and Cleopatra of the eighteenth century, two brilliant lovers ruling a vast empire, sharing a tumultuous passion. They made love passionately at night—and Potemkin seems to have had more sexual stamina than even Orlov—and worked together on political projects throughout the day. Their stunning political partnership alarmed Frederick the Great, who grumbled, "A woman is always a woman and in a feminine government the cunt has more influence than a firm policy governed by reason."[56]

"They love each other for they are exactly alike," wrote one courtier.[57] But perhaps not exactly alike, for Catherine faced west, toward Voltaire and the Enlightenment, while Potemkin faced resolutely east. Born in Ukraine, he had an in-depth knowledge of the languages and customs of the Cossack and Tatar tribes. Like them, he was a man of black earth, crystal streams, and sudden storms; the passions of the wild steppes coursed through his veins. Like Russia, he was a man of startling incongruities. "Prince Potemkin is the emblem of the immense Russian Empire," wrote the prince de Ligne, the Austrian envoy. "He too is composed of deserts and goldmines."[58]

Potemkin boasted countless talents; in addition to statecraft and warfare, he was a gifted musician, poet, theologian, and architect. Sometimes his bright fire burned itself out, and he collapsed suddenly on a divan where he remained for days at a time. Sunk into a deep depression, he would play with loose diamonds, dropping them from one cupped hand into the other, looking with childlike wonder at how they caught the light as they fell. Then with a burst of energy, he would spring up from his couch and work tirelessly for days on end without a moment's sleep. Recognizing his brilliance, Catherine soothed and encouraged him when he was depressed. When he was buoyant, the two of them argued, fretted, reconciled, and finally agreed on policy.

Sometimes Potemkin enjoyed torturing Catherine by refusing to make love to her. She would wait up, hoping to hear his footfall padding down the hall, the creak of her door, to feel the flood of warmth that came with his presence. When he did not come, forgetting all pride, she would creep to his apartments and find the doors locked. "I come to your room to tell you how much I love you, and I find your door locked!" she scribbled in a note.[59] Once she sadly wrote him, "The subject of our disagreements is always power and never love."[60]

For Potemkin, the unattainable was most desirable. The already attained was dull. After eleven years of worshiping a shining image, he suddenly found himself with a plump, sexually insatiable middle-aged woman, abject in her love for him, completely, irrevocably, and boringly conquered. Potemkin would always love Catherine as the personification of Mother Russia, his eternal mistress and only true love. But by 1776 he sought a plan to extricate himself from her bed. She had not wearied of him yet, but the day might come, and Potemkin had no intention of being pensioned off as another useless cast-off lover.

Moreover, he longed to burst forth from the constraints of the relationship and make his own path in the world, to win political power and riches outside of St. Petersburg. He found himself in the usual position of a queen's favorite—his mistress's son and heir heartily detested him. Paul hated all his mother's lovers, but particularly resented Potemkin for coruling with Catherine. He, Paul, with Romanov blood reportedly flowing in his veins, should have helped rule the empire. If Catherine, who was ten years older than Potemkin, should die before him, Potemkin could reckon with the confiscation of all his property, and probably prison and death.

Grand Duke Paul had grown up twitching, paranoid, and a devoted admirer of Frederick the Great of Prussia—oddly similar to Peter III. Though she indicated in her memoirs that Saltikov was Paul's father, perhaps Catherine simply couldn't bear the thought of creating a child with Peter. On the other hand, perhaps Paul, hearing stories of Peter's behavior, strove to imitate it to prove he was legitimate. Paul's paternity is still hotly debated among Russian historians.

Paul suffered from epileptic seizures and night hallucinations in which he saw his murdered father seeking revenge on his murderer, Catherine. Paul grew up terrified that his mother would kill him, too, just as Peter the Great had killed his son and heir. According to the French chargé d'affaires, at the age of ten Paul asked "why they had killed his father and why they had given his mother the throne that rightfully belonged to him. He added that when he grew up, he would get to the bottom of all that."[61] Eyeing his mother's lovers coldly, Paul promised "hardness and vengeance" the moment he took the throne.[62] For her part, Catherine found her son repulsive, unappetizing, like "mustard after dinner."[63] She called him "*die schwere Bagage*," heavy baggage.[64]

Potemkin, keenly aware of Paul's hatred, and tiring of Catherine's urgent embraces, needed to shift the love affair onto the footing of deep friendship and political partnership. He began by persuading the empress that their relationship involved far more than the two of them. Their love existed in the realm of the sublime; it was a shining spiritual partnership, far above mere groping in bed. In a sexual relationship, he pointed out, they spent time quarreling, valuable time that they could give to Russia. Such quarrels would be acceptable with meaningless lovers, but not with each other.

Sadly Catherine realized that in order to keep him at all, she had to let him go. In St. Petersburg Potemkin would always have to share power with the empress. So she sent him to govern various imperial provinces, and in 1783 he landed in the Crimea, a former Turkish province on the north of the Black Sea. There he ruled alone, sending the empress reports of his decisions. He held his own court, something in between the Oriental magnificence of the sultan's palace and the filth and disorder of a barnyard. Here visitors would find him wearing a silk caftan, reclining on a divan, with a harem of half-dressed odalisques around him, a one-hundred-twenty-piece orchestra playing in the background and a turbaned boy fanning him with ostrich feathers.

Within five years Potemkin had built the Black Sea fleet, which he immediately turned on the Turks to utterly defeat them. He added new Muslim territories to the empire as so many jewels to Catherine's crown. Potemkin gestured and cities sprang from empty fields, cities such as Sebastopol and Odessa. He built a silk stocking factory, sending the first pair to Catherine, and planted thirty thousand vines for wine. When he promised free land, oxen, and plows to settlers, hundreds of thousands of Europe's poor and disenfranchised arrived in his new towns. Within three years the population of his territories skyrocketed from 204,000 to roughly 800,000. Respectful of ethnicity and religious beliefs, Potemkin invited priests, rabbis, and Muslim mullahs to serve at his court.

In his southern empire Potemkin indulged his taste for showmanship. At heart he was a wizard, an impresario, a ringmaster of visual delights. Cannons boomed when he entered a town; maidens crowned him with garlands and strewed rose petals in his path. Wherever he traveled he was met with fireworks, pageants, military parades, and mock naval battles. Potemkin took mistresses by the dozen, including several of his own nieces. Secure in the knowledge that she truly possessed his heart, Catherine showered gold and diamonds on his girlfriends.

Serenissimus, the Prince of Princes, as he was now known, was Russia's most brilliant statesman since Peter the Great. But Potemkin's string of successes sometimes brought depression in their wake. "Can any man be more happy than I am?" he asked one evening at dinner. "Everything I have ever wanted, I have; all my whims have been fulfilled as if by magic. I wanted high rank, I have it. I wanted medals, I have them. I loved gambling, I have lost vast sums. I liked giving parties, I've given magnificent ones; I enjoy building houses, I've raised palaces. . . . In a word, all my passions have been sated, I am entirely happy!"[65] And then he swept all the valuable china plates on the floor, smashing them to bits, raced off to his bedroom, and locked the door. Potemkin suffered bitterly from having nothing left to want. For when dreams turn into reality, there is an empty spot where the dreams used to be, and Potemkin had no dreams left.

Meanwhile, in St. Petersburg, Catherine had to find a new favorite. She started a new system in which a doctor checked out all prospective candidates for venereal disease. If the young man seemed healthy, he would then be taken to bed by Catherine's good friend Countess Prascovya Bruce, and rated on his appearance, sexual technique, and the size of his penis. The *éprouveuse* as she was called, or tester, would then inform the empress of her findings. Those who passed the test were sent on to Catherine for further testing before she selected a favorite. We can imagine that many a nervous young man was too terrified to rise to the occasion. His entire future and that of his family were at stake, based solely on the hardness of his penis.

The first favorite to pass this barrage of tests was thirty-seven-year-old Peter Zavadovsky, whom Catherine appointed her personal secretary. Handsome, dark, and courteous, Zavadovsky worked assiduously on her personal correspondence, and within a month of his arrival at the palace he was promoted to major general.

But it would take more than a Zavadovsky to make a woman forget Potemkin. A French diplomat remarked that Zavadovsky was "probably no more than an amusement."[66] But he was not as amusing as Catherine had hoped. Though he had somehow passed the sexual performance tests, once he landed the position of favorite Zavadovsky suffered from premature ejaculation. Catherine wrote him, "You are Vesuvius itself. When you least expect it, an eruption appears. . . ."[67]

He was unambitious, wanting neither riches nor honors, just her love, and bemoaned the fact that in attending to affairs of state she had so little time for him. Zavadovsky threw jealous tantrums about Potemkin, and Potemkin stormed about Zavadovsky. In 1777 Potemkin informed Catherine that he would never return to court unless Zavadovsky was dismissed.

Catherine begged him to relent. "Do not make me do anything so unfair," she implored him. But Potemkin remained stubborn and Zavadovsky had to go.

He was devastated. "Amid hope, amid passion full of feelings, my fortunate lot has been broken like the wind, like a dream which one cannot halt; (her) love for me has vanished," he said.[68] Like Vasilchikov before him, he retired grumbling to his estates laden with gifts—four thousand serfs, eighty thousand rubles, and a silver dining service for sixteen. "You must agree, my friend," wrote the French chargé d'affaires in St. Petersburg, "that it's not a bad line of work to be in here."[69] Three years later, Catherine brought Zavadovsky back to court and gave him a government position. She made him legal guardian of Count Bobrinsky, her child with Gregory Orlov.

Before Zavadovsky's dismissal, Potemkin decided that *he* would select Catherine's lovers, those who would not foment against him, those who would serve as his creatures. The successful candidate would offer an abundance of physical beauty and a corresponding lack of brains. A German courtier told Frederick the Great that Potemkin chose them "expressly to have neither talent nor the means to take direct influence."[70]

The day Zavadovsky left, his successor, Peter Yoritz, moved into his apartments. The new lover boasted a splendid physique and fiery temperament but was illiterate. He remained in favor ten months and then the empress told a visiting Potemkin, "Last night I was in love with him; today I can't stand him anymore."[71] The spurned suitor was appeased with a life pension, several rich estates, and seven thousand serfs.

Catherine celebrated her fiftieth birthday in 1779 with banquets, fireworks, and sighs. Her youth was now vanished beyond any pretense. She felt girlish only during the sex act when, in a passionate tangle of arms and legs and hard thrusts, she could feel youth, feel passion, forget her corpulent aging body. And when she did look in the mirror, did she truly believe she saw a woman who could still inspire love and lust? A woman for whom men would rage and fight, even if she had not worn a crown? Yes, she was old and heavy and wrinkled but there was something special there still, wasn't there? A gleam in the eye, a flash of a smile, something still magical that rose above mere physical beauty? *Wasn't there?*

Potemkin quickly found a successor to Yoritz. This time he chose an elegant fellow with chiseled Greek features who resembled a young Apollo. Twenty-four-year-old Ivan Korsakov played the violin and sang love songs to Catherine for hours. In June 1778 the British ambassador wrote, "Potemkin, who has more cunning than any man living, has introduced Korsakov at a critical moment. . . ."[72]

Korsakov, knowing he was out of his league intellectually, decided to impress courtiers with his new library. The bookseller asked, "What books would His Lordship wish to possess?" To which the startled young man replied, "Oh, you know, big volumes on the bottom shelves and small ones on the top, like the Empress has."[73]

But the new lover, who had been tested by Madame Bruce and received excellent grades, was far more interested in the trim and subtle *éprouveuse* than in the gross and hungry empress. One day after a year with Korsakov, the empress found the two of them together in bed. Both were requested to leave St. Petersburg.

Potemkin already had another one waiting in the wings. Alexander Lanskoy was a twenty-four-year-old guardsman from an impoverished but noble family. Charming, handsome, and incredibly tall, he was incredulous to hear that Prince Potemkin had plucked him from obscurity and appointed him his new aide-de-camp. Potemkin had been aware of Korsakov's affair with Madame Bruce well before the empress found out, and rather than relinquishing the position to a rival faction, he decided to groom Lanskoy in advance and slide him in at the right moment. When Catherine, dejected at her lover's infidelity, turned to Potemkin for sympathy, he introduced her to Lanskoy, who was overcome with love for her. Catherine, for her part, was delighted at finding a young man who would be the support of her old age.

Within weeks Alexander Lanskoy was promoted to general and became the empress's personal aide-de-camp. The young man who had only five shirts to his name suddenly found himself with one hundred thousand rubles to spend on his wardrobe, and seven million rubles in gifts. Though not possessed of the physical stamina of Catherine's other lovers, Lanskoy aroused her maternal instincts. Modest and gentle, he was truly devoted to her and refused to take part in political intrigues. He enjoyed helping Catherine lay out gardens and design buildings.

Catherine was grateful to have the sympathetic Lanskoy with her when Gregory Orlov, the powerful lover who had given her the crown, was stricken by insanity. He had married his teenage cousin and brought her to court in 1778. Catherine had generously welcomed the girl, given her a splendid toilet set, and made her a lady-in-waiting. But his wife's early death from consumption in 1781 threw Orlov into madness. His brothers had to physically force him away from her tomb where he had remained for days, sobbing, refusing to eat or sleep.

On one occasion he escaped his brothers' watchfulness and appeared at court, dirty and unkempt with bulging eyes. Hearing of his arrival, Catherine insisted on seeing him. Orlov, howling like a wounded animal, saw the corpse of Peter III rise before him seeking vengeance. "It's my punishment!" he cried.[74] Catherine spoke gently to him before his keepers trundled him off. Then she took to her bed, utterly devastated by the sight of her once magnificent lover reduced to this. Gregory Orlov died in 1783, suffering perhaps from the insanity which announced the last stages of syphilis.

By 1782 Lanskoy was experiencing his own health problems; his nocturnal duties with the empress so exhausted him that he began taking sexual stimulants. In 1784 he caught diphtheria, which would not have proved fatal, according to his doctor, if his constitution had not already been weakened by his excessive use of aphrodisiacs. He died quickly, and those who came to offer condolences to the empress found a locked door and heard heart-wrenching sobs coming from behind it. Only Potemkin could help Catherine in her grief. He was called for and, riding day and night, arrived in only a week. The door to the imperial bedroom was opened, then locked behind him. Servants heard the two of them wailing for hours.

But Potemkin's grief could not have been that excessive. He told a British friend, "When things go smoothly my influence is small but when she meets with rubs, she always wants me and then my influence becomes as great as ever."[75]

By the time of Lanskoy's death, the empress had cultivated the reputation of an unbridled nymphomaniac. Menopause had not slowed her down one whit, and her reputation for the benevolent statecraft she practiced in the day was tarnished by the pleasures she enjoyed at night. Rumors portrayed Catherine having sex with stallions and bulls because men could no longer satiate her.

But though Catherine enjoyed sex, she was no nymphomaniac. After Lanskoy's death she refused to even consider a new lover for months, although Potemkin continually shoved grinning candidates in Catherine's direction. Seeing the coveted position remain vacant, many ambitious families pushed their muscular teenaged sons forward at court. These youths, wearing the mortgages of their family estates on their backs, were trained to puff out their chests and flash the empress a dazzling smile as she passed. One visitor noticed that "during the church service for the court, lots of young men, who were even the slightest bit handsome, stood erect, hoping to regulate their destiny in such an easy way."[76]

The new favorite could quickly earn enough money to found a noble dynasty. Going up the secret staircase to the apartments of the imperial paramour for the first time, he would find as much as ten thousand rubles in cash on the sofa waiting for him. But it was a twenty-four-hour-a-day job, requiring frequent vigorous lovemaking with a stout middle-aged woman, and brilliant conversation at all other times. Catherine stifled her lovers, suffocated them, and rarely let them out of her sight.

But finally her interest was awakened by one of Potemkin's studs. Thirty-one-year-old Alexis Yermalov was rough and good-natured, with a wide flat nose. Though honest and devoted by nature, Yermalov allowed his sudden rise to go to his head.

Prodded by the anti-Potemkin faction, he decided to unseat his mentor. He was soon complaining to the empress of Potemkin's corruption, accusing him of pocketing bribes and diverting money which she had sent to the south for other purposes. The truth was that Potemkin floated in so much money he often mixed his private and government bank accounts, borrowing from one to pay the other. He was so rich he seemed to be above bribery, certainly above pocketing paltry sums.

Potemkin, furious, refused to defend himself against Yermalov's allegations. When his friend the French ambassador asked why, he thundered, "So also you say that I am working for my own destruction, and that after all the services I have rendered, I should defend myself against the allegations of an ungrateful boy. But no little whippersnapper will bring about my downfall, and I do not know of anyone who would dare to do so."[77]

In June 1786, during a ball celebrating the anniversary of the empress's accession to the throne, Potemkin strode in. The music stopped. The crowd parted as the powerful figure, gleaming with diamonds, Europe's highest decorations clattering on his broad chest, strode straight up to Yermalov who was playing at the gaming tables. Everyone in the vicinity fled except Yermalov, pinned to the spot by the gaze of his former benefactor. Potemkin threw the table over; cards and chips were sent flying through the air.

"You cur, you white nigger, you monkey, who dare to bespatter me with the mud of the gutters from which I have raised you," Potemkin bellowed. Yermalov bravely put his hand to his sword hilt but found himself soaring backward. Potemkin had slugged him. No one dared pick up the crumpled figure on the floor. Catherine, who had left the ball early, was astonished to see Potemkin roaring into her apartments without knocking. Courtiers in the hall heard him shouting, "It's either he or I. If this nonentity of nonentities is allowed to remain at court, then I quit the state's services from today."[78]

Trembling with the excitement that Potemkin always provoked, Catherine readily gave up Yermalov, who after seventeen months was beginning to bore her anyway. Moments after

Potemkin's temper tantrum, the court was regaled with the vision of a smiling Serenissimus leading the empress by the hand back to the ball. Catherine slept three hours later than usual the next morning, presumably with Potemkin.

Yermalov received notification of his dismissal that evening but walked away staggering under the weight of his retirement gifts—4,300 serfs, 130,000 rubles in cash, a silver dinner service, and the polite suggestion to live abroad for five years.

Within days of Yermalov's dismissal, Potemkin placed another young man in the imperial bed, twenty-six-year-old Alexander Momonov, predictably handsome and charming. He was, alas, easily bored with the empress's stifling devotion and fretted at the tight leash she kept him on. Momonov stayed on in his position only because of his loyalty to Potemkin, whom he idolized, and not because of the exceptional financial rewards. In the first eighteen months Momonov was given 27,000 serfs, a salary of 180,000 rubles a year, and a table budget of 36,000 rubles. The empress made him adjutant general and a count of the Holy Roman Empire.

Despite the cash and honors heaped upon them, the vapid young men who came and went in the empress's bed did not awaken the most vicious jealousy at court. That was reserved for the insolently powerful Potemkin, reigning like a sultan in his southern kingdom. Many courtiers were furious at reports of cities springing up from dust at the prince's command. Rumors spread that his vaunted success was nothing short of a pack of lies. And so Potemkin arranged for his show of shows, the empress's nine-month voyage to visit her new southern provinces and see for herself. To ensure that all Europe learned of his achievements, he arranged for a slew of foreign diplomats to accompany the empress. Even Emperor Joseph II of Austria agreed to join part of the expedition.

The expedition embarked on January 7, 1787. Wrapped in luxurious sables, Catherine cast quick glances out the windows of her gilded coach. She saw the beauty of her country but none of the misery of its serfs. As she had written Voltaire earlier, "The soil of the country was so productive and the rivers so rich in fish that the Russian peasant was happier and better fed than any other in the world."[79] Certainly the Russian peasant should have been happy and well fed in such a land of natural riches, if the Russian peasant's master had not taken his happiness and food away from him.

Well aware of the power of visual images, Potemkin spruced up the towns and villages through which the empress would travel. Roads were repaired, trash removed, cottages painted, and undesirable characters temporarily imprisoned. When his enemies stewing in St. Petersburg heard reports that his successes were true, they were furious. It had all been a mirage, they growled, a façade, a series of grandiose optical illusions. The magician Potemkin, they declared, had built a series of stage sets which he transported from place to place, just ahead of the empress's caravan, along with the same plump cheerful peasants to stand in front of them. Potemkin villages.

Joseph II was awestruck by Potemkin's achievements. Looking closely at the gleaming new buildings, he saw not façades but shoddy construction. "But what does this matter," he asked, "in a country which exists on slave labor and where anything which crumbles can be built again? Money is limitless and lives are of no account. In Germany and France we would not dare to attempt things which they risk here every day without encountering a single obstacle or hearing one word of complaint."[80]

In August the party boarded a luxurious galley specially made by Potemkin to cruise the Dnieper River, the border between Russia and Poland. Docking in the town of Kanieve, Catherine reluctantly met with King Stanislaus, the lover she had not seen in nearly thirty years. At fifty-six, Poniatowski was still handsome. He was one of those men who, though insipid in youth, grows more handsome with age. His eyes sparkled with confidence, his salt-and-pepper hair gave him the air of wisdom; the lines in his face spoke of experience. But Catherine did not find him attractive. After her decades of exciting sex with domineering men, she found Poniatowski weak, dull, and unbearably sincere. How could she ever have loved him?

Ever the romantic, if Stanislaus had hoped for some rekindling of ancient passions, he was disappointed. Disappointed in her appearance, for one thing; where was the shapely young brunette he had loved? Disappointed in her manner, for another; polite but coolly distant. In a private conversation, Stanislaus asked for a new constitution for Poland. Catherine refused; she wanted Poland to remain weak. Dinner was difficult; the empress looked embarrassed, the king depressed. After dinner the empress refused to attend the ball Stanislaus had prepared for her, even though he had built a special ballroom just for the occasion. As for Stanislaus, his shimmering memories had vanished. "I don't know her anymore," he said sadly.[81] She had not set a crown on his head, but a dunce cap. While guests danced at the king's ball, Catherine stood on the deck of her galley and watched the fireworks. "The king bores me," she told Alexander Momonov.

But without a doubt the most bored traveler on the journey was not Catherine but Momonov himself. During the interminable months of travel in closed sleighs or onboard the imperial galley, Momonov was dying of boredom and called his job "imprisonment."[82] Though the empress constantly tried to bribe him into contentment, he complained bitterly. When Catherine confided to Potemkin her many grievances against her spoiled lover, Serenissimus replied with characteristic gusto, "Eh, Little Mother, spit on him!"[83]

Catherine, seeing Potemkin in his own kingdom, glittering like a maharaja, his fleet bobbing in the Black Sea firing their guns for their sovereign, could not help comparing him with the bored and boring Momonov. She wrote Potemkin impassioned letters, and he responded with gratitude and devotion. But not with passion. As dirty and careless as he often was with his own appearance, he was fastidious with his women and was only aroused by slender blooming girls, not tubs of wrinkled flesh.

Once Catherine and her entourage spilled out of their carriages in St. Petersburg, the Turks, alarmed by Potemkin's naval maneuvers during his three-ring circus for the empress, attacked. Potemkin, barely convalescing from the greatest, biggest, longest-lasting show on earth, was totally unprepared. His men were scattered, manning far-reaching outposts. Potemkin quickly recruited tens of thousands of soldiers from across Europe. One young Corsican officer volunteered but was summarily turned down because he insolently demanded too high a rank. His name was Napoleon Bonaparte.

In the first year of the Turkish War, Potemkin suddenly sunk into a dark swirl of apathy and could not be roused to defend, much less attack. Many wondered whether he was in the pay of the Turks. The fact was that his health had been deteriorating for several years from a rich diet, sexual excess, overindulgence in alcohol, and recurring bouts of malaria. Now, in his deepest depression, he was waited on by seven hundred servants as his one-hundred-twenty-piece orchestra played. The Prince of Princes regaled himself with a harem of women chosen from his officers' wives. He had an underground palace built for one of his mistresses, and each time he approached orgasm, he tugged on a bellpull to signal the cannoneers to fire. When the woman's husband heard the cannon, he yawned, "What a lot of noise about nothing."[84]

Back in St. Petersburg, Momonov wrote Potemkin imploring him to release him from his onerous duties as Catherine's lover. Potemkin replied angrily, "It is your duty to remain at your post for the duration of the war, and don't be a fool and ruin your career."[85]

By the spring of 1789 Alexander Momonov was suffering from sexual exhaustion, complaining he could no longer perform. He confessed to Catherine that he was in love with another woman. Wiping away her tears, she summoned his beloved and realized that the young woman was heavily pregnant. Catherine suggested they marry immediately and told the trembling girl—who had been fearing exile in Siberia—that the imperial wedding gift would be a country estate and one hundred thousand rubles. The bride promptly fainted. On the day of the wedding, the empress dressed the girl's hair with a diamond coronet and presided over the wedding supper. "God be with them!" she said wistfully. "Let them be happy."[86]

A few days after the wedding the empress took a new lover. Twenty-two-year-old Plato Zubov had not been selected by Potemkin but thrust in at the right moment by the prince's enemies when he had returned to the war. Catherine gave Zubov one hundred thousand rubles, made him a general, and appointed him her personal aide-de-camp. The new lover quickly lifted her sadness over Momonov's betrayal. "I am healthy and merry and have come alive like a fly," she wrote Potemkin.[87]

Catherine and Zubov were an incongruous pair. She was a barrel-shaped toothless grandmother; he was young, slender, and the handsomest of all her lovers since Orlov. His face was a study in elegant curves with its high cheekbones, refined jawline, and small cleft in the middle of his chin. His eyes were deep and hooded, his nose aristocratic, his lips perfectly shaped. One of her advisers, looking at the two, remarked, "The empress wears him like a decoration."[88] Others eyeing the pair believed that Zubov earned every last penny of his pay.

Catherine's favorite was expected to hold levees for visitors, favor seekers, and supporters, but Zubov's levees were nothing short of a demonstration of arrogance. Comte Antoine de Langeron reported, "Every day, starting at eight o'clock in the morning, his antechamber was filled with ministers, courtiers, generals, foreigners, petitioners, seekers after appointments or favors. Usually, they had to wait four or five hours before being admitted. . . . At last the double doors would swing open, the crowd would rush in and the favorite would be found seated before his mirror having his hair dressed, and ordinarily resting one foot on a chair or a corner of the dressing table. After bowing low, the courtiers would range themselves before him two or three deep, silent and motionless, in the midst of a cloud of powder."[89]

Grand Duke Paul's tutor, the Swiss-born Charles Masson, twittered, "The old generals, the great men of the Empire, did not blush to ingratiate themselves with the least of his valets. Stretched out in an armchair in the most indecent, careless attire, with his little finger in his nose and his eyes fixed vaguely on the ceiling, this young man with his cold, vain face, scarcely deigned to pay attention to the people around him."[90]

Courtiers had to put up not only with Zubov's rudeness, but with his monkey. This nasty little creature jumped on visitors' shoulders and plucked off their wigs, at which they were required to chuckle politely.

Having finally won the war against the Turks, Potemkin returned to a triumphal hero's welcome in St. Petersburg. Zubov fidgeted with jealousy. Courtiers rushed to see the face-off between the empress's lovers, and most placed their wagers on Potemkin. As Serenissimus descended his carriage and marched into the palace, a servant behind him carried his hat, which was so loaded with diamonds it was too heavy to wear.

When the empress and Potemkin faced each other once more, both were sadly changed. Potemkin had been under tremendous strain from the Turkish War and suffered from exhaustion and depression. Catherine had become so obese that she took up two seats at the theater. Her legs were so swollen that she could hardly walk, and architects installed gently sloping ramps over the palace stairs. Worse, the former brilliance of her mind was dimming. Tired and cranky, she increasingly left political matters in the inept hands of Zubov. At court Potemkin's friends advised him to oust the arrogant Zubov and resume his position in Catherine's bed. Potemkin was horrified at the thought.

But he did try to warn Catherine of the danger of allowing the feckless, stupid Zubov to take over state affairs. Catherine loudly proclaimed that the boy was a budding political genius who only required a bit of training to mature. "I am doing a great service to the state by educating young men," she said with a straight face.[91] Too tired to fight further, Potemkin gave up. Russia was now in the hands of a conceited youth whose sole recommendation was the sexual satisfaction he gave an old woman.

Turning to something at which he excelled, Potemkin gave a show—one last, brilliant show that would be talked about for decades after his death—Potemkin's ball. Fountains ran with wine. Three thousand guests were invited to dance in a room lit by 200 chandeliers; the fragrant gardens shimmered with the light of 140,000 lanterns, 20,000 candles, and fireworks bursting overhead. Draped in Persian silks, a dark-skinned African sitting on a mechanical golden elephant called the guests to dine as the elephant's trunk, studded with diamonds, rose and fell.

After dinner Potemkin led Catherine into the Winter Garden and presented her with a valuable statue bearing the inscription "To one who is Mother, and more than Mother to me."[92] At the end of it all Potemkin fell on his knees before Catherine and, kissing her hand, wept. Was it joy? Sadness? Fear? Loss of all the beauties of youth? Or knowledge that the end was coming? She, too, wept.

Before he left St. Petersburg for the south, a countess asked him what he planned to do when Catherine died. "Don't worry," he replied. "I'll die before the Sovereign. I'll die soon."[93]

Potemkin left St. Petersburg in the scorching heat of summer to make peace with the Turks in the south. In the town of Jassy, burning with malarial fever, ravaged by liver failure and pneumonia, he insisted that he continue his journey despite the grave warnings of doctors. But on the second day of travel he suddenly cried to stop. "I'm dying," he groaned. "There is no point in going any further. I want to die on the ground."[94] On the Russian soil from which he had sprung. They laid a mattress on the side of the road. Within an hour the mighty Cyclops was dead. The orchestra had ceased playing, the lights had faded, and the curtain had fallen. Potemkin's show was over.

Potemkin "lived on gold," said one court wit, but "died on grass."[95] Indeed, everyone found his death as remarkable as his life.

Between her sobs the empress kept asking, "Whom shall I rely on now?"[96] And, "Prince Potemkin has played me a cruel turn by dying! It is me on whom all the burden now falls."[97]

Grand Duke Paul announced that Potemkin's death meant there was one less thief in the empire. Plato Zubov was also elated, though he feigned sympathy with the empress. "It is his fault I am not twice as rich as I am," he told his friends peevishly.[98] The large shadow of Potemkin which had loomed over him had suddenly disappeared. Zubov immediately pestered Catherine to give him Potemkin's honors and riches. He further requested the top government positions for foreign affairs.

Catherine was tired, fading slowly, and found it easier to give her lover whatever he wanted. Charles Masson, in comparing the empress's two lovers, wrote, "Potemkin owed almost all his greatness to himself. Zubov owed his only to Catherine's decrepitude."[99]

In 1793 Catherine sent the Russian army into Poland and carved it up as if it were a pie, doling out slices to Prussia and Austria and keeping a large share for herself. In 1795, after a reign of thirty-one years, King Stanislaus abdicated. Catherine confined him to a Russian palace; she gave thousands of acres of Polish land and thousands of Polish serfs to Zubov, who was now the richest and most powerful man in Russia.

Yet success had its price. Catherine's sexual needs grew stronger with age. One courtier reported seeing Zubov, having just serviced the empress, returning to his rooms "prostrate with fatigue and pitiably sad, throwing himself upon his couch, and drenching his handkerchief with scent."[100]

Catherine gave Zubov the lead role in the delicate negotiations for the marriage of Paul's thirteen-year-old daughter Alexandra to young King Gustavus IV of Sweden in September 1796. But Zubov mangled them horribly, neglecting to address the issue of religion. The Swedes insisted the bride become Protestant; Catherine insisted she retain her Orthodox faith. Zubov insisted to both sides that it was a small matter, easily cleared up.

When the Swedish ambassador told a stunned Catherine that under no circumstances would a queen of Sweden be permitted to profess the Orthodox faith, she grew so angry that she had a slight stroke. Zubov still argued that the betrothal ceremony should go forward, that the Swedish king would lose his honor if he didn't follow through. At the last minute Gustavus would surely sign the wedding contract allowing her to remain Orthodox. Unaware of Zubov's ploy, the king of Sweden came to St. Petersburg for the betrothal, believing his bride would convert.

The blushing princess, arrayed in a white gown, waited in a drawing room with hundreds of guests. But the king, who at the last minute had been handed documents to sign that would allow the girl to keep her religion, never showed up. Hours passed; the would-be fiancée wept quietly. In the half century since she had come to Russia, Catherine had never once lost her formidable dignity in public. But now, publicly humiliated and probably suffering brain damage from her recent stroke, Catherine vented her anger at the Swedish representatives, swearing at them like a fishwife and reportedly banging one of them over the head with her scepter, twice.

On the morning of November 5, 1796, Catherine rose and put on a white silk dressing gown. Her ladies commented on how remarkably youthful she looked. Settling down to her desk with her secretaries, she asked them to leave for a few moments and visited her private room with the chamber pot. She never came out. After waiting nearly an hour, her alarmed maids and valets opened the door and found her on the floor, felled by a stroke. She lived for two days without recovering consciousness. According to witnesses, Zubov looked like a man whose "despair was beyond comparison."[101] And well should he despair, for the new emperor hated him with particular venom.

Catherine's enemies became Paul's friends; her friends, his enemies. He liberated Stanislaus Poniatowski from his refined prison and invited him to live in a marble palace in St. Petersburg. The former king, who still had a spring in his step and a sparkle in his eye, was the toast of the town, the guest of honor at the best dinner parties. Yet some noticed an air of sadness about him as he promenaded from one social event to the other with his silver-tipped walking stick. He died suddenly in 1798, a bachelor to the end. He was, perhaps, one of those rare individuals who falls in love only once, and when his mate departs, remains true to the memory of those long-ago golden nights.

If Paul had rewarded Poniatowski, he had a score to settle with Potemkin who, though dead, could still be punished. The emperor decreed that his bones should be dug up and dispersed and his grave monument smashed. Soldiers sent to do the job destroyed the monument but could not bear to disturb their general's bones. They pretended they had carried out the emperor's orders, but let Potemkin rest in peace.

Paul's most bizarre act of vengeance was his mother's state funeral. He decreed that the ceremony should be not for her alone, but also for his father Peter III, who had been murdered thirty-four years earlier. The ornate casket with Peter's remains was placed next to Catherine's open casket for the viewing. It was a macabre reunion, a bloated corpse and a dusty skeleton lying next to each other. The bodies of Catherine the Great and her murdered husband were buried together as if they had been the most loving couple in the world. Over them hung a banner: "Divided in life, united in death."[102]

Still stewing about the long, magnificent reign of his mother, in 1797 Paul changed the law regarding the imperial succession. Women, he decreed, would be disqualified from ruling. Never again would another Catherine the Great tell men what to do. This law remained in effect until the end of the Russian Empire in 1917.

Paul's hallucinations and paranoia increased each year. He was stabbed to death in 1801 by a group of conspirators that included Plato Zubov. As in the case of Peter III, when it came time to punish the mad emperor's murderers, there came from the Russian people a deafening silence. Paul's gifted son Alexander would lead Russia through the Napoleonic Wars and into the future.

Was Catherine great? A woman of her time, she devoted her life to making her country powerful rather than her people happy. Today we could not imagine a great monarch keeping her people in miserable servitude. We could not admire palaces built on the broken and bleeding backs of helpless slaves.

Perhaps the quality that made Catherine truly great was an intensely personal quality—her understanding of the weakness of human passion. Hypocrisy was not one of her failings. An unwise love affair, an unwelcome pregnancy, well did she understand these, and never did she judge. Generous in the face of romantic betrayal, she paid off her former lovers and their mistresses handsomely.

In her memoirs she wrote candidly, "Nothing in my opinion is more difficult than to resist what gives us pleasure. All arguments to the contrary are prudery."[103] Catherine thought society's preoccupation with female chastity greatly exaggerated, and she laughed at stories of her nymphomania. Though she enjoyed sex, her work took precedence. "Time belongs not to me, but to the Empire," she often said.[104]

She never permitted off-color jokes in her presence and maintained a strict decorum throughout the day; she gave in to her passions at night behind tightly closed doors. Deeply in love with all of her favorites, she practiced serial monogamy. Hers was a healthy sexuality, straightforward and uncomplicated, with no feigned shame or attempts at concealment. Hers was a sexuality which threatened the customs of the day.

The legend of her sexual appetites increased until it rewrote the story of her death. Catherine the Great died by impalement on a horse penis, it was said. According to a slightly varied version, the impalement didn't kill her; it was the horse being lowered into position on top of her and suddenly falling that crushed her. That, then, was a suitable punishment for a woman's unabashed sexual freedom. Perhaps Catherine's loudest laugh would have been reserved for the horse story.

"In love she was indulgent," wrote one courtier, "but in politics implacable; ambition was her ruling passion, and she made the lover subservient to the Empress."[105]

Catherine's greatest success was in convincing her subjects that she was as Russian as they were, and not a petty upstart German princess. One day she said to her doctors, "Bleed me to my last drop of German blood so that I may have only Russian blood in my veins."[106] And indeed, of all her many lovers, the greatest, longest-lasting love affair of her life was with Russia.

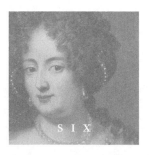

SIX

EIGHTEENTH-CENTURY EUROPE: POWER, PASSION, AND POLITICS

With mine own tears I wash away my balm,
With mine own hands I give away my crown,
With mine own tongue deny my sacred state,
With mine own breath release all duteous oaths;
All pomp and majesty I do forswear.

—WILLIAM SHAKESPEARE

THE EIGHTEENTH CENTURY WAS A SEA OF FEMALE DEBAUCH-ery dotted with islands of prudery. To avoid tainting her cherished purity, Queen Charlotte of Great Britain banned from court those individuals who had the merest whiff of scandal attached to their names. As a result, the smallness of her court was outdone only by its dullness. This plain-faced German princess gave her husband, George III, fifteen children, and luckily for her, George was equally horrified at the thought of adultery. Many courtiers pointed sadly to this unnatural fidelity to an ugly wife as the cause of the king's madness; in 1788 George began foaming at the mouth as he shrieked his obscene desires for the queen's maids of honor.

Empress Maria Theresa of Austria was not so fortunate in the fidelity of her husband. Though Francis of Lorraine, Holy Roman Emperor, regularly did his duty by the empress, giving her sixteen children, he had a proclivity for actresses and ladies-in-waiting. Hoping to dampen her husband's enthusiasm for other women, in 1747 the empress formed the Chastity Commission to investigate reports of adulterous sexual activity. After six months and a handful of convictions of prostitutes, dancers, and their customers, the commission was laughed out of existence. Francis's diddling continued unabated.

Russia, first and foremost, was the land where female sovereigns openly enjoyed the sexual prowess of strapping young men. But by the latter part of the eighteenth century, western European queens were following suit.

MARIA LUISA OF PARMA, QUEEN OF SPAIN

"The Earthly Trinity"

When the future Carlos IV of Spain married the fourteen-year-old Maria Luisa of Parma in 1765, she almost immediately began having affairs with courtiers. Her husband seemed unconcerned, but his outraged father, King Carlos III, exiled every man upon whom the princess's eyes alighted with favor. On one occasion the prince begged his father to bring the young man back because "his wife Luisa was quite unhappy without him, as he used to amuse her amazingly." "Booby!" the king snapped, turning away in disgust.[1] Under his breath he added, "All of them alike—all of them whores!"[2]

Maria Luisa heaved a sigh of relief when old King Carlos died in 1788; he had been prepared to exile to a remote province her most recent lover, a spirited eighteen-year-old guardsman named Manuel Godoy. The latest object of the queen's affections was tall and strongly built, with a shock of thick black hair, dreamy dark eyes, and cheeks so naturally rosy that many incorrectly believed he wore rouge. There was a sensual, sleepy look to him that absolutely inflamed women. Now, with such a compliant husband as king, Maria Luisa could keep Godoy by her side and have sex with him whenever she wanted.

At twenty-seven, the newly minted queen had dark auburn hair and large black eyes sparkling with sensuality. She was neither ugly nor beautiful; with her alert expression, thin lips, and long flared nose, she rather looked like an attractive dog. Her sex drive was insatiable, and the only man who ever came close to satisfying her was Manuel Godoy, who was reported to be a roaring lion in bed. As a reward for services rendered to Spain, the queen had her husband make Godoy prime minister and give him the exultant title Prince of the Peace.

Over time, both Godoy and Maria Luisa took other lovers and quarreled heartily about them, yet still maintained their sexual relationship. Once during a procession the favorite actually slapped the queen's face. The king, walking ahead, turned around to ask what the noise was, and the queen merely murmured that she had dropped a book.

When the queen took on a new lover named Manuel Mallo, King Carlos, seeing Mallo in a beautiful carriage pulled by four magnificent horses, wondered aloud how the fellow could afford to keep such a splendid equipage. Godoy replied loudly enough so the queen could hear him, "Sire, Mallo doesn't have a penny in the world, but everyone knows that he is kept by an old and ugly woman who robs her husband to pay him." When the king burst out laughing and asked the queen her opinion, she said haltingly, "Oh, well, Carlos, you know how Manuel is always joking."[3]

In 1796, after a particularly stormy scene, Maria Luisa reluctantly agreed to appoint Godoy's new mistress, the sleek and sinuous Josephina Tudo, as her lady-in-waiting. But Godoy, not satisfied with his luscious mistress and powerful queen, had even greater ambitions. He tried to arrange a marriage with Madame Royale, the daughter of the late Marie Antoinette. When Hapsburg laughter at this suggestion echoed all the way from Vienna to Madrid—stopping at every court in between—Godoy had to make do with the king's cousin Maria Theresa of Bourbon, the countess of Chinchon. Though married to a Bourbon, Godoy brazenly advertised that he was maintaining a ménage à trois and received guests at dinner with his wife sitting on his right and his mistress on his left.

Nor did Godoy limit his amorous adventures to the queen, his wife, and his mistress. He engaged in sex with women who threw themselves at him during his evening receptions. "A girl arriving with her mother always went in to the Minister without her," reported the French ambassador J. M. Alguier. "Those who went in came out again with heightened color and rumpled dresses, which they would then smooth down in full view of everybody. . . . Every evening the same scene was enacted in the very palace itself, the Court looking on and the Queen's apartments being not twenty yards away; the latter would rage and scream and threaten, only in the end to admit herself beaten."[4]

Observers at the time and historians ever since have wondered how the king could remain unconcerned about the love affair his wife so openly conducted with Godoy. Some courtiers believed that he was actually unaware of it. The French ambassador reported, "The thing that must strike those most who watch Charles IV in the bosom of his Court is his blindness where the conduct of the Queen is concerned. He knows nothing, sees nothing, suspects nothing. . . . Neither the warnings he has received in writing nor the intrigues going on all around him, nor the marks of favor lacking both pretext and precedent, nor the attentions which violate all usage and decency, nor even the existence of two children who bear, as is obvious to all, a striking resemblance to the Prince of the Peace—nothing has availed to open the King's eyes."[5]

King Carlos, Queen Maria Luisa, and Godoy called themselves "the earthly trinity." In 1808 after a palace revolt which made Crown Prince Ferdinand king of Spain, the trinity and the new king raced to France, both sides hoping to get Napoleon's support. But the emperor promptly put the whole squabbling group in elegant French confinement for several years, while Napoleon's brother Joseph climbed onto the vacant throne of Spain. After Napoleon's demise, Ferdinand once again became king. The trinity, meanwhile, had retired to Italy.

The queen's love affair with Godoy lasted thirty-one years until her death in 1819. When Maria Luisa breathed her last, it was Godoy at her side, not her husband, who was visiting his brother, the king of Naples to go hunting. Within days of her death, Carlos himself gave up the ghost.

Godoy was devastated. He had lost both royal patrons within a fortnight; at fifty-one he was hale and hearty with expensive tastes and no money. Maria Luisa had left him a generous inheritance, but her son, King Ferdinand VII—who had always hated his mother's lover—forced him to renounce it. However, Ferdinand, bristling at the thought of Godoy holding the title Prince of the Peace, offered him a large sum of money to give it back to the Spanish crown. Godoy agreed.

In his last years Godoy gravitated to Paris, that magnet for older men with money and an eye for the ladies. The country boy who had conquered a queen and ruled a nation was now an elderly gentleman with white whiskers and a jaunty walk. Only his voluptuous lips and dreamy eyes were the same. He died in 1851 at the age of eighty-four.

MARIA CAROLINA OF AUSTRIA, QUEEN OF NAPLES: THE WHITE GLOVE TRICK

Oddly similar to his brother, King Carlos of Spain, King Ferdinand of Naples cared little about his wife's lovers as long as he could chase stags. His wife, Maria Carolina, an Austrian archduchess and sister of Marie Antoinette, had dark blue eyes, chestnut hair, and an unquenchable thirst for politics. In her quest for political power, she was fortunate that her husband had a strange sexual fetish for her arms. She could convince him to do anything she wanted by slowly removing her long white gloves. According to Count Roger de Damas, "His brain becomes exalted when he sees a glove well stretched over a beautifully shaped arm. It is a mania he has always had and which has never varied. How many affairs of the greatest importance have I seen settled by the Queen's care to pull her gloves over her pretty arms while discussing the question which engrossed her! I have seen the king take notice of this, smile, and grant her wish."[6]

Once, when she did not get her way despite cajoling, threatening, storming, imploring, *and* the white-glove trick, she bit her husband's hand so hard he had a scar for quite some time.

Realizing her own political wisdom was not sufficient to run a nation, in 1779 she nominated an English visitor, the ex-naval officer Sir John Acton, as chief adviser. Sir William Hamilton, the British ambassador, reported, "He was forty-two, an experienced man of the world, enterprising, cosmopolitan and a bachelor. After a few conversations with him, Maria Carolina was convinced that she had found a perfect collaborator. . . . She regarded him as her own discovery. Together they would create a really independent kingdom. Acton set to work with cool thoroughness, patience and a systematic energy almost unknown in Naples."[7]

She also fell head over heels in love with him. Tall, lean, with an intelligent face and dignified bearing, the very proper Sir John seemed oblivious to the queen's charms, which made her passion burn more brightly. She finally conquered him, however, and rewarded him with the war department and, soon after, the finance ministry, where he became prime minister in all but name. Last, he became a field marshal and general of the Neapolitan armed forces. The right foil to the queen's melodrama, the taciturn Sir John ruled Naples with calm strength.

But the queen's long white arms had ceased to pull Acton's puppet strings by the late 1780s, when he began to work openly against her cockamamie political ideas. He was in the possession of steamy titillating letters she had written him and checked her scheming by threatening to release them. To punish him, she took countless young lovers. Unconcerned with her sexual escapades, Acton intervened only when he saw a young man delving into politics. Acton would inform the king of his wife's love affair, and the lover would be exiled. Ironically, Acton became the king's best friend and the queen's greatest enemy. The former lovers studiously avoided each other.

The queen fumed against Acton as the man "whose wickedness has altogether surpassed what I could have imagined, and I admit that this black ingratitude is deeply distressing to me and disgusts me more and more with this world."[8]

Throughout the tumult caused by the Napoleonic wars, Acton stood by the royal family. He arranged their escape from revolutionary forces and lived with them in their Sicilian exile while Napoleon's sister and her husband, the Murats, ruled Naples. But finally, plagued by old age, poor health, and the queen's temper tantrums, he retired and the lethargic king permitted his wife to rule once more. We can assume she went right to her glove drawer.

MARIE ANTOINETTE OF AUSTRIA, QUEEN OF FRANCE

"Adieu, My Heart Is All Yours"

When seventeen-year-old Marie Antoinette of Austria, for three years the wife of the heir to the French throne, made her first official entrance into Paris in 1773, she was met by the thunderous applause of wildly cheering crowds. "Madame, you have here a hundred thousand lovers," a city official told her.[9] But they would, over time, dwindle down to one.

On a glittering cold January night in 1774 she met him at a masked ball in Paris. Such balls had been the rage for over a century because masked women could flirt outrageously without being recognized. Incognito, even the noblest women teased unknown men and sometimes had sex with them in carriages or gardens, willingly raising their skirts but never their black velvet masks. There were reports that some men had sex with their own wives at masked balls and never knew it.

Eighteen-year-old Count Axel Fersen of Sweden, sent by his powerful father on a European tour to polish him up, was enchanted when a lovely masked girl approached him, placed her hand ever so gently upon his sleeve, and began to flirt. After a time, she raised her mask and others gasped to see the dauphine, or crown princess, Marie Antoinette. The dauphine should have been presiding over her elegant court at Versailles, not attending a shocking masked ball in Paris. But she had been forced to marry a man she found repulsive, a man who after five years of marriage was still unable to consummate it. She vented her frustrations in dancing, gambling, and shopping.

Marie Antoinette looked straight into the grave blue eyes of young Count Axel Fersen and laughed out loud before disappearing into the crowd. The following day Fersen attended a ball at Versailles where he danced continuously for five hours, the eagle eyes of the dauphine watching his graceful movements. A few days later he reported in his diary, "I go only to the balls given by Madame la Dauphine."[10] Possibly he had already fallen in love. For four months he stayed at Versailles, and it is likely that he saw her often at court events.

Slender gallant Fersen must have contrasted favorably to Marie Antoinette's husband, Louis. The baron de Frénilly wrote of the dauphin, "He was a good man, a good husband, pious, chaste, virtuous, just, humane, but without wit, without character, without will, without experience, a heavy mass badly carved, stout, lumbering, brusque, coarse, common in speech and trivial in manner; it was necessary to take thought, and to close one's eyes, to do him justice."[11]

Shortly after Fersen reluctantly left Versailles to visit London, old King Louis XV succumbed to smallpox. The dull-witted dauphin was now King Louis XVI of France. Louis was miserable in the knowledge that just as he made a terrible husband, he would make an awful king. Iron strength, unrelenting ego, and unquenchable thirst for glory were the qualities required by a king. Poor Louis was kindhearted, moral, modest, and indecisive. When asked what adjective he would like to see attached to his name, Louis replied with a heavy sigh, "I would like to be known as Louis the Severe."[12]

The queen, for her part, said that her goal was not to be a great queen; she wanted to be the most fashionable woman in France. Marie Antoinette, though beautiful and sparkling enough to fill a decorative role at the French court, boasted even less intelligence than her plodding husband. Unlike him, she was not smart enough to realize her own limitations. Decisive and confident, Marie Antoinette prided herself on her political genius, easily swaying her weak husband.

In August 1778 Axel Fersen returned to Versailles. At twenty-two he was an experienced lover and sophisticated courtier. In a crowd of clucking favor seekers, Fersen alone was reserved, discreet, thoughtful. A French nobleman, the duc de Lévis, reported, "His manners were noble and unaffected. His conversation was not very animated, and he showed more judgment than wit. He was circumspect with men and reserved with women, serious without being sad. His face and his manner were perfectly suited to the hero of a novel, though not of a French novel, for he had neither the brilliance nor the frivolity."[13]

The queen's page Alexandre de Tilly said that Axel was "one of the handsomest men I ever saw, though with an icy countenance, which women do not dislike if they can hope to give it animation."[14] One of his spurned lovers wrote that "he had a burning soul beneath a layer of ice."[15]

As for Marie Antoinette, much had changed since she had last seen Fersen. In the intervening four years Louis had finally conquered his impotence and the queen was pregnant. But she was still not in love with her husband. Upon seeing her former admirer, the queen's face lit up. Smiling broadly, she cried, "Ah! But here is an old acquaintance!"[16]

Fersen wrote his father, "The Queen, who is the most beautiful and amiable princess I know, has had the kindness to ask often about me. . . ."[17] Hearing that as a captain of the Swedish king's light horse he owned a gorgeous pale blue and white uniform, she made him promise to wear it. When Fersen walked toward her one day resplendent in his military attire, she was leaning on the arm of her first equerry, the comte de Tessé, who "was made aware, by a movement of her hand, of the strong emotion caused by that sight."[18]

By autumn she was seen to be giving Fersen more attention than any other courtier. She played the harpsichord for him and sang. She often invited him to her private apartments where, in a small group, she would play cards with him, or perhaps draw him aside for a private chat. "My stay here becomes more agreeable by the day," he wrote his father gleefully in December. "It's a charming place!"[19]

On December 19, 1778, Marie Antoinette gave birth to a daughter. Though a girl could not inherit the French throne, and Louis was eager to try for a boy, the queen spurned his attentions and focused on her devoted Swede. It is likely that the burgeoning love affair was not yet physical; it consisted of bright eyes and slow smiles, the inexpressible delight of being together.

But after a time, Fersen looked about him and realized his love was futile, even dangerous. Hoping a change of scene would ease his pain, he volunteered to serve France in the American Revolutionary War. Perhaps, with an ocean between them, he could forget her.

In April 1780 the Swedish ambassador Gustaf Creutz wrote to King Gustavus III of Sweden, "I must confide to Your Majesty that young Count Fersen has been so well treated by the Queen that several people have taken umbrage at it. . . . Young Count Fersen conducted himself admirably in these circumstances by his modesty and reserve, and above all by the decision he took to go to America. . . . The Queen couldn't take her eyes off him during the final days; when she looked at him they were filled with tears. . . ."[20]

On October 17, 1781, Fersen was present when the British commanding general, Lord Charles Cornwallis, surrendered to General George Washington at Yorktown. As the only English-speaking aide to the French commanding general, Comte Jean de Rochambeau, he served as interpreter for Washington and his French allies. But Fersen found his duties uninspiring and believed that France was wrong to help the Americans rebel against their lawful king. To his horror, he realized that Americans were not even gentlemen. "Money is their god," he wrote, scandalized. "Virtue, honor, these are nothing to them beside the precious metal."[21] Worse, after the glories of Versailles, he found himself stewing in the Virginia capital of Williamsburg for several months, "a wretched hole."[22] Nonetheless, for his invaluable services General Washington rewarded Fersen with America's most distinguished decoration, the Cross of the Cincinnatus.

Heaving a tremendous sigh of relief that the American expedition was behind him, Fersen arrived in Paris June 23, 1783, to a hero's welcome from the jubilant queen. It is likely that the two became lovers that summer. During his absence, the queen had finally done her duty by giving the kingdom a prince in October 1781; she could now indulge more freely in a love affair, as spurious children would not likely inherit the throne. Tired of her repulsive husband, tired of waiting for the man she truly desired, she must have brought out her substantial arsenal of charms to win over the hesitant lover. Fersen, modest and reserved, as chivalrous as a medieval knight, had resigned himself to worshiping an unattainable highborn lady, *une dame belle et cruelle*, a gorgeous stone statue. But like Pygmalion, he found his cold statue turn to warm flesh in his arms and step down from her pedestal.

Outwardly, nothing changed. The queen showed warmth and interest in the Swede, that was all. Fersen remained cool and correct toward her in public. In his diary entry of July 15 he noted for the first time that he had gone to Versailles for an audience with the queen and stayed *chez Elle*. Whenever Fersen wrote in his diary the word *chez* followed by the name of a woman, it meant he had spent the night with her. And *Elle* became a secret code name for the woman whose name must not be spoken. They probably met in the private rooms above the queen's bedchamber, reached by a secret staircase, and usually reserved for a lady-in-waiting when the queen was ill or pregnant. Most likely he slept in the *méridienne*, a cozy octagonal room which contained a large sofa set in a curtained alcove. During that long hot summer when most courtiers were away at their country homes, Marie Antoinette had plenty of opportunity to entertain her secret lover.

But even a man as discreet as Axel Fersen needed to unburden his heart to someone, and he chose his discreet sister, Sophie, in Sweden, who began to correspond secretly with the queen herself. In these letters to Sophie, Fersen refers to the queen either as *"Her"* or "Josephine." Marie Antoinette's third name was Josèphe.

On July 31 he wrote Sophie, "I can hardly believe I'm so happy. I've more than one reason for that, which I'll tell you when we meet."[23] He added, "I never want to tie the conjugal knot. . . . I cannot belong to the only person I want to belong to, the only one who truly loves me, and so I don't want to belong to anyone."[24]

Surely with his burning soul beneath the crust of ice, Fersen made a more passionate lover than clumsy Louis, who never excelled at the art of lovemaking. Marie Antoinette, for her part, had been denied sex for the first seven years of marriage and then forced to copulate with a man who repulsed her. Now, for the first time, she found sex and love. We can picture them in her tiny secluded love nest, the pent-up passion exploding in rapture, intertwined arms and legs, warm lips and flesh, a tangle of hair, the aroma of perfume and sweat and sex.

But after the perfect summer, family responsibilities called Fersen home. He eagerly returned to Versailles in June 1784 in the entourage of the king of Sweden. Hearing King Gustavus had arrived, poor Louis dressed so quickly that he put on stockings of different colors and only one shoe buckle, then went flapping out, puffing and breathless, to meet his fellow sovereign. King Gustavus, known for his impeccable dress and reserved demeanor, must have eyed the French king with veiled laughter.

But Fersen had eyes for only one person, the queen. Required to accompany Gustavus every waking moment, Fersen pled illness to be able to meet Marie Antoinette secretly. Wrenching himself away after a visit of only a few days, Fersen did not know that he had most likely left something of himself to comfort her. Nine months after his visit Marie Antoinette had a son, the future Louis XVII.

Fersen bounced back to Versailles whenever he could. By May 1787 he was with the queen once again, making notes in his diary about lodging "upstairs" with his royal mistress. Despite Fersen's vaunted discretion, the entire court was well aware of the affair.

The comte de Saint-Priest wrote, "Fersen proceeded on horseback to the park, beside the Trianon, two or three times a week; the Queen, alone, did the same, and these rendezvous caused a public scandal, despite the modesty and reserve of the favorite, who never revealed anything by his outward appearance."[25]

On September 27, 1788, the king was seen receiving a packet of mysterious letters while he was out hunting. One courtier reported, "He went into a copse to read them and soon he was seen sitting on the ground, his face held in his hands and his hands resting on his knees."[26] An equerry rushed forward and saw the king crying. Louis ordered him to go away and sat sobbing miserably as tears rolled down his cheeks. He announced that he was ill and needed help in mounting his horse. But by the time he arrived at the palace, he had composed himself. No one knew what documents had upset him so terribly, but it is possible they were intercepted love letters of Marie Antoinette and Axel Fersen. Worse, at this time the dauphin was dying slowly of tuberculosis, and Louis would have been deeply upset to receive evidence that the duc de Normandie, the next king of France, was the son of the Swedish count.

June 3, 1789, the dauphin died. Fersen hastened to Versailles to comfort the queen. Swathed in black, she was still grieving on July 14 when a howling mob stormed the Bastille prison twenty miles away in Paris. It was a hot, uneasy summer, with revolutionary politics heating up to a rolling boil. Louis wanted to agree to a new constitution ensuring greater rights to his people; his wife insisted on the divine right of kings and vowed never to cede an inch.

On October 5 a mob surrounded Versailles with cannons, and Fersen personally stood guard outside the queen's rooms. At six the next morning, the shrieking rabble raced into the palace hard on the scent of blood, the queen's blood, the hated Austrian woman who had danced in diamonds while they starved. Fersen escorted the queen to the comparative safety of the king's apartments, while the mob, furious at not finding her, tore her guards to pieces. Brandishing the severed heads on pikes, the angry crowd forced the royal family to ride to Paris. Even then Fersen would not leave the queen but trailed behind her.

In Paris the royal family lived under house arrest at the Tuileries Palace. Fersen closed his Versailles apartment and rented one close to the queen. It was no longer easy to see each other. On December 29, 1789, Marie Antoinette wrote to her friend Madame de Polignac, "I have seen him; for, after three months of grief and separation, although we were in the same place, the person and I managed to see each other safely once. You know us both, so you can imagine our happiness."[27] On December 27 he wrote to his sister, Sophie, "At last on the 24th I spent the whole day with *Her.* It was the first; imagine my joy—only you can feel it."[28]

Marie Antoinette and Fersen made great efforts to conceal their relationship from Louis to avoid hurting him. But Louis was not as stupid as he seemed. Though jealous of the charming Swede and painfully aware of the romance, he decided to pretend their relationship was platonic. Perhaps it was his way of saying he was sorry for being a terrible king and a terrible husband, that he loved her enough to ensure her happiness at the expense of his own.

In 1790 Fersen began making careful plans for the royal family's escape. He borrowed money from friends, much of it to secure men and horses to stand guard just over the French border and train their guns on any pursuers.

In December the queen bought for her escape a huge lumbering coach that held seven people; painted green and yellow, it boasted white velvet upholstery and green taffeta blinds. A courtier sniffed, "It was an abridged edition of the Chateau of Versailles, only the chapel and the musicians' balcony were lacking."[29]

Luxury aside, it would have attracted attention by its sheer size. Fersen had proposed two small swift traveling carriages, but the queen refused to travel in a vehicle so unworthy of her exalted station. He wanted to hire real drivers, men who knew the routes and the lingo and, unaware of the identities of their passengers, would not attract attention. But the queen haughtily demanded that she be served only by gentlemen.

Worse, she insisted on bringing along a wardrobe fit for a queen. Her lady-in-waiting Jeanne-Louise Campan recalled, "It was with distress that I saw her occupied with details that seemed to me useless and even dangerous, and I pointed out to her that the Queen of France could find chemises and dresses wherever she went. My remarks were fruitless; she wanted to have a complete outfit not only for herself, but for her children. I went out alone and in disguise to buy and have made this trousseau."[30]

Worst of all, the queen refused to leave until her hairdresser from happier days, Monsieur Leonard, dressed her hair for the voyage. The little man was kidnapped for this purpose, taken to the palace in his bedroom slippers, forced to dress her hair, and returned to his home. For this, he was later guillotined.

Fersen intended to accompany the royal family, but Louis refused to have his wife's lover along on the ride. On May 29 Fersen wrote sadly to a friend aware of the plot, "I shall not accompany the King, he didn't want me to."[31] The Swede would leave France via another route.

On the evening of June 20, Fersen, dressed as a coachman, waited next to his coach outside the palace, chatting to other coachmen and offering them snuff. One by one the members of the royal family arrived. Early in the morning of June 21 he drove them to a staging post outside of Paris, where he took his leave and set off alone. Traveling lightly and swiftly, Fersen soon arrived in safety.

But the heavy coach of the royal family broke down, and repairs went so slowly that the troops waiting for them at the border assumed the escape had been abandoned and left. In need of fresh horses, lost on the country roads, the coach finally reached a staging post where a cavalryman named Drouet looked into the carriage and recognized the king. In hot pursuit, revolutionary soldiers captured the royal family at the town of Varennes and took them back to Paris as prisoners. When Madame Campan saw the queen two days later, "She took off her nightcap and told me to see the effect grief had had on her hair. In a single night it had turned as white as that of a woman of seventy."[32]

On June 23 Fersen wrote in his diary, "Learned that the King was captured. Details not very clear; the troops didn't do their duty, the King lacked firmness and will." That night he wrote his father, "Everything is lost, my dear father, and I am desperate. The King was arrested at Varennes, 16 leagues from the frontier. Think of my misery and pity me. . . ."[33]

Because of their flight, members of the royal family had lost all their privileges. Guards remained in their rooms day and night, even when the queen was on the chamber pot. On July 4 she sent a coded letter to Fersen. "I can tell you I love you and I have only time for that," she scribbled. "Adieu, most loved and loving of men. I embrace you with all my heart."[34]

In April 1792 the guillotine was set up in the Place de Grève, its first victim a thief. But soon afterward enemies of the state and aristocrats were forced to kneel before this altar to a bloodthirsty new god. The courtiers of Versailles remained haughty to the end. One day when entering the cart that would take them to the guillotine, an aristocrat bowed and allowed a lady to pass before him. The jailer yelled at him for wasting time. "You can kill us when you like," replied the nobleman disdainfully, "but you cannot make us forget our manners."[35]

Puffed up with pride in her political genius despite the prison cell where her genius had landed her, Marie Antoinette was up to her elbows in intrigue, sending secret letters to foreign courts asking for forces to invade France. Contemptuous of her captors, she wrote letters in code and in invisible ink, then handed them to helpful friends or servants who smuggled them out of prison. But Louis refused to ask foreign governments to cross French frontiers and shed French blood. "God's will be done," he often sighed. "I would rather pass for weak than for wicked."[36]

It was Marie Antoinette's misfortune that her powerful mother, Empress Maria Theresa, had died in 1780 and her favorite brother, Emperor Joseph II, in 1790. If her mother or Joseph had still been alive, they would have used horrifying threats, backed by the substantial firepower of the Austro-Hungarian Empire, to rescue her. But now her younger brother, Leopold, who had never been close to her, was emperor. More ambitious than loyal, Leopold hoped to use the chaos in France to his political advantage, perhaps taking chunks of France for himself. Fersen was aware of this, writing her, "He is deceiving you. He will do nothing for you . . . he will abandon you to your fate and let the whole kingdom fall to complete ruin."[37]

The European powers had already begun to devour Poland, and they now turned to fresh meat—France, historically the strongest, richest, and most populated country in Europe. Now France was weak and fractured; now was the time to circle in for the kill. Britain, salivating at the thought of grabbing the French colonies in North America, demanded that France be flattened to "a veritable political nonentity." Leopold, baring his fangs and snarling, claimed Flanders, Artois, and Picardy for Austria, and, indifferent to his sister's fate, insisted that France be "crushed by terror." Frederick William II of Prussia claimed Alsace Lorraine, and Catherine the Great of Russia complacently advised everyone to take what they wanted, leaving France "a second-class power which need no longer be feared by anybody."[38]

It is ironic that European nations tied to France by centuries of marriages and treaties were so eager for its destruction and unconcerned about the welfare of the royal family, and the one country truly interested in a rescue attempt was the United States. Perhaps the new nation wanted to express its gratitude to the king and queen for providing invaluable aid in the war for independence.

The American ambassador to France, Gouverneur Morris, carefully arranged an escape attempt. But Louis, who had given his word of honor to his captors that he would not try to escape again, hesitated. Morris later explained, "The measures were so well arranged that success was almost certain, but the King (for reasons which it is pointless to detail here) gave up the plan on the very morning fixed for his departure, when the Swiss Guards had already left Courbevoie to cover his retreat. His ministers, who found themselves gravely compromised, all tendered their resignation."[39]

It was Louis's last chance. In December 1792 he was on trial for his life. The American ambassador wrote to Thomas Jefferson, "It is strange that the mildest monarch who ever filled the French throne, one who is precipitated from it precisely because he would not adopt the harsh measures of his predecessors, a man whom none can charge with a criminal or cruel act, should be prosecuted as one of the most nefarious tyrants who ever disgraced the annals of human nature."[40]

Knowing the king would be condemned and executed, Fersen wrote Sophie, "Poor, unfortunate family, poor Queen—why can't I save her with my blood! It would be the greatest happiness for me, the sweetest joy for my soul."[41]

As expected, Louis XVI was condemned to die on the guillotine for crimes against the people of France. On the evening of January 20, 1793, he was allowed to spend ninety minutes with his family and broke the news. As his wife and children sobbed uncontrollably, Louis remained strong. He sat the dauphin on his lap and made him promise not to seek revenge on those who had condemned him. To blunt the pain of the final parting, Louis promised he would return to say good-bye at seven A.M. the next day, knowing full well that he would not come.

The next morning, before he left the prison, he said, "Crimes have been imputed to me, but I am innocent, and I shall die without fear. I desire that my death may bring happiness to the people of France, and may preserve them from the misfortunes that I foresee."[42]

Accompanied by sixteen hundred soldiers, Louis was rolled through Paris on a cart to what is now the Place de la Concorde. The crowds were strangely quiet. Most doors were closed, the windows shuttered. The king who could not rule well at least insisted upon dying well and, as he approached the scaffold, refused the indignity of having his hands bound. The executioner argued and Louis finally allowed him to use his own handkerchief instead of the rope. He next had to climb a six-foot ladder without the use of his hands and wobbled unsteadily. Some spectators, ashamed for him, believed it was out of fear, but the king, despite the rigors of prison, still had an ungainly bulk. Fat Louis. Louis the Pig. Once on the scaffold he marched resolutely to the front and began to speak, but the drummers intensified their staccato beat, drowning out the king's last words.

He took his place, laying his head on the guillotine. With the noise of gathering thunder the heavy blade came hurtling down and severed it. There was some cheering but also much grief among the French for the murder of their king. In her prison Marie Antoinette heard the cheers and held her son closer to her.

Days later Fersen wrote that he was haunted by "the image of Louis XVI mounting the scaffold. . . . Often I curse the day I left Sweden, that I ever knew anything but our rocks and our firs. I would not have had, it is true, so many joys, but I'm paying dearly for them at the moment, and I would have spared myself many pains. I cry often all alone, my dear Sophie. . . ."[43]

In March 1793 Marie Antoinette had a last chance at escape— the commissioner in charge of the royal prisoners was prepared to smuggle her to the coast and put her in a boat for England. But as it was impossible to rescue her children at the same time, the queen refused to leave them behind. "I could enjoy nothing if I left my children," she wrote, "and this idea leaves me without even a single regret."[44]

Because France had become too dangerous for him, Fersen moved to Brussels, 210 miles away from Paris, hoping to make another rescue attempt. No Scarlet Pimpernel, Fersen was frustrated at every turn. Moreover, his generosity in paying for the earlier escape was catching up with him, and he found himself living on very little money. "Never mind, it was for *Her*," he wrote, "I had to."[45]

The eight-year-old dauphin, now called Louis XVII by royalists, was taken from his mother and given to a cobbler who beat him, plied him with alcohol, and tried to get him to masturbate to provide evidence against the queen's incestuous proclivities. Having lost her son, Marie Antoinette was also separated from her daughter and taken to a different prison. Waiting at the doorstep for their prisoner, her new jailers became concerned that she did not emerge from her carriage for some time. After she finally did venture out, they looked inside and saw that the floor was coated with blood. Once in her cell, the queen kept losing alarming amounts of blood. It is likely that she was dying of uterine cancer.

In a cold chamber with no fire, the queen began to show symptoms of tuberculosis. The sheets on her narrow bed were filthy, and she had a single dirty blanket with holes in it. Dressed in black to hide the blood, she expected to be murdered in her cell or led to her execution at any moment. One day, walking through a door she struck her head on the doorway. Asked if she were hurt, she replied, "Oh no—nothing can hurt me any more."[46]

On September 4 Fersen wrote to Sophie, "I often reproach myself even for the air I breathe when I think she is shut up in a dreadful prison. This idea is breaking my heart and poisoning my life, and I'm constantly torn between grief and rage."[47]

In October 1793 Marie Antoinette, the Austrian whore, as she was called, was charged with aiding and abetting the enemies of France to launch an invasion, which was true. Many of the letters she had had smuggled out of prison had been intercepted and decoded. To drag her despised name through the mud even further, she was also accused of sexually abusing her son, which was untrue. The terrified little boy had been beaten until he testified against her. Found guilty of all charges, she was sentenced to be guillotined.

She was, without the aid of the guillotine, already a dying woman, eaten up by tuberculosis and cancer and the grief that fed their growth. In her final letter, she wrote to her sister-in-law, Madame Elizabeth, of her dead husband: "I hope to show the same firmness as he did in his last moments. . . ."[48] She continued in a mysterious passage which must have referred to Fersen: "I used to have friends. The idea of being separated from them for ever and their grief is one of the greatest sorrows I shall carry to my grave; may they know at least that I thought of them until my last moment."[49] On her prayer book she wrote,

"My God, have pity on me! My eyes have no tears left to weep for you, my poor children. Adieu, adieu!"[50]

Hours later, Marie Antoinette, dressed in a simple white dress with her hands tied behind her back, was loaded into a tumbrel which drove her from her prison to the foot of the guillotine. In preparation for the sharp blade, her hair had been cut. Those golden curls, once piled high with diamonds, feathers, and bows, were now a raggedy mess of dirty white tendrils. As the cart lurched forward through howling crowds, her priest said, "Have courage, Madame." "Courage!" she almost spat. "It is to live that requires courage, not to die."[51]

She was shoved roughly up the steps. Louis would have been proud of her, for, like him, she showed no fear. Even at that moment Marie Antoinette was still the most fashionable woman in France, leading the fashion right up to the guillotine where thousands more fashionable women would follow. Moments later her head was held up by the executioner. Her body was dumped in an unmarked grave near that of her husband. It was October 16, 1793.

Upon hearing the news that she was, at last, beyond hope of his rescue, Fersen was devastated. "I seemed to feel nothing," he wrote in his diary.[52] The next day he went out riding alone. When he returned he wrote, "That she was alone in her last moments without consolation, with no one to talk to, to give her last wishes to, is horrifying. The monsters from hell! No, without revenge, my heart will never be satisfied."[53] He kept a list of the names of the judges who had condemned her. As the years passed, he checked off the names of those who had died; with exquisite irony, most of them were guillotined.

Two months after the queen's execution, he wrote to Sophie of the bungled night of Varennes two years earlier: "I would have been much happier if I'd died on June 21."[54] He was not yet forty, yet his life was over. His remaining years would not be living, but existing, dragging himself reluctantly through each day, until death assuaged his pain.

When a dejected Fersen finally returned to Stockholm, his sister handed him a scrap of paper that the queen had somehow smuggled out to Sophie shortly before her execution. "Adieu," it said simply. "My heart is all yours."[55] A ray of light pierced the darkness of his soul; this pitiful scrap of wrinkled paper seemed to be a message from *Her* in heaven.

In June 1795 another blow hit Fersen; the death in prison of the ten-year-old Louis XVII, the boy who was perhaps his son. "This event caused me real pain," he wrote sadly. "He was the last and only interest left to me in France."[56]

In December 1795 the seventeen-year-old dauphine, Marie Antoinette's daughter, was exchanged for French prisoners and returned to Vienna to live with her mother's family. Fersen followed her to Vienna and tried to meet with her Austrian relatives to ask for reimbursement of his expenses for the escape to Varennes. Ignored by the imperial circle, Fersen finally left in dejection. He paid all the capital and interest—the crushing burden of one million livres—out of his inheritance.

Before Marie Antoinette died, she destroyed most of her papers and letters. Many of Fersen's diaries and copies of his letters to the queen were passed down in his family. But when his great-nephew Baron Rin de Klinckowstrom published Fersen's letters in 1877—in an era of Victorian prudishness—he edited them heavily, removing most of the first and last lines where amorous expressions were likely to have been inserted. After publication Klinckowstrom burned them. By this time Marie Antoinette's reputation had been established as sainted mother and holy martyr, and the publication of her adulterous love letters, salted with references to hot sex, would have been unthinkable.

Fersen never married, remaining committed to his memories of love with the queen. He had a successful political career in Sweden, and in 1797 was sent as Swedish ambassador to the Congress of Rastatt to treat with Napoleon. The little Corsican, however, "refused to deal with a man who had slept with the Queen of France."[57]

The world was rapidly changing, and Fersen did not truly belong to the new one. "He who has not known Paris before 1789 has never known the true sweetness of living," wrote the French statesman Charles Maurice de Talleyrand long years after the revolution.[58] It had been an age of soft silks and powdered wigs, where sweet strains of the minuet echoed through gilded rooms flickering in candlelight, an age in which every aspect of living was an exquisite art form. This most civilized of civilizations had been drowned in a sea of blood, and after the mess had been mopped up, nothing would ever be the same. Talleyrand was not the only one to find the light harsher, the music louder, the women less graceful. Axel Fersen would have agreed.

In 1810 the middle-aged Crown Prince Karl August of Sweden suddenly died of a stroke. Rumors circulated that Axel Fersen, who had disliked the prince, had in fact poisoned him. Alarmed at the growing revolt against Fersen, his friends warned him to steer clear of the funeral procession; but as grand marshal, Fersen insisted that he lead it according to custom. Halfway through the procession, a mob tore him from his carriage and bludgeoned him to death.

Handsome Axel, who had danced so gracefully at Versailles, was now reduced to butcher's offal in the streets. As a youth he had once written with a clear vision of his future, "I'm not one of those men who will find happiness."[59] It must have been a relief to die, to cross over the inviolable wall of separation toward *Her.* Lying in the street, as the lights dimmed, the cries subsided, and the pain diminished, perhaps he saw a radiant girl with golden hair who, laughing, touched his arm.

CAROLINE MATILDA OF BRITAIN, QUEEN OF DENMARK

"I Would Marry Him I Loved, and Give Up My Throne"

"To be unfaithful to a husband one has been forced to marry is not a crime," said Queen Caroline Matilda of Denmark in 1770.[60] And yet the penalty she would pay for her infidelity was a heavy one.

In 1766 the fifteen-year-old British princess, great-granddaughter of Sophia Dorothea of Celle and sister of King George III, was forced to marry the seventeen-year-old King

Christian VII of Denmark. Matilda—as she was known—wept when she heard of the marriage, wept all the way on the long journey from England to Copenhagen, and upon her arrival wept more when she learned that something was rotten in the state of Denmark.

During the marriage negotiations, the Danish ambassador had advertised Christian with great praise. "The amiable character of the Prince of Denmark is universally acknowledged here," he said.[61] But in reality the amiable prince knocked over citizens in the street and beat up the night watch. "In his way of living he is regular and sober," the ambassador continued, "eats heartily, but drinks little or no wine."[62] He neglected to mention that Christian was a staggering alcoholic by the time he hit his teens. "He is now impatient for the accomplishment of this marriage," the ambassador continued.[63] But in fact the king dreaded the accomplishment of the marriage. Christian's "application was equal to his capacity," George III was told. This last was, in fact, true. Both were at zero.[64]

In an effort to make a man out of the delicate prince, Christian's tutors had beaten and tortured him until he turned eleven, when he was given a kindhearted Swiss tutor named Elie Salomon François Reverdil. But by then, the damage had been done. The little prince had learned to escape from his tutors' brutality into a fantasy world of strange dreams spiced by paranoia and sexual degradations. All of Reverdil's patience and compassion could not coax Christian back out into the real world. When Christian was informed that his father had died and he was the new king, he eagerly inquired if that meant he would never be beaten again.

The new monarch was unbearably bored by his royal responsibilities. No national business could be transacted without his signature, and his signature on a decree made it law immediately. In contrast to other European nations where parliaments and constitutions limited royal power, the Lex Regia of 1665 declared that Denmark was the personal property of its monarch, who held absolute unquestioned power and was accountable only to God. The Danish council was an advisory board which the king could dismiss at will. Christian VII of Denmark, idiot, whoremonger, alcoholic, had more power than any other eighteenth-century European monarch.

The king would leave piles of state papers unread for days while he crawled around on the floor with his companions playing practical jokes. When he encountered ladies drinking tea, he would invariably push the raised cups into their faces, sometimes burning them badly. One day he dropped pastries out of his window onto the head of a visiting bishop. Another time, when his aunt was sedately sipping coffee, Christian jumped out from beneath her table, his face blackened with soot, howling like a wolf. The terrified matron tipped backward in her chair which crashed to the floor, her diamond-buckled feet waving in the air.

This was to be the husband of England's fairest flower. But it mattered little to the power brokers of Britain and Denmark if the groom was an alcoholic imbecile. The princess was sold off to firm up traditional ties between the two nations, to check the power of France and strengthen the Protestant religion. It was rumored that someone would have to rule Denmark through Christian, and George III hoped that his sister would be that person, pushing the dazed king firmly toward a British alliance instead of a French one.

But Matilda had been kept far from the intriguing court of her grandfather George II. Raised in the seclusion of Kew Palace with her widowed mother and seven brothers and sisters, she had learned to raise vegetables in her little garden, to dance and embroider and speak French. This wide-eyed girl, with no political education whatsoever, was expected to rule a nation.

When Matilda was introduced to her husband, she found a tiny boy whose head barely reached her shoulder. On the surface Christian had learned to charm. Slender and perfectly proportioned, he was like a white-wigged doll in silk stockings. His face was long and narrow with slightly protruding blue eyes. He had a long aquiline nose, a finely molded mouth, and a chiseled jaw. His high forehead gave him, ironically, a look of superior intelligence. His flaxen hair was so pale it required no white hair powder. This tiny puppet of a king, mercurial, sometimes violent, offered occasional flashes of brilliance. When calm, he was good-hearted, though often confused. He danced gracefully and could talk prettily enough, reciting poetry and theatrical speeches in between violent temper tantrums.

Entranced by the appearance of his blushing bride, the king, in a fit of exuberance, rushed forward to embrace her. The ministers responsible for the marriage heaved a collective sigh of relief. The marriage would be a great success.

After meeting her husband, Matilda was introduced to Dowager Queen Juliana Maria, Christian's stepmother. The stiff matron, caked with piety, had one goal in life—that her son Prince Frederick, Christian's younger half brother, would inherit the throne. Because Prince Frederick clearly suffered from even greater mental aberrations than his brother, Juliana would rule the country in his name. As queen, Juliana had reportedly tried to poison Christian in his nursery, but a faithful maid, seeing the queen mix something into the prince's breakfast, threw away the noxious brew and warned the king. Juliana shrieked in protest at the accusation, but a watch was kept on Christian's food.

Ambition pulsated relentlessly behind Juliana's soft smile, beneath her deceptively feminine pink silk gowns. Adept at concealing her ambition, she manifested it only in her eyes, hard sharp eyes, quick to shift from right to left to focus unblinkingly on new prey. And when Matilda arrived, Juliana saw new prey. This healthy buxom princess would, no doubt, ruin all Juliana's plans by having children. The pious dowager queen declared she was simply delighted with Matilda, but beneath her parchment skin, her blood boiled.

Within a few days of the wedding, Christian decided he didn't like being married and that it was, in fact, unfashionable for a man to love his wife. He returned to the brothels of Copenhagen with his debauched friends, ripping up taverns and attacking citizens on the streets. Matilda was pointedly neglected by her new husband, the courtiers following his lead. She had not been permitted to bring a single friend from Britain into Denmark and had been forced to bid a tearful farewell to those ladies who had accompanied her from London to the Danish border. Now, all alone, the bride sat mute and dejected for days on end. Casting her glance about her magnificent rooms, she longed for the wet vegetable garden where she had cheerfully rooted and dug with her brothers and sisters.

The French, who had initially been alarmed that Christian had married an English princess, were delighted that the marriage was off to such a bad start. "The Princess has made little impression on the King's heart," wrote the French ambassador gleefully to Louis XV, "and had she been even more charming, she would have met with the same fate. For how can she please a man who quite seriously believes that it does not look well for a husband to love his wife?"[65]

Christian's ministers, looking on in despair at Matilda going to bed alone each night, informed His Majesty that the lack of an heir would convince his people he was not so much fashionable as impotent. Boasting platinum blond hair, a dazzling complexion, lovely features, and "a bosom such as few men could look on without emotion," Matilda inspired the sexual fantasies of every man at court except her husband.[66] When his friend Reverdil begged the king to treat Matilda as a wife deserved, Christian replied, "A person of royal blood seems to me—when one is in bed with her—rather worthy of respect than of love."[67]

Once, at least, the king rose to the occasion, for in April 1767 Matilda became pregnant. But Christian's mental health was deteriorating so rapidly that Reverdil suggested a pleasant distraction, a tour of the Danish duchies, an idea which the king embraced with delight. During the royal progress, Christian met a German doctor named Johann Struensee who had been investigating mental disorders. Tall, well spoken, with a soothing and modest address, Struensee made an immediate impression on the king. Christian insisted on taking him along for the rest of the tour and, finding his company indispensable, promised him a minor post at court.

At thirty, Struensee was a large man who carried his weight well. His well-shaped head perched solidly on broad shoulders with no sign of a neck. His was a broad face made up of refined angles, a high wide forehead, powerful cheekbones, a strong jaw and chin. His aquiline nose, far too long to be considered handsome, gave his appearance a hawkish strength. Only his lips, full and fleshy, betrayed his sensuality. He left his thick light brown hair unpowdered. Cautious, and discreet, he was graceful for his bulk, dancing and fencing well, stepping silently on agile feet.

Struensee had stewed in the town of Altona for over a decade, tending to the poor, seducing women, and dreaming of adventure. "If my lady patronesses will only contrive to get me to Copenhagen, then I will carry all before me," he once proclaimed.[68]

Settled into the Christiansborg Palace in Copenhagen, Struensee mixed potions to cure Christian's hangovers, a surefire way of winning his devotion. His sensible conversation had a calming effect on the king's nervous excitement. Modest and humble, Struensee won over courtiers who saw him as no threat to the existing power structure. Those who chose to look more deeply, however, would have seen that his quiet demeanor curbed a fierce raw power waiting to explode.

When the king sank into a weeping depression, too incapacitated to leave his bed, even the birth of Matilda's healthy son, Prince Frederick, could not rouse him. Christian's official doctors were helpless, and his ministers feared that if the populace discovered the king's mental state, the result would be rebellion, possibly civil war. As a last resort, a courtier suggested that Dr. Struensee, who had stayed quietly in the background at the palace, try to effect a cure. And the German's ministrations— fresh air and exercise, less alcohol, a healthful diet combined with his own calming manner—worked wonders. But Struensee knew the improvement was temporary and that Christian would swing wildly between excitable good spirits and black despondency until he descended into irrevocable madness.

In October 1769 Matilda came down with an alarming illness which was probably venereal disease, bestowed upon her by her husband from a syphilis-riddled whore. She sank into a deep depression and wished for death. Given the delicate nature of her ailment, the queen was unwilling to undergo a physical examination. Bedridden, she moaned pitifully in her pain. Weeks passed until even Christian was concerned enough to insist that she consult Dr. Struensee, who had proved invaluable in curing his own illness.

The first consultation lasted two hours, during which the doctor won Matilda's respect and admiration. Self-confident and sensible, Struensee listened intently to the queen and coaxed her from her apathy. She commanded him to visit her the next day and again the next. Sometimes she would call for him three or four times a day, with each visit lasting one or two hours. All the while he would sit next to her bed respectfully and talk calmly to her. Suddenly, in the midst of the insanity and cruelty that oppressed her, the queen had found a friend. More than that, she was falling in love.

Struensee knew that depression was a worse enemy than the queen's physical discomfort. "Your Majesty does not require medicine so much as exercise, fresh air and distraction," he advised.[69] He suggested that Matilda go riding, a sport rarely pursued by Danish ladies. The queen had never sat on a horse in her life but quickly became a fearless horsewoman.

She also took up the shocking exercise of walking. Danish ladies didn't walk. They were carried in sedan chairs or rolled about in carriages. Suddenly Matilda was seen walking through Copenhagen visiting her charities. The result was a striking improvement in her appearance. She had gained weight from lounging around on palace sofas and in palace beds. Now she shed the extra poundage, and her skin glowed with radiant good health.

Once Matilda had regained her health and her friendship with Struensee seemed firm, he began the next phase of his plan—to reconcile her to the king and convince her to become politically active. He dolefully informed her that Christian had few days of sanity left and would soon fall into an abyss of madness from which he would not return. Power would be grabbed by someone at court, and it might very well be Matilda's enemies, Dowager Queen Juliana, for instance, and her cabal of scheming ministers. Before Christian plunged into total insanity, Matilda should grasp the reins of power for the good of Denmark.

By May of 1770 Matilda was spending several hours a day with her doctor and often dismissed her ladies when he arrived. One day that month, Struensee told Reverdil, he was reading to Matilda in her boudoir, laid the book aside, and began to make love to her. The queen was not unwilling. We can picture her, subjected to the spastic embraces of a cackling syphilitic imbecile, giving herself to this strong intelligent ox of a man. How she must have melted as she inhaled the aroma of his skin, felt the strength of his powerful arms.

Finally, this was love. Finally, this was sex. Finally, this was happiness. Ripened into womanhood, Matilda was no longer a whining girl miserable with her husband. The man whom she had hoped to love, to rule with, had become a sick child needing to be cared for, petted, calmed. Warmed by her love for Struensee, Matilda could afford to be generous to her nervous fretting poodle of a husband.

Curiously, as soon as his wife betrayed him, Christian became quite fond of her and even fonder of Struensee. Perhaps in the sane corners of a predominantly mad mind, Christian wanted Matilda to find the happiness he could not provide. He even confided to a shocked Reverdil that he was quite happy about his wife's love affair with Struensee who so completely fulfilled her needs.

The king's health declined precariously; at the age of twenty Christian looked like a withered old man of seventy. Even his lust shrank away with the last vestiges of sanity. He made his dog, Gourmand, a councilor and granted him a salary paid from the royal treasury. But perhaps this last act was not so very mad. Gourmand was the only councilor who did not spy, plot, or intrigue against his master.

Christian was only comfortable in the company of Matilda and Struensee and became uneasy when they left him. As these two took government control away from him, Christian was delighted to find that no one wanted to talk politics to him anymore; no one made him attend boring council meetings. He could live unmolested in his own world of twisted fantasies. He loved to sign papers, however, flourishing his quill pen as if it were a saber and attacking the document with great gusto. In his mind, in the act of signing his royal name Christian was the equal of his idol, Frederick the Great of Prussia.

Matilda was so happy in her love for Struensee, with her husband's approval and even encouragement, that she did not bother to hide the affair. Reverdil lamented, "This princess hardly took her eyes off him, insisted on his presence at all gatherings, and allowed him, publicly, to take liberties which would have ruined the reputation of any ordinary woman, such as riding in her coach and walking alone with her in the gardens and woods."[70] For her, it was an innocent relationship, the kind of marriage she had longed for. And by having an affair she was, after all, only imitating her mother.

When the German princess Augusta of Saxe-Gotha found herself not queen of England, as she had imagined, but the widowed Princess of Wales, she lived a retired life at Kew Palace with her eight children. Family friend and adviser John Stuart, marquess of Bute, was in almost constant attendance, often in locked rooms with the princess dowager. A handsome man known for his shapely calves wrapped in white silk stockings—that benchmark of eighteenth-century male beauty—Lord Bute seemed to conduct his love affair openly, coming and going from Kew as he pleased.

Moreover, Catherine the Great of Russia had lovers. But Matilda failed to see the crucial differences—her mother had been a widow living in quiet retirement; Empress Catherine was the most powerful woman in the world in her own right. Matilda lacked the political insignificance of the one and the political might of the other.

Sometimes the odd trio of king, queen, and queen's lover would walk together or ride in a carriage, Matilda and Struensee engaged in deep conversation, Christian never interrupting, never understanding, only happy to be with his friends and protectors. Struensee dined with the royal couple in their private apartments several times a week. Soon he was given his own apartments in all the royal palaces and a large salary.

So far Struensee's role at court had been to look after the

health of the king, queen, and crown prince. But now Matilda appointed him official reader and private secretary to the king, which automatically made him a councilor.

The nobility, noticing the foreign doctor's sudden rise, began to feel threatened even as Struensee removed his mask of affected humility. "Had he but been of the nobility!" lamented the compassionate Reverdil. "But Struensee, physician, reader . . . and thus of the second rank, was not yet a high Court official."[71] And therein lay the rub for many at court. A native nobleman making love to the queen might have been tolerated. A parvenu foreigner, never.

Almost more shocking than Matilda's love affair was her sudden appearance in men's dress. Encouraged by Struensee to flout tradition, Matilda began wearing men's buckskin breeches, vest, and coat, her feet encased in knee-high military boots. Instead of piling her hair high on her head according to the fashion of the times, she wore it in a long braid falling down her back. In this outlandish costume she cast aside her ladylike sidesaddle and rode astride, as men did. Seeing a lady's legs wide open—even if a horse's back filled the space between them—was a shocking and vulgar sight in the eighteenth century.

At the annual Copenhagen archery festival, Danes were treated to the sight of their queen, dressed like a man, hitting the bull's-eye while their king sat crouched with a vacant stare. "She is the better man of the two," many remarked.[72]

To avoid prying eyes and stiff palace etiquette, Christian, Matilda, and Struensee moved to the secluded palace of Hirscholm, a lovely baroque confection on an island not far from Copenhagen. Christian delighted to walk in the gardens with his wife and her lover, and play with his dog and the little African boy who had become his playmate. While the king played, the queen's lover worked all day preparing documents for Christian to sign. In September 1770 Struensee—having obtained the king's signature—replaced the popular prime minister Johann Bernstorff with himself. He issued orders that all communications between the king and his ministers be in writing and that private audiences with the king be abolished. Struensee had given himself complete power to run Denmark. And his burning desire was to bring Denmark, still mired in medieval customs and laws, into the modern world.

Struensee reduced the burdensome salt tax and halved the price of wheat. The funds that came in from a tax on saddle and carriage horses of the rich were enough to build a children's hospital for the poor. He opened up the royal parks and gardens—previously reserved solely for the nobility—to the citizens who delighted in walking and picnicking in them.

He had streetlights put up in Copenhagen and allowed everyone—not just the nobility—to carry torches at night. He had the houses numbered and the streets cleaned. A new law prohibited the police from entering houses without a search warrant. But his appreciative subjects—the poor—were powerless and their approval meant nothing.

Struensee outraged the clergy by removing the customary fine on citizens who worked on Sundays. He further infuriated the church by guaranteeing illegitimate children the same rights as those born within marriage and by prohibiting the punishment of unwed mothers. As a result, unwanted children were no longer exposed or murdered. He built a maternity ward attached to a foundling hospital where children could be dropped off, no questions asked. The pillory—in which adulterers were locked as a jeering populace threw rotten vegetables at them—was removed. From their pulpits, pastors railed against Struensee and his mistress the queen.

When Struensee tackled the problem of the national debt, he eliminated thousands of court posts and their corresponding salaries. Naturally, those who lost their positions became his enemies. He further enraged the nobility with the novel concept that all men were equal before the law, and that a title would not allow a murderer, rapist, or thief to escape justice.

Struensee abolished the council and exiled its members to their country estates. Furious, these powerful nobles banded together in an effort to remove the intruder and regain their ancient privileges. They found a friend in the person of Dowager Queen Juliana who, once she dislodged Matilda and Struensee, would rule as regent until Christian's son came of age at fourteen. Clutching her Bible, Juliana expressed herself outraged at the decadence of the court and denounced the adulterous queen.

Struensee lost the support of the armed forces in a disastrous effort to reorganize them. He alienated the legal profession by dismissing corrupt judges and streamlining the courts of law, thereby rendering superfluous countless clucking lawyers. He angered the diplomatic community by decreasing salaries and benefits. He simplified taxation and reorganized pensions and titles. For every individual pleased with the new laws, there were several others who had lost their livelihoods. Struensee, for all his vision, succeeded in alienating every important segment of Danish society.

Lord Robert Gunning, George III's ambassador to Denmark, wrote of his alarm at the unrest caused by Struensee's laws. "There is scarcely a single family or person in these dominions of any considerable rank, property or influence, who has not been disobliged, disgusted and (as they think) injured," he warned, "and whose disaffection, there is reason to apprehend, only waits for a favorable opportunity of manifesting itself."[73]

Matilda, thrilled at the progress her lover was bringing to Denmark, often compared herself to Catherine the Great. And indeed, the two women had much in common. Both had been trundled into foreign countries and married to imbeciles at the age of fifteen, then abandoned in vicious and dissolute courts. But Matilda lacked Catherine's slicing intelligence and brilliant political acumen. The Russian empress laughed heartily to hear of Matilda's comparison. Aware that Struensee was behind Denmark's sudden cooling of relations with Russia, Catherine icily observed, "Give them enough rope and they will hang themselves."[74]

Struensee had plenty of rope. His power came from his connection to the queen, a connection which he advertised to the increasing resentment of influential forces at court.

During Christian's spells of clarity, which were fewer and farther between, Struensee and Matilda paraded him in front of his subjects in carriage rides and poked him in the ribs to wave to the people. They pushed him onto the palace balcony and nudged him again. Their goal was to give the illusion of a king in charge. But many who saw the blank stare on their king's face assumed the royal physician was drugging him. They feared Struensee might do him in and rule Denmark with Matilda.

In fact, Christian's mental condition continued to sink rapidly. Many times he was found wandering the palace corridors lost and disoriented. Struensee assigned a keeper to watch over him. Matilda held levees alone, seated on a throne, speaking with courtiers, ministers, and ambassadors. One day the king, who had eluded his keeper, stumbled in. A respectful silence ensued. Christian began to recite a poem, finished with a shrill ripple of laughter, and ran off. Trembling, Matilda continued the levee as if nothing had happened.

One day as Reverdil and Christian walked in the gardens, Christian confessed that he had been contemplating suicide. "But how can I do it without making a scandal?" he inquired. "And if I do, shall I not be even more unhappy? Shall I drown myself? Or knock my head against the wall?" The next day, as the two were rowing on the lake, Christian said, "I should like to jump in—and then be pulled out, very quickly. I am confused. There is a noise in my head. I cannot go on."[75]

On July 1, 1771, the queen gave birth to a daughter in great secrecy in her island palace of Hirscholm. Struensee held the queen in his arms throughout the labor and personally delivered the baby, whom they named Louise Augusta. Contrary to royal tradition, no announcement of her pregnancy had been made in the months before the birth, asking the people to pray for the safe delivery of the queen and her child. The Danish people were amazed by the news that they suddenly had a new princess.

When the birth was announced, the press, which had been freed from censorship by Struensee, decried their benefactor who "had shamelessly dishonored the King's bed, and introduced his vile posterity" into the royal family.[76] In response to these accusations, Struensee issued a proclamation with Christian's signature stating that the child had indeed been fathered by the king. Christian actually believed Louise Augusta to be his and had great fun planning the christening.

Shortly after the birth, Struensee made himself privy councilor and a count. The poor physician from Altona luxuriated in the trappings of royalty. He bought himself a new gilded coach of regal appearance and ordered for his servants uniforms of scarlet and white adorned with diamond badges.

Despite his unheard-of success, sometimes Struensee suffered from a melancholy foreboding. He often told his friends that he wanted to leave court, that he was exhausted from his round-the-clock issuing of decrees. When asked why he did not leave, Struensee replied, "Where else could you be Prime Minister, the King's friend and the Queen's lover?"[77]

The harvest of 1771 was scant. The merchants of Copenhagen were suffering, as Struensee had exiled most of the free-spending nobility to their country estates. The clergy decried the country's woes as clear evidence of God's displeasure at wickedness in high places. Warned on all sides of rising discontent and possible rebellion, Struensee simply shrugged. George III became so alarmed at his sister's affair with the detested prime minister that he sent their mother, Dowager Princess Augusta, to Denmark to lecture her sternly. But Matilda abruptly ended her mother's scolding with a scathing reference to Augusta's own lover, Lord Bute. Furious, the princess dowager rumbled away in her carriage, never to speak to her daughter again.

When Matilda's ladies begged her to send Struensee away, she only answered, "How fortunate you are, to marry where you wish! If I were a widow, I would marry him I loved, and give up my throne and my country."[78]

Dowager Queen Juliana had been hard at work amassing copious evidence of Matilda's love affair. Four of the queen's servants willingly became Juliana's highly paid spies. They wrote down the time at which Matilda and Struensee drove out alone in a carriage and the time they returned—usually several hours later. Each night they sprinkled powder on the secret staircase that led from Struensee's apartments up to Matilda's rooms. The next day they could see a man's footprints in the powder, footsteps that reached the queen's bed itself. The spies examined the sheets—unkempt, thrown about—and gloated over the stains. Struensee's valet, paid to rifle through his coat pockets, found a special prize—a man's handkerchief with semen stains.

Sometimes after Struensee left the queen's room, her maids entered and saw her naked in bed. While dressing Matilda, her ladies exclaimed over the bruises on her throat and breasts. She would only laugh and say it was nothing. In the evening, spying at the keyhole, they saw the prime minister massaging the bruises.

Armed with indisputable proof of adultery, Juliana organized a highly placed group of conspirators. Many were nobles who had lost power and money at Struensee's hands and bore him a seething resentment. One of them was Count Schack Karl Rantzau, a close friend of Struensee's from Altona, who felt slighted that the prime minister had not adequately rewarded him with a high-level position. The conspirators set the date for the coup in the wee hours of January 17, following a masked ball at court. They hoped that the noise and drunkenness of the ball would cloak their treasonous plot until it was too late.

As a diversion for the discontented, Struensee had ordered that the ball be particularly ornate. It was held in a theater, the boxes newly regilded and hung with purple curtains. Hothouse flowers and colored lanterns added to the festive atmosphere. At ten P.M. Struensee arrived wearing a blue velvet coat and rose satin breeches. On his arm he wore the queen, dressed in a gown of white brocade embroidered in pink roses, a sparkling cascade of diamonds dripping down the length of her bodice. In the royal box, Christian sat down to cards while Struensee and Matilda opened the dance.

Reverdil later recalled how beautiful the queen looked that evening as she stepped the minuet, and how powerful and commanding Struensee. She was more in love with him than ever, and for his part he believed the threat of revolution had passed.

At midnight the supper was over, and Christian was led back to his rooms. Matilda and Struensee danced until three A.M. With their departure the ball was over and guests ambled out. The lamps were guttering, the flowers wilted. Wine goblets were overturned, red stains soaking the snowy white tablecloths. Plates were heaped with bones, and chairs were askew. Here was a mask on the floor, its sightless eyes staring at the ceiling. There was a silken cape dropped by a tipsy reveler. Matilda and Struensee, warmed by wine and dancing, went to the queen's apartments and made love by the fire's glow. Sweet and urgent, their shadows dancing on the wall, the lovers clung to each other. It was to be the last time.

Juliana, meanwhile, strode briskly through dark palace corridors. She knew that to effect a coup she must first force Christian to sign the arrest warrants of Struensee and his allies, and then take possession of the king himself. For whoever had Christian ruled Denmark. When she roused the sleeping monarch, Christian sat up with a shriek. "For God's sake! What have I done? What do you want?" he cried. Juliana told him that a revolution was forming against Struensee and the queen, and the people were going to storm the palace.

The king burst into tears. "Terrible, terrible," he moaned. "Where shall I go? What should I do?"

"Sign these papers," Juliana urged, "and Your Majesty's life will be saved."

Christian looked at the papers but, seeing his wife's name, cast aside the pen and tried to get out of bed. Juliana pushed him back and forced the pen back into his hand. Suddenly docile, he signed everything—the arrest warrants of his wife, Struensee, and their friends, and the appointment of two of the conspirators to supreme command.

The order for Matilda's arrest stated, "Madame, I have found it wisest to send you to Kronborg, as your conduct obliges me to do so. I am very sorry, it is not my fault, and I hope for your sincere repentance. Christian."[79]

Juliana bade her stepson to dress quickly and hustled him off to the security of her own apartments. There she harangued him on the dangerous plots of Struensee and Matilda to murder him and rule Denmark themselves. It took only moments to convince him that those he had loved most were actually his bitterest enemies, and he signed a pile of new orders repealing all of Struensee's laws.

With the king safely in hand, officers were sent to arrest the dictator. Roused from a deep slumber by men storming into his bedroom, Struensee had trouble clearing his head of wine and music and sleep. Given two minutes to dress, he flung on the clothes he had worn at the ball. "What crime have I committed?" he asked.[80] But there was no answer.

In prison, Struensee was sent to the cell used for the most violent criminals. Faced with a cold dark room furnished only with a pallet and chamber pot, Struensee lost his composure, ranted at the jailer, rushed past him, and tried to reach the door. Informed of his tirade, the prison governor had him chained to the wall.

When the soldiers first stomped into Struensee's rooms, which were directly below Matilda's, she heard the noise but thought it was more after-the-ball revelry. She sent one of her ladies down to Struensee's rooms to request quiet, as she wanted to sleep. The lady never returned, and Matilda fell asleep.

At 4:30 A.M. another lady woke the queen urgently whispering that the hall was full of uniformed men. "Count Rantzau is there, with several officers," she said. "He demands admittance in the King's name." "In the King's name!" Matilda gasped. She realized what was happening—a coup. She ordered her woman to slip downstairs by the secret staircase to warn Struensee. "The Count has been arrested," cried the woman upon her return. "I am betrayed—lost!" Matilda moaned. "But let them in—traitors! I am ready for anything they may do."[81]

Count Rantzau, followed by several officers, entered Matilda's antechamber, took out Christian's letter, and read it aloud. Matilda grabbed it to see for herself and threw it on the floor, crying that the king had had nothing to do with the letter.

Count Rantzau sat down and stretched his legs. "I must beg your majesty to obey the king's orders," he said. "His orders!" she cried, laughing bitterly. "He can know nothing of them—your villainy has made use of his madness. No, a queen does not obey such a command!"

The count motioned the soldiers to grab her. The soldiers held back. "Where is Count Struensee?" the queen asked. "There is no longer any such person," came the reply.

Seeing a path clear to the door, Matilda raced past the soldiers and out of the room, running for her life down to Christian's apartments, and banged on the door. But the doors had been locked by Juliana an hour before, and Christian was nowhere to be found. Five officers were close on her heels and seized her, but she flung them off with such violence that her dress was ripped from top to bottom, leaving her half naked. Count Rantzau appeared and, looking her up and down, said sarcastically, "Your Majesty must excuse me, but my duty forces me to resist your charms. Pray dress yourself."[82]

The count agreed to allow the six-month-old Princess Louise Augusta to accompany her mother to prison. The child was still nursing and, after all, was not related to the royal Danish family in any way. But Matilda's son, Frederick, the heir to the throne, was the property of the crown of Denmark and this child she would never see again.

And so Matilda, holding her infant, accompanied only by a nurse and a maid, entered the carriage that would take her to prison. She sat facing a guard with his sword drawn. Thirty soldiers rode around the coach. Her destination, the royal castle of Kronborg, also called Elsinore, was the gloomy fortress of mists and ghosts that Shakespeare had used as the setting for *Hamlet*. The trip lasted three hours, during which the coach passed the island palace of Hirscholm, the romantic idyll where she had romped with Struensee, where he had held her hand as she gave birth to his daughter. She sat silently, in shock.

She entered the fortress expecting to use the royal apartments, but spiteful Juliana had assigned her to a small octagonal turret room, its foundations beaten by icy waves. It had no fireplace and no shutters to keep the January winds from penetrating the thin glass. It was furnished only with a low bed, two stools, and a prie-dieu for her devotions. Matilda sat on the bed and wept.

Her thoughts flew to Struensee. "Is he in chains?" she asked her attendant, tears sliding down her face. "Has he food to eat? Does he know that I am imprisoned here?"[83] The woman answered that she did not know, secretly made notes of Matilda's interest in her lover, and sent them to Juliana.

Fearing the retribution of the British Empire, Juliana moved Matilda to the state apartments of Kronborg, gave her better meals, and allowed her to walk in the palace gardens. But the rumblings from Britain came from its outraged people, not from its king. George III, well aware of his sister's adultery, did not step up to fight for her. George saw no reason to interfere with the punishment his sister so richly deserved for her behavior. He ignored all her impassioned pleas and later burned her correspondence. Queen Charlotte went into retirement out of pure shame, she said, for her sister-in-law. After hearing the news of her daughter's arrest and disgrace, Matilda's mother, the princess dowager, who had been ill for some time, stated that she never wanted to hear Matilda's name spoken again. "I have nothing to say," she said, "nothing to do, nothing to leave," and died.[84]

Chained to the wall, Struensee tried to commit suicide by bashing his head against the stones. Unwilling to lose such a valuable prisoner who had yet to confess to his adultery with the queen, Juliana put him under a suicide watch, forced him to wear an iron cap, and had his meat cut by a man who fed it to him one piece at a time.

During two days of interrogation, Struensee denied an illicit relationship with the queen even under threat of torture. The third day he was told of Matilda's arrest and imprisonment and her confession of adultery. This last was, in fact, a lie. But hearing of her confession, Struensee lost his cool manner, covered his face with his hands, and began to cry. Through his hands, mingled with sobs, the commissioners heard him mumble, "The person I loved best in the world. . . . What have I done . . . disgrace . . . shame."[85]

When Struensee composed himself, he said he did not believe that the queen had confessed, that it was a trick. Then they showed him a counterfeit confession, apparently signed by the queen, which thoroughly betrayed him. He read it and said sadly, "It is true. Our intimacy began in the spring of 1770, and has continued ever since."[86] He then began to supply details of the relationship and said that they had first had sex in the queen's cabinet, a small room in her apartments.

"I plead guilty to the charge," he said, "and I would gladly suffer any agony as long as the Queen and my friends could be spared."[87]

Holding Struensee's confession, the commissioners converged upon Kronborg and sat down in the guardroom with paper and quills at the ready to interrogate the queen. Their hopes of finding a weepy pliable girl were dashed when Matilda walked in arrayed in royal robes and crowned with regal composure. When she refused to answer questions, she was told that if she did not do so, they would take her infant daughter from her. But still she sat imperturbable and said nothing.

One of her inquisitors said, "Your majesty having refused to acknowledge your guilt, it is my duty to inform you that Count Struensee has confessed to your having committed adultery."[88]

"Impossible!" cried the queen. "And if he has, I deny it!" They read her the confession, and she stated that it was a forgery. But when she examined it, she recognized the signature of her lover and found herself horribly betrayed. She sank back and covered her face with her hands. Her interrogator continued, "Madam, if this confession be true, no death can be cruel enough for such a monster." When he told her that Struensee had already been condemned to die, the queen fainted. Her ladies revived her, and she tried to rise but found she lacked the strength. At length she whispered, "If I were to confess, would the King spare Struensee? Could I save his life?"

The commissioner replied, "Surely, Madam, that would be adduced in his favor, and thereby alter the situation. You have but to sign this," and he pushed a confession in front of her. She hesitated but a moment, wondering if this were some trick, then suddenly resolved, she signed. The queen had to be carried back to her bed as the commissioners, their work done, collected their quills and papers, pushed their chairs back, and strode satisfied from the hall.

And so both Matilda and Struensee were convinced of each other's treachery. Perhaps this blow was crueler than the loss of their exalted positions or the sorrows of prison. Betrayed by the one each loved best, that was the greatest agony.

At her trial, Matilda was given an experienced lawyer but was not permitted to testify in her own defense. Nor was she allowed to mention the king's insanity or his apparent acquiescence in the affair. Her lawyer vociferously denied her guilt and claimed that her confession of adultery had been signed under duress. But for ten days the king's witnesses rattled off their stories of stained handkerchiefs, rumpled sheets, and footsteps in sprinkled powder. Matilda brought not a single witness.

Matilda was found guilty and divorced from Christian. Oddly, the decree which proclaimed her adultery also asserted the legitimacy of both her children. Declaring one child a bastard would cast doubts on the legitimacy of the other. Although Louise Augusta grew up the spitting image of Struensee, with a face of elegant angles and a feminine version of his bird-of-prey nose, in the eyes of the law she was the legitimate daughter of King Christian VII.

When Matilda's lawyer returned to Kronborg to give her the sad tidings, she sighed and said, "I expected as much—but what will become of Struensee?" When the lawyer told her that Struensee was fated for execution, she trembled and began to cry. "Tell him," she said, weeping, "that I forgive him for the wrong he has done me."[89]

Christian, chafing under the tutelage of the wicked stepmother whom he had always hated, grew restive and rebellious. She had taken away his dog, for one thing. And for another, she had done something with his wife. Christian kept asking her where Matilda was. The more irritated Juliana became at this question, the more often he peppered her with it. To pacify the people who were concerned that Christian had merely traded in one keeper for another, Juliana had him stand on the palace balcony. But his expression was blank as if he did not know where he was. He neither bowed nor waved but stood stiffly until he was pulled in.

One day, asked to sign a paper, the king had a moment of clarity. "Christian VII, by the Grace of God King of Denmark," he wrote, "in company with Juliana Maria by the Grace of the Devil."[90]

Despite his persistent questions, no one would tell the king the whereabouts of Matilda. One day, overhearing that she was imprisoned in Kronborg, Christian escaped from his apartments, ran to the royal stables, and called for a carriage. But just as he was stepping inside, he was captured and taken back to his rooms. His shrieks could be heard throughout the palace, and in between them he asked for Struensee.

Struensee was preparing himself for execution. He would not face death alone. Another prisoner, Count Enevold Brandt, was found guilty of treason. Brandt had been the king's reluctant keeper and had once grown so exasperated with his lunatic charge that he had thrashed him soundly. Now he was to pay the price for raising his hand against his king, though his greatest offense was his friendship and support of Struensee. The executions of Struensee and Brandt were set for April 28, 1772. To show her joy at the executions, the night before, Juliana made Christian and the entire court attend a gala opera performance and a palace feast.

The scaffold was twenty-seven feet high so that with the aid of a telescope Juliana could see the executions and grisly dismemberments from her window in the tower of Christiansborg Palace. Years later, when Juliana insisted on staying in that tiny room instead of the state apartments, she explained, "These rooms are dearer to me than my most splendid apartments, for from the windows I saw the remains of my bitterest foes exposed upon the wheel."[91]

Dressed in the rose-colored breeches and blue velvet coat he had worn at that last masked ball, Struensee mounted the scaffold and waded through Brandt's blood. Brandt's hand had been chopped off before his beheading, the very hand that had dared strike a king. "Now for the fat one!" Juliana shrieked from her tower with glee.[92] Kneeling in the gore, Struensee placed his right hand—the hand that had dared defile a queen—on a small block. When the executioner struck off his hand, Struensee popped up and writhed in convulsions, blood spurting from the stump. The executioner's assistant had to push his head onto the block for the fatal blow. And when it struck, the virtuous old queen yelped for joy.

Juliana's only regret, she told her friends, was that Matilda had not joined the others on the scaffold. She could not see Matilda's hand and head struck off, her body split from throat to groin, her intestines pulled out and nailed to a wheel, her limbs severed and nailed next to her intestines, her head jammed on a pike and left to rot in a field beyond the city. That would have made for a perfect day indeed.

Aside from Juliana, there was no cheering from the fifty thousand spectators as Struensee's head was lopped off. Suddenly Struensee was the martyr, the folk hero, the visionary who had led Denmark into the modern world. Dowager Queen Juliana was the despised dictator. In the weeks following the execution, the Danish people resented her wholesale dissolution of Struensee's laws, and riots broke out in the streets of Copenhagen. To quell the tumult, Juliana was forced to reinstate some of his edicts.

Unaware of the execution, Christian wailed for Matilda and Struensee. When the king was told firmly that Struensee was dead—as a result of his own signature on the death warrant—and Matilda had been divorced for adultery, Christian began to cry and asked for them again. He sobbed that Matilda was still his wife and could not be kept from him.

When the English ambassador visited Matilda and told her of her lover's execution, she fainted, and upon being revived, sat numbly in her chair for several hours, a bloodless marble statue of a queen, unmoving, unfeeling. But after her initial shock and grief, there were practical considerations to attend to. Matilda needed to find a place to live in refined disgrace. With the Danish people clamoring in the streets for Matilda to replace Juliana as queen regent, the old queen was suddenly eager for the young queen to leave Danish soil.

Matilda assumed that she would return home to a quiet life in England, back to digging in her garden, perhaps, with friendly faces, English faces, around her. When Queen Charlotte refused to have an adulteress living on her territory, contaminating the purity of her young daughters, George decided to keep his sister in his German dominion of Hanover. And so Matilda heard that she would be going to Celle, to a palace that had remained empty for nearly seventy years since the death of Sophia Dorothea's father in 1704.

Matilda was eager to leave the chilled ramparts of Kronborg. For weeks her eyes were fixed on the gray and gloomy sea, looking for the English ship that would take her away from the country she now despised. Finally, three ships were spotted. But Matilda's elation was tempered by the knowledge that she must part with her daughter, Louise Augusta. This child, now acknowledged as a Danish princess, was property of the Crown. She would have a privileged life, but no mother.

For three days Matilda spent every moment playing with her daughter. But she could not bring herself to say that final farewell. At the hour of departure, she kept kissing the child good-bye, then turned around to pick her up and kiss her again. The little girl cooed, thinking it a delightful game. But Matilda knew it was unlikely that she would ever see her daughter again, that the child may very well be raised to despise her mother's memory. Finally forced to leave, Matilda cried, "Let me go. Now I have nothing! Nothing!"[93] She staggered down the hall, outside the castle, and onto the ship, and the ship's cannon, proudly announcing the boarding of a royal princess of Britain, drowned out her piteous sobs.

On her sad journey, Matilda had no idea of the growing support for her in three nations. Many British subjects despised George III for abandoning his sister, a victim of jackals at an evil court. Heedless of her adultery, the Danes angled to get her back to replace the wicked Juliana as regent. The German town of Celle offered her a festive welcome as if she were still a queen.

In Celle, Matilda led a quiet but active life. She gave card parties, plied her needle, attended church, and worked with her gardeners. Riding no longer attracted her—it reminded her too much of Struensee—and the lack of exercise resulted in a tremendous weight gain. Though many noticed a deep sadness lurking just beneath her pleasant demeanor, she never complained and always tried to be cheerful. Receiving no news of her own children, she gave parties for the town children and adopted an orphan, a four-year-old girl named Sophie, whom she took into the palace to live with her. Little did she know that a group of conspirators was plotting her return to power.

Gloating and vindictive, Juliana had made many enemies; powerful groups were agitating for Matilda to replace her and needed to make her aware of their plans. But surrounded by spies, Matilda was hard to reach. Finally a twenty-two-year-old conspirator named Nathaniel Wraxall presented himself as a traveling Englishman and was allowed to meet her. In whispers he informed her of the plot, to which she immediately agreed. Wraxall then left for London in a futile attempt to get official support from George III.

When Wraxall again visited Matilda, she declared herself ready at a moment's notice to go to Copenhagen and take up the government—if she obtained at least written permission from George III to leave Celle. When she and the conspirators had entered Copenhagen, they would sneak into the palace, find Christian, and have him sign a paper authorizing their coup. As the interview ended, Wraxall noticed that Matilda looked astonishingly beautiful in her crimson satin gown, her powdered hair coiffed high. Perhaps hope for the future had given a sparkle to her eye, a flush to her cheeks. She was halfway out the door when she paused and looked as if she were about to speak. Then she turned around and disappeared.

Wraxall set off once again for London just as an epidemic—scarlet fever or typhus—broke out in Celle. Matilda's young page died, and the next evening Matilda suddenly jumped up and announced that she would see the boy's body before burial. Her attendants begged her not to—viewing the body of an epidemic victim was often an indirect means of committing suicide—but Matilda raced to the room where the child was laid out and stood next to the open casket.

The next day her adopted daughter, Sophie, became ill. Terribly distressed at the possible loss of another child, Matilda paced for hours in her garden. She returned to her rooms exhausted, and over dinner developed a sore throat and fever. Her physicians believed she would recover, but she seemed to have no will to live. Perhaps she had hoped to catch the infection after all. On May 11, 1775, she was told that little Sophie was out of danger. "Then I can die happy," she said, closing her eyes.[94] She never opened them again. Within days she was dead. She was twenty-three.

It was an easy, simple death after a life of insanity, adultery, betrayal, and imprisonment. Her pastor wrote, "I never remember so easy a dissolution, or one in which death lost all its terrors. . . . She fell asleep like a tired traveler."[95]

And so Matilda found her freedom, but not in the way the conspirators had intended. Upon hearing the news of her death, Dowager Queen Juliana attended a ball that evening. In London, Wraxall was devastated to hear the news; he had been stewing for weeks in the hopes that he could meet privately with George III, but the king had made no response to his urgent requests.

When Matilda's son, Frederick, was sixteen—two years past the time Juliana was legally obligated to hand over her power—he grabbed his imbecile father and made him sign a document appointing him, Frederick, regent. There was quite a scuffle among Juliana's supporters trying to pry the little imbecile king from the strong grip of the crown prince, but Matilda's son won the day. King Frederick VI ruled as one of Denmark's best-loved monarchs. Juliana retired from court and died in 1796, and for many years visitors spat on her grave.

Hearing of his sister's death, George III refused her request to repose in Westminster Abbey next to her ancestors. But perhaps, after all, it is more appropriate that she lies next to Sophia Dorothea in St. Mary's Church crypt of Celle.

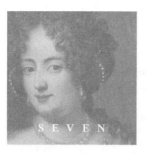

SEVEN

THE NINETEENTH CENTURY: AUDACITY AND OUTRAGE

Of all my lands is nothing left me but my body's length?
Why, what is pomp, rule, reign, but earth and dust?
And live we how we can, yet die we must.

—WILLIAM SHAKESPEARE

※

THE NAPOLEONIC QUEEN

"Liberty Is in Her Mouth,
Equality in Her Heart and Fraternity in Her Garters"

NAPOLEON BONAPARTE PRIZED FEMALE CHASTITY JUST A LITTLE BELOW
military might. It was his great misfortune to have two wives who
betrayed him—Josephine before he became emperor, and the
Austrian archduchess Marie Louise after his abdication—as well
as three sisters and a stepdaughter who embarrassed him with
their love affairs.

While Napoleon was still a rising general, he fell desperately
in love with Josephine de Beauharnais, a charming widowed
aristocrat rescued from the jaws of the guillotine when the revolutionary government fell a day before her scheduled execution.
Napoleon pressed her to marry him, and Josephine, knowing
that her fading looks and rotten teeth signaled the end of her lucrative career as a high-class prostitute, reluctantly agreed. She

told friends that she "had to overcome a feeling of repugnance before I could bring myself to marry 'the little general.' "[1]

On campaign, Napoleon wrote her passionate love letters. Mentioning her "little Black Forest," he wrote, "I kiss it a thousand times and I await impatiently the moment of being inside."[2]

But Napoleon was not the only man wandering around in the little Black Forest. When her husband was fighting in Italy, Josephine had a torrid affair with a lusty aide-de-camp named Hippolyte Charles, a muscular young man with dancing blue eyes and bouncing black curls. In July 1798 the Paris gossip reached Napoleon, who was now waging war in Egypt. Absolutely devastated, he openly took mistresses himself. When he returned home the following year he was prepared to divorce her. Faced with her abject pleas for mercy, he forgave her, content merely to torture her with recounting details of his mistresses' private parts for the rest of their marriage.

In 1811, having divorced Josephine to marry the eighteen-year-old Hapsburg archduchess Marie Louise, Napoleon finally had the son Josephine could never provide him. But in 1814, toppled from his self-made throne, Napoleon waited impatiently on the island of Elba for his wife to join him. Emperor Francis II of Austria, horrified that his daughter would remain tethered to the bane of Europe, sent an attractive equerry to bring her back to Vienna—by way of several luxurious spas where revitalizing waters helped love blossom, if not health. The emperor's plan worked perfectly. Marie Louise bore General Adam von Neipperg three illegitimate children in secrecy. As soon as Napoleon died in 1821, she married her lover.

Napoleon's sister Elise, whom he made queen of Tuscany, took poets and artists as lovers, but with enough discretion so as not to ruffle the imperial plumage. However, his sister Caroline, whom he made queen of Naples, was less discreet. English newspapers reported, "Liberty is in her mouth, equality in her heart and fraternity in her garters."[3]

Pauline, the most beautiful Bonaparte sister, caused Napoleon the greatest irritation. Bored with life as the wife of Roman prince Camillo Borghese—who was unsatisfying in bed and perhaps gay—Pauline agitated to return to the delights of Paris. Napoleon refused and Pauline plotted her revenge. She commissioned the renowned sculptor Antonio Canova to make a statue of herself, posing languishing on a chaise lounge almost naked, wearing only a thin veneer of drapery over her hips, her breasts thrusting proudly outward. Europe was scandalized, and thrilled. Napoleon was furious, and Pauline was delighted at his fury. Having advertised her wares in the form of the statue, she could now take her pick of Europe's most hot-blooded men, and soon there was a revolving door into her bedroom—elegant courtiers, soldiers throbbing with virility, famous actors, and talented musicians.

Even Josephine's blushing daughter, Hortense, wretchedly married to Napoleon's brother King Louis of the Netherlands, bore two illegitimate children. The child born in 1809—who grew up to become Emperor Napoleon III of France—Hortense pawned off on Louis, who vociferously denied to the pope and all the courts of Europe that the child was his. Realizing she couldn't foist the next one on her husband, in 1811 she had a child in secrecy who was raised by her lover's mother.

Napoleon's irritation at his female relatives, however, was tempered by his delight in watching his fiercest enemy, Britain's prince regent, suffering the messiest, most scandalous marriage of any monarch ever.

CAROLINE OF BRUNSWICK, QUEEN OF BRITAIN

"I Never Did Commit Adultery but Once"

In 1795 the British envoy Lord Malmesbury traveled to the German duchy of Brunswick to escort Princess Caroline to London as the bride of George, Prince of Wales. Thirty-two-year-old George had agreed to marry a German princess only because he was up to his ears in debt, and Parliament offered him a substantial bribe if he would finally do his royal duty and wed. He had, in fact, already married a devout Catholic widow, Maria

Fitzherbert, who had refused him sex outside of matrimony. The marriage was secret; if the heir to the British throne was known to have wed a Catholic, he would have lost his inheritance. Pushed into a corner by his debts, George decided to commit bigamy.

Taking in the princess at a glance, Malmesbury was alarmed. Though pretty in a frowzy-blonde way, Caroline didn't care about her attire. She prided herself on dressing quickly, throwing on any old garments that were soiled, ripped, and didn't match. Her stockings, Malmesbury reported sadly, were "never well washed, or changed often enough."[4] He was forced to introduce her to a bar of soap and a toothbrush. Malmesbury shuddered when he thought of the fastidious, fashionable prince who awaited her, the prince who spent hours each morning on his toilette, carefully bathing, shaving, and coiffing himself, then sometimes spending another hour fastening his starched white cravat *just so*.

Malmesbury was further alarmed when the duke of Brunswick confessed his concern at his daughter becoming Princess of Wales. The duke begged Malmesbury to instruct her "not to ask questions, and, above all, not to be free in giving opinions of persons and things aloud."[5] Both men were worried by "the apparent facility of Princess Caroline's character—her want of reflection and substance—(we) agree that with a steady man she would do vastly well, but with one of a different description, there are great risks."[6] Both knew that George, Prince of Wales, was a far cry from steady.

On April 3, 1795, Prince George stood apprehensively in a drawing room of St. James's Palace, waiting to be introduced to his bride. When he first saw her, he was so traumatized by her looks and demeanor that he wiped his brow, whispered "I am not well," and called for a stiff drink. Malmesbury suggested that perhaps a glass of water would be more helpful.[7]

But the prince said with an oath, "No; I will go directly to the queen," and stumbled away.[8] When Malmesbury returned to the princess, she asked, "Is the prince always like that? I find him very fat and not nearly so handsome as his portrait."[9]

Indeed George, tall, blond, and blue-eyed, would have been devastatingly handsome if he had been able to control his appetite. But the spoiled prince was unable to deny himself anything—a glass of wine, a pork chop, a woman, an expensive mansion. His excesses had spoiled his finances and were already spoiling his looks.

Given George's revulsion for the bride, the wedding could easily have been called off; they had not been married by proxy. But there were, after all, pressing debts to pay. As the prince walked up the aisle, Lord Peniston Melbourne wrote, he "was like a man doing a thing in desperation," as if he were "going to execution, and he was quite drunk." Other wedding guests noticed that the groom had "manifestly had recourse to wine or spirits."[10]

George managed to rise to the occasion with his wife three times during the first two nights of marriage. He wrote a friend, "She showed . . . such marks of filth both in the fore and *hind* part of her . . . that she turned my stomach and from that moment I made a vow never to touch her again."[11] For her part, the princess later told a friend, "Judge what it was to have a drunken husband on one's wedding day, and one who passed the greatest part of his bridal night under the grate, where he fell and where I left him."[12]

Fortunately for George, he had already made Caroline pregnant during his halfhearted efforts. Caroline was dumbfounded to learn of her condition; she expressed profound surprise that such a speedy and insignificant coupling would produce a child. As for George, he was delighted that an heir was on the way, and he never did touch Caroline again.

George exulted in torturing his pregnant wife; he locked her in her rooms while he went all over town socializing with his mistress Lady Jersey. He gave Caroline no money for expenses and insisted that Lady Jersey, who went out of her way to be obnoxious to his wife, eat dinner with her every night. Finding that Caroline delighted in spending time with her newborn, Princess Charlotte, George had the child taken away from her.

When Caroline complained, George called her "the vilest

wretch this world was ever cursed with, who I cannot feel more disgust for from her personal nastiness than I do from her entire want of principle," and further described her as "a very monster of iniquity."[13]

When the king, fearing the rising scandal, suggested a reconciliation, and Caroline seemed willing, George declared that he must have a separation, adding that he would "rather see toads and vipers crawling over his victuals than sit at the same table with her!!!"[14]

The couple separated and Caroline went to live in a large home at Blackheath near London. She and the prince saw each other a few times a year at palace events and rarely spoke. By 1799 the princess, giving up all pretenses of loyalty to the husband who had so publicly abandoned her, was flirting openly with ministers and courtiers who visited her there. She had an affair with a junior minister, George Canning, the famous artist Sir Thomas Lawrence, the naval hero Sir Sidney Smith, and another naval officer, Captain Thomas Manby.

The Prince of Wales, who had set spies on his wife, was well aware of Caroline's love affairs. Moreover, among the several poor children she looked after was an infant named Willy Austin whom she had adopted in 1802 and whom some believed was, in fact, her own. In 1805 Caroline was informed that she was being investigated for a "charge of high treason, committed in the infamous crime of adultery."[15] Her household staff was led away to be questioned.

On the witness stand, one of Caroline's servants asserted that he had found Sir Sidney Smith wandering around the house at three or four A.M. On another occasion the servant was surprised to find Sir Sidney in the house at ten A.M., though no one had let him in that morning. But surely the worst testimony came from Caroline's former footman, Samuel Roberts, who solemnly asserted, "The Princess is very fond of fucking."[16]

One witness, Lord Francis Moira, spoke of a box that a friend of Captain Manby's had opened at the captain's lodging. Inside he saw a portrait of the Princess of Wales "with many souvenirs hanging to it," including a leather bag holding "hair of a particular description and such as his friend said he had been married too long not to know that it came from no woman's head."[17] One of the commissioners suggested good-naturedly that the hair in the bag be compared with the suspected source of the hair, and only then could it be admitted as evidence. Naturally, this did not take place.

Caroline's former friend and neighbor Lady Charlotte Douglas, who had since become her adversary in a property case, reported that the princess had confessed to being pregnant by a lover. She would hide her pregnancy, Caroline supposedly said, by tying a cushion behind her, under her high-waisted gown, to balance out the increasing girth in front, and make it seem that she was gaining weight all over. When Lady Douglas visited Caroline in January 1803, she saw the princess with "an infant sleeping on a sofa." "Here is the little boy," the princess said. "I had him two days after I saw you last; is it not a nice little child?"[18]

It is likely that despite her enmity toward the princess, Lady Douglas's statements were true. Caroline had probably been playing one of her bizarre jokes, taking great delight in shocking her prudish neighbor Lady Douglas with stories of a pregnancy and showing her one of the orphans she cared for. Caroline was, after all, the same woman who a decade later, after a private audience with the pope, told an inquiring friend that her interview had gone very well indeed and "You will see evident symptoms of it in nine months' time."[19]

Other servants, however, denied that their mistress had been pregnant or had committed adultery. They testified that little Willy Austin was visited frequently by his mother, the same woman who had originally arrived with the infant in her arms. The commissioners soon had Mrs. Austin herself on the witness stand, and she swore that Willy was her child. They then found a birth record of Willy Austin, born to Samuel and Sophia Austin on July 11, 1802.

The entire sordid affair contained rumor and innuendo, shrieking accusations and outraged denials, and the testimony of fired servants who bore their former mistress a grudge. On July

14, 1806, the lord commissioners stated, "There is no foundation for believing that the child now with the Princess is the child of her Royal Highness, or that she was delivered of any child in the year 1802; nor has anything appeared to us which would warrant the belief that she was pregnant in that year, or at any other period within the compass of our inquiries."[20]

But it was clear that Caroline had been indiscreet in her flirtations and had allowed men to visit her regularly, not always in the presence of virtuous ladies. The princess was issued stern instructions to be more discreet in the future.

But this recommendation was not likely to win Caroline's favor. Shortly after she was cleared of adultery, she began an affair with the elegant fifty-seven-year-old Lord George Rivers, a relic of the eighteenth century who still powdered his hair. A maid later declared that one afternoon she had seen "the pillows of the sofa on the floor, the floor covered with hair powder."[21] By 1809 Caroline was having an affair with a politician, Lord Henry Fitzgerald.

As she ate, and drank, and made love to fill up the emptiness where a devoted husband should have been, her looks took a turn for the worse, as did her taste in clothes. One gentleman remarked "that the Princess is grown very coarse, and that she dresses very ill, showing too much of her naked person. . . ."[22]

In 1814 Caroline, bored to tears with her life in London, decided to travel across the continent. She shook the dust of England from her sandals, joyfully leaving the scene of so many years of bitter humiliation. As she left Britain, Caroline said wistfully that she hoped her eighteen-year-old daughter, Charlotte, as "great and powerful as she may be, will not tyrannize over anyone, because they have not the good fortune to please her."[23]

Caroline went about Europe thirsting to meet the famous, the talented, and the notorious, and few refused her. When traveling to Italy, she needed a courier to ride ahead to the towns she intended to visit and make hotel reservations for her entourage. An Austrian general in Milan recommended his personal assistant, the handsome thirty-year-old Bartolomeo Pergami. Measuring a full six feet three inches tall, Pergami had curly black hair and whiskers, flashing dark eyes, a broad chest, and a bold swaggering charm. When Caroline arrived in Naples, she was introduced to her new courier and immediately fell in love.

She barely bothered to hide her love affair with Pergami and even tried to look like an Italian. Her greatest physical assets had always been her fine golden hair and white complexion; now she wore a thick black wig and painted on thick dark eyebrows and rouge so heavy that she resembled a painted puppet. Attending dinners and balls in Italy, she grew heavier and danced wildly, "with a frivolity hardly fitting her age and figure," according to one witness, her dress often slipping off her shoulders.[24]

The Prince of Wales, through his network of spies, kept a close watch on her activities, hoping for undeniable proof of her infidelity. If such evidence remained elusive, proof of Caroline's increasing eccentricity manifested itself almost daily. When her cousin the duke of Baden saw her one hot day, she was wearing half a hollowed-out pumpkin shell on her head. It kept her cool, she said.

In Naples, Caroline traveled about in a coach made in the form of a conch shell. It was led through the streets by a small child dressed as Cupid in flesh-colored tights, leading two tiny ponies. In the vehicle sat a rotund, black-wigged, berouged woman in a sheer gown, the skirt of which barely hung past her chubby knees. Next to her sat Willy Austin, now a gangly lad of thirteen whom all Naples believed to be her son and whom she called "the little Prince."[25] Her astonishing carriage was preceded by Pergami on horseback, blazing forth in a military uniform that made him look like a circus ringmaster.

The princess and her entourage took a ten-month Mediterranean voyage to Tunisia, Sicily, Egypt, and Istanbul. She entered Jerusalem as Jesus had, astride an ass. After this adventure, she returned to her house in Lake Como with a colorful suite of Turks, Arabs, and Africans, as well as shadowy Italians—friends and family of Pergami. Pergami's mother worked as the princess's laundress, perhaps so no one else could testify later about stained sheets.

In 1816 Princess Charlotte married Prince Leopold of Saxe-Coburg, who later became the king of Belgium. The following year Charlotte died giving birth to a dead son. Caroline was devastated; not only had she lost her only child, but her hopes for a brighter future as queen mother, reinstated to her royal status, had died with Charlotte.

The only link between them buried, George saw no reason for delaying his much-longed-for divorce. In 1818 he wrote his lord chancellor, "My whole thoughts (are turned) to the endeavoring to extricate myself from the cruelest as well as the most unjust predicament that even the lowest individual, much more a Prince, ever was placed in, by unshackling myself from a woman who has for the last three and twenty years not alone been the bane and curse of my existence, but who now stands prominent in the eyes of the world characterized by a flagrancy of abandonment unparalleled in the history of women, and stamped with disgrace and dishonor."[26]

But his ministers explained that the precarious state of the nation, riddled with rebellious factions, ruled out such an unpopular move. The British people would not take to a womanizing monarch divorcing the mother of his dead child. Furthermore, despite the reams of evidence accumulated over the years, nothing proved inconclusively Caroline's adultery with Pergami.

George sent a commission of experienced lawyers to Milan to try to dig up *irrefutable* evidence. The Milan Commission, as it came to be known, found cast-off servants willing to talk. Although the commissioners high-mindedly declared bribes would not be paid, working-class people demanded at least travel expenses and recompense for lost wages.

While George was eagerly digging up evidence of his wife's adultery, he had never ceased committing adultery himself. His mistress Lady Jersey, who had so offended Caroline upon her arrival in England, had given way to Lady Hertford, who by 1820 had been replaced by Lady Conyngham. Along the way there had been adventures with actresses, singers, and dancers. The virtuous Mrs. Fitzherbert, George's secret Catholic wife, had made a dignified retreat from the field in 1811.

As the investigation into Caroline's conduct inched forward, in January 1820 old mad King George III finally died. Caroline, whether her husband liked it or not, was now queen of England. King George IV, who had been planning his coronation for more than forty years, was horror-stricken at the thought that this nightmare of a wife could claim to be crowned beside him. Indeed, whenever the new king went forth he heard, to his grinding chagrin, cheers for good Queen Caroline.

According to British tradition, each Sunday ministers asked their flock to pray for members of the royal family by name. Caroline had always been mentioned as Princess of Wales. But the new king positively forbade any church prayers for Caroline as queen. Though George was head of the Church of England, he was not head of the Kirk of Scotland, and the Scots prayed twice as fervently for her, a fact which irked George mightily. Often the king couldn't sleep at night as he lay in bed imagining Scottish prayers for his detested wife winging their way heavenward.

Caroline, by nature easygoing and forgiving, was furious that her name had been removed from the liturgy. Moreover, while she visited Rome, the Vatican, which had always given her royal honors, stopped doing so at the request of the British government. She vowed to fly to England like a Fury and take revenge on her errant husband. Wisely leaving Pergami and her Italian suite in Italy, she landed at Dover in June 1820. At her arrival guns fired off a royal salute, and the streets were crowded with supporters, some of whom, seeing young Willy Austin, called three cheers for "Mr. Austin, her majesty's son!"[27]

Thousands had waited since early morning to welcome her, dressed in their Sunday best, crying "God save the Queen!" Arriving in Canterbury, she found the town illuminated with torches and ten thousand eager citizens cheering her. Cannons were fired and bonfires lit. This fulsome welcome, however, certainly had more to do with their loathing of the king than their love for the queen. She had become an icon of oppression at the hands of a tyrant king, just as the people felt oppressed at his hands. The cheers followed her all the way to London.

In the face of such broad support, Caroline generously offered to live abroad in return for a reasonable allowance and the restoration of her name to the liturgy. But George would not budge. No prayers for her. Moreover, he wanted a divorce. He brought forward the Milan Commission documents to both houses of Parliament to consider a bill of pains and penalties to exile Caroline, take away her titles, and dissolve her marriage with the king due to her adultery with Pergami.

Both the king and queen had very dirty laundry, and it was a catastrophic idea to wash it before the British public, advertising all its stains, stench, and filth by means of an eager British press. As one member of the House of Commons said of this messy case, either the king was betrayed, or the queen insulted. Either way, no good would come of it.

The British public remained firmly on Caroline's side. When a boatload of Italian witnesses for the prosecution landed in Dover, they were attacked by furious fishwives who beat them with sticks and scratched their faces until they could retreat to safety. Hearing the news, other boats bearing witnesses turned back.

As queen, Caroline had found decorum with lightning speed. No more pumpkins on her head or dresses cut so low that her breasts dangled out of them. She looked the picture of middle-aged respectability in her high-necked gowns of black or white satin, her long dark cloaks trimmed with ermine, and her modest bonnets. On August 17 the queen rode in triumph to her trial at the House of Lords. Among the 258 peers judging her were two of her former lovers, the husband of the king's current mistress, and the son of his former one.

The first days of opening statements, legal wrangling, oratorical effusions, and political grandstanding passed tediously in the sticky August heat. One day the queen was observed to be sleeping deeply during a speech. Lord Henry Holland promptly wrote an epigram:

Her conduct at present no censure affords
She sins not with courtiers but sleeps with the Lords.[28]

Interest picked up when Caroline's former servants took the stand. Several testified to having seen Pergami creeping about corridors at night half naked holding a candle, holding the princess on his lap, or sitting next to her in bed. Hotel maids described stained sheets and Pergami's slippers in the princess's bedroom.

A Swiss chambermaid related that one night, when Pergami had been out of town on business, she had bedded down with her mistress. But in the middle of the night Pergami returned and threw the maid out of the room, taking her place. "I have also seen Pergami in the princess's room when she was at her toilette, when she had no skirts on," the maid continued. "Pergami turned round and said, 'Oh! How pretty you are. I like you much better so.'"[29]

A servant named Giuseppe Rastelli had the most shocking evidence. He reported that while riding past the princess's carriage on horse, he looked in the window and saw Caroline and Pergami, both sound asleep, her hand resting lovingly on his private parts.

On cross-examination all of the servants admitted to being well paid for their time and living expenses in England or to being dismissed by the princess for poor work performance, admissions which served to destroy the value of their testimony. Caroline's defense attorney, Henry Brougham, relentlessly discredited witnesses and pointed out inconsistencies in testimony, ripping the prosecution's case to shreds. "Was it not a curious thing that these people, all of them poor," he thundered, "should be brought over to England to live in luxury and idleness and should be in receipt of great rewards?"[30]

Brougham derided the government's evidence as the "tittle-tattle of coffee-houses and alehouses, the gossip of bargemen on canals and . . . cast-off servants."[31] He described the Milan Commission as "that great receipt of perjury—that store house of false swearing and all iniquity."[32]

In the heated debates which followed the concluding statements of both sides, the general feeling was echoed by Lord Ellenborough who, admitting "the queen was the last woman any one would wish his own wife to resemble," felt forced to vote against the bill.[33]

As Brougham later said, "The strength of the Queen's case lay in the general demurrer which all men, both in and out of Parliament, made, viz., admit everything to be true which is alleged against the Queen, yet, after the treatment she had received ever since she first came to England, her husband had no right to the relief prayed by him, or the punishment sought against her."[34]

Perhaps Caroline had put it best herself in a letter written to her husband which she sent to a newspaper for publication. "From the very threshold of your Majesty's mansion the mother of your child was pursued by spies, conspirators, and traitors . . . ," she wrote. "You have pursued me with hatred and scorn, and with all the means of destruction. You wrested me from my child. . . . You sent me sorrowing through the world, and even in my sorrows pursued me with unrelenting persecution. . . ."[35]

After closing arguments, the bill to condemn the queen would have three readings, each one followed by a debate and a vote. The vote of the third reading would be the judgment of the case. On November 6, after one of the longest debates in British history, 123 lords voted for the bill to condemn the queen and 95 against it. After discussion, a second reading of the bill resulted in 108 for condemnation and 99 against. The government then withdrew the entire bill before a third reading could officially vindicate Caroline. And yet she was already vindicated; the British peers wisely chose to punish hypocrisy rather than adultery.

For five nights the major British cities were illuminated in support of the queen's victory and the king's defeat. George was so stunned that he talked of abdicating and leaving the country forever.

A few days after the trial, a Sicilian, Iacinto Greco, who had served as Caroline's cook in 1816 during her visit to Syracuse, arrived with shocking new evidence. He reported that after dinner one evening he opened a door and saw "the Princess on the sofa at the further end of the saloon—Pergami was standing between her legs which were in his arms—his breeches were down, and his back towards the door—at which I was. I saw the Princess's thighs quite naked—Pergami was moving backwards and forwards and in the very act with the Princess."[36] Pergami looked back and saw the cook, and the next day he was fired.

When asked why he had not come forward sooner, Greco replied that his wife had told him that the English would cut off his head. But his testimony arrived too late and could not be used against the freshly vindicated queen.

The trial over, the king could now make plans for his coronation. Much to his irritation, he had not obtained the desired divorce and Caroline was still queen of England. On May 5, 1821, the king was told, "Sire, your bitterest enemy is dead." "Is she, by God!" George replied, his face beaming with joy.[37] But it was, alas, only Napoleon who had died, not Caroline. And Caroline made it known that she would attend the coronation and ruin it by demanding that she, too, be crowned.

But at his coronation on July 19, Caroline made the mistake of planning a grand entrance once everyone was seated and the ceremony about to begin. Hearing of this, George had all the doors locked once the guests were inside and hired prizefighters to stand guard. Hammering on the door with her fist Caroline cried, "The Queen—open!" The pages opened the door a crack, and the sentries inside stood resolutely with crossed bayonets. According to an eyewitness seated in the hall, Caroline "was raging and storming and vociferating. 'Let me pass; I am your Queen, I am Queen of Britain.'" The lord high chamberlain sent his deputy who, with a voice that rang throughout the entire abbey, cried, "Do your duty, shut the Hall door," and the pages slammed the great door shut in the queen's face.[38]

His Majesty King George IV, puffed up with wine, pork chops, and pride, held in his monstrous bulk with a specially designed contraption of whalebone and corset strings. He strode through his coronation magnificently, gleeful in the knowledge that his wife was fruitlessly banging on the doors of Westminster Abbey.

That night Caroline invited several friends for supper. Her friend Lady Anne Hamilton wrote, "Her Majesty put on the semblance of unusual gaiety, but the friends who were around her observed that though she labored hard to deceive them, she only deceived herself, for while she laughed, the tears rolled down her face—tears of anguish so acute that she seemed to dread the usual approach of rest."[39]

The fiasco of the coronation had finally crushed the unflappable Caroline. Her stomach had been troubling her for months. Within days of her defeat she suffered an obstruction and inflammation of the bowels and her doctors soon concluded that she was dying. When informed of this, she calmly instructed that her body rest not in England, the land where she had never truly rested, but be returned to Brunswick with a simple plate affixed to her coffin: "Caroline of Brunswick, the injured Queen of England."[40] She died on August 7, 1821.

With regard to her love affairs, Caroline once quipped, "I never did commit adultery but once, and I have repented of it ever since. It was with the husband of Mrs. Fitzherbert."[41]

ISABELLA II, QUEEN OF SPAIN:
THE LUST THAT LOST THE THRONE

In the 1820s, when the convulsions of the French Revolution and its aftermath had subsided, Europeans looked around and didn't like what they saw—thirty years of bloodshed, war, suffering, and shocking immorality personified by Maria Luisa of Spain, Maria Carolina of Naples, Napoleon's three sisters, and the rowdy Queen Caroline of Britain. Unable to control the political upheavals of nations, they realized that one aspect of life they could control was family life. A tidy home harboring a sturdy husband, a chaste and motherly wife, and several bouncing rosy-cheeked children. Yes! That was much better than guillotines, marches on Russia, and the disgusting licentiousness of men and women of the preceding generation.

Since human nature had not changed along with human morals, male adultery was not to be given up, but to be kept politely concealed to avoid causing scandal or hurting the wife's feelings. The husband, pretending to visit a gentlemen's club, would instead visit his mistress and no one would be the wiser. The wife, of course, would not commit adultery at all. The ideal woman didn't even enjoy sex with her husband, but sacrificed herself now and then upon the altar of wifely duty.

While those in former centuries often shrugged off female adultery, especially if the adulteress had reformed her ways, the nineteenth-century woman, once fallen, could never hope to redeem herself socially. If she was repentant, God might forgive her, but society never would.

In 1846 the sixteen-year-old Queen Isabella II was forced to marry her cousin, the twenty-four-year-old Don Francisco d'Assisi, duque de Cadiz. The bridegroom had a shrill falsetto voice and was thought unfit to marry, a polite way of saying he was homosexual. Don Francisco was slightly built with a faint trace of moustache, and he moved strangely, like a mechanical doll. He had a feminine fascination for perfume, jewels, and fine fabrics. His frequent baths were eyed with suspicion. What normal man would insist on being so clean? Pale-faced and dark-haired, his features were attractive enough, and he was certainly elegant. But an observer could detect not the faintest trace of testosterone. The royal doctor, having examined the prince, declared optimistically that he did not think him impotent.

Isabella's mother Queen Cristina told the French ambassador, "To be sure, you have seen him, you have heard him; his hips, his movements, his sweet little voice. Is it not a little disturbing, a little strange?"[42]

Isabella was devastated to hear the choice and said she would be happy to marry Francisco if only he were a man. Seeing the virile Spanish grandees swashbuckling about court, she could not help but compare them with her weak, skinny, effeminate husband-to-be. Wallowing in tears, the little queen at first absolutely refused the marriage but was finally bullied into it by her ministers. Neither was Don Francisco pleased that he, who was disgusted at the thought of sex with a girl, would have to satisfy the seething passions of a fat giddy teenager.

For the wedding ceremony, the groom's sunken chest and narrow shoulders had been carefully padded to lend his figure a bit more dignity. When the priest declared they were one flesh, both the bride and groom were sobbing loudly.

The queen later recalled, "What shall I say of a man who on his wedding night wore more lace than I?"[43] Over the years Isabella had several children whose paternity was attributed to various Spanish officials, military men, and a strolling player. Her son the future Alfonso XII was reportedly fathered by an American dental assistant. But at each baptism, Don Francisco proudly held the infant aloft on a silver salver, the traditional gesture of acknowledging a child as his own.

Though Don Francisco's position was humiliating, he sometimes managed to view it with humor. When the queen's troops were sent to control a mob, Isabella bravely announced, "If I were a man, I would myself lead my soldiers to the fray." To which her husband reportedly quipped, "And so would I if *I* were a man."[44]

But if her husband accepted her infidelities, the Spanish people did not. In 1868 popular unrest forced her to find sanctuary in France. The outraged Spaniards, who had tolerated Queen Maria Luisa's Manuel Godoy eighty years earlier, refused to tolerate Isabella's Carlos Marfori, the son of a cook whom the queen appointed governor of Madrid and chief of the royal household. Times had changed.

In their Paris exile, the ill-matched royal couple dropped all pretenses and separated. The slovenly Isabella took countless lovers, and the dapper Francisco raised countless poodles, all named after his wife's lovers. He took up landscape painting and gave elegant dinner parties. The former king and queen saw each other only on their birthdays when, over a cup of coffee and a

cigarette, they would enjoy a good chat which inevitably degener-
ated into a raging argument over past grievances. They would
part in anger until the next birthday when they would do it all
over again. On his deathbed at the age of eighty, Francisco insisted that Isabella stay far away from him so he could die in
peace.

VICTORIA, QUEEN OF BRITAIN: MRS. BROWN

In contrast to the scandals of Queen Isabella II of Spain, the
marital devotion of Queen Victoria and Prince Albert of Great
Britain created a sense of reverence and respect among their
people. Sexual fidelity, domestic pleasures, an ever-increasing
nursery, as well as tireless devotion to state affairs—these were
qualities the British pointed to with pride in their sovereign.
The queen's one affair of the heart was platonic, as all Victorian
love affairs were supposed to be.

After the sudden death in 1861 of her beloved Albert at the
age of forty-two, the queen, deeply depressed, withdrew from
society. And society, after being deprived of the monarch's presence for several years, withdrew its approval of the queen. After
three years of brooding in black, Victoria was roused from her
torpor by a towering specimen of testosterone in a kilt.

John Brown, a farmer's son, had worked as a groom for over a
decade at Balmoral Castle in Scotland where the royal family va-
cationed every August. In 1864, when Victoria's doctor advised
her to take up riding to lose weight, it was John Brown who took
her out every afternoon. The queen developed quite a crush on
the handsome Scot. His eyes were as blue as a clear Scottish sky,
his face as chiseled as the rocky granite outcrops of the High-
lands, his hair and beard a curly red-gold. Perhaps Brown's best
feature was his gorgeous muscular legs, perfectly formed, strong
and sinewy, flashing beneath his kilt.

The dour widow, in her eternal black silk, her gray hair
scraped up tightly in a knot on her head revealing pendulous
jowls, inspired terror and trepidation among her own children.

But when Brown spoke with all the bluntness of his race, the queen loved it. He told her she was getting fat, and she chuckled. "Hoots, then, wumman," he yelled, while fixing the strap of her bonnet, "can ye no hold yerr head up."[45]

Once, when the queen met Brown for her daily ride, he cried, "What are ye daeing with that auld black dress on again? It's green-moulded."[46] Victoria, black silks rustling over her enormous crinoline, promptly went to her room to change her gown.

By February 1865 she decided Brown could never leave her side. She created a new post for him, "The Queen's Highland Servant," a position in which he would take orders only from the queen herself. His menial tasks—cleaning her boots and looking after her dogs—were given to other, lesser servants.

His sudden rise in the world had a corresponding effect on his arrogance; he routinely outraged the dukes and lords who served the queen. On one occasion Brown, poking his head into a palace billiard room, cast his icy blue gaze on the assembled courtiers and cried, "All what's here dines with the Queen."[47] He was even impudent to the most powerful ministers, once cutting off Prime Minister William Gladstone with "Ye've said enough."[48]

One day at Balmoral, Brown stomped into the room of the queen's assistant private secretary, Arthur Bigge, and informed him, "You'll no be going fishing. Her Majesty thinks it's about time ye did some work."[49]

The queen's devotion to this ruffian completely confounded genteel courtiers. The moment they complained about him, Victoria would send them packing. They were forced to accept John Brown, but not without grumbling.

In 1866 Lord Edward Derby scolded, "Long solitary rides, in secluded parts of the park; constant attendance upon her in her room; private messages sent by him to persons of rank . . . everything shows that she has selected this man for a kind of friendship which is absurd and unbecoming in her position."[50]

Queen Victoria's daughters, kept at arm's length by the imperious personage who was their mother, realized that Brown enjoyed an intimacy with her that they never knew. Shrugging, they laughingly called Brown "Mama's lover."[51]

Brown became known as "the Queen's stallion."[52] Rumors circulated that the queen was pregnant with his child but that this was no sin—the two had secretly married. Many referred to the queen—out of her hearing, of course—as "Mrs. Brown."[53]

It is likely that Victoria flaunted her devotion to Brown because their relationship was purely platonic, and as such, she had nothing to hide. She even told him that no one loved him more than she, and he gruffly replied he felt the same about her.

When riding out, Brown sat solidly on her carriage box, strong as Samson, eagle eyes searching the crowds for any threat to the queen. He steadied runaway horses, once grabbed a pistol from an assailant's hand, and picked her up in his strong arms when the carriage overturned. He stood guard at her office door, barring the way for those who would disturb her.

In March 1883 John Brown woke up at Windsor Castle feverish and with a swelling on his face. When he died a few days later, the queen was inconsolable. It was almost like losing Albert all over again.

"I have lost my *dearest best* friend who no-one in this World can *ever* replace," she wrote to her grandson. To Brown's sister-in-law she wrote, "Weep with me for we all have lost the best, the truest heart that ever beat. My grief is unbounded, dreadful and I know not how to bear it, or how to believe it is possible. . . . Dear, dear John—my dearest best friend to whom I could say everything & who always protected me so kindly. . . . I have no strong arm now."[54]

Years before her death in 1901, the queen had arranged her funeral to the last detail and extracted a promise from her friend Sir James Reid that a photo of John Brown, and a lock of his hair, be placed in her left hand. Reid, not wishing to shock the family who were coming in for the final viewing, discreetly placed flowers over the hand so no one would see that Queen Victoria was being expedited to eternity with a photo of her rumored lover, the surly Scot.

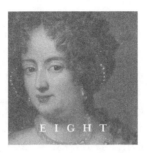

EIGHT

THE TURN OF THE TWENTIETH CENTURY: STRUGGLE FOR EQUALITY

For what is wedlock forced but a hell,
an age of discord and continual strife?

—WILLIAM SHAKESPEARE

THE END OF AN ERA

BY THE TIME OF VICTORIA'S DEATH IN 1901 WOMEN WERE agitating for equality. Many were attending college and even pursuing careers. Suffragettes marched for voting rights. The life of average citizens had greatly improved over that of their ancestors. Indeed, citizens now lived better than any king or queen could have imagined only a century earlier. Even modest homes boasted plumbing, heating, and electricity. Trolleys and trains whisked passengers across town for pennies. Laws had become more humane and just, and most working people earned a wage that kept them comfortable.

But life in the palace had not essentially changed in centuries. Though palaces, too, boasted electricity and plumbing, daily life had ossified over time and still revolved around age-encrusted ceremonies. If health care had improved, the deadly viruses of envy, greed, and revenge—the main ingredients of every royal court since the dawn of time—were all still thriving. And there was little room for self-expression, individuality, or personal choice, shocking new concepts heartily enjoyed by the masses. Princesses of the late nineteenth century could look with envy on daughters of wealthy merchants who chose their friends, hobbies, and husbands according to their own inclinations—young women who wallowed in luxury on a palatial scale, without the ancient residue of moldy hatred and mildewed greed.

Royal brides of the late Victorian period began to expect more from marriage. No longer the passive brood mares of earlier generations, these women actually insisted on happiness in their married lives. And, if their husbands couldn't provide it, they would find lovers to make life in the gilded cage more enjoyable.

Two late-nineteenth-century princesses—Louisa of Tuscany, who married Prince Frederick Augustus of Saxony, and Marie of Edinburgh, who married Prince Ferdinand of Romania—were faced with palace oppression, weak husbands, and nasty elderly monarchs. Both reacted in the same way—by taking lovers. But the more impulsive of the two would lose her marriage, her children, and her name, falling into obscurity. The more intelligent would manipulate her way to becoming a great queen ruling a crucial nation in times of the most challenging adversity.

A third princess yoked to a weak and vacillating monarch fell under the hypnotizing spell of a man so hated he unleashed a firestorm that destroyed her family and her country.

LOUISA OF TUSCANY, CROWN PRINCESS OF SAXONY

"Harmless Friendships"

Ninety years before Lady Diana Spencer burst onto the international scene as wife of the future king of Great Britain, a Hapsburg princess started along a similar path of popular acclaim and personal tragedy.

At the age of twenty-one Princess Louisa of Tuscany was considered a prime candidate for a royal marriage, even though her father had lost his duchy decades earlier when the Italian kingdoms were unified into one. She boasted Hapsburg blood, dark blond hair, and sparkling brown eyes; a slender yet shapely figure; and a bubbly personality. Though no great beauty, the princess was wooed by numerous princes. Of all her suitors, she preferred the handsome twenty-six-year-old Prince Frederick Augustus of Saxony, tall, blond, and blue-eyed.

Similar to "Shy Di" before she married Prince Charles, Louisa played her part as a sweet and modest young woman throughout the courtship. The prince and his family did not know that beneath Louisa's beaming countenance lurked a soul seething with dissatisfaction.

Louisa's parents, who had fallen so irrevocably from grandeur into mediocrity, were thrilled that their daughter would be the future queen of Saxony. They pressed her to accept the suit and, smitten by the dancing blue eyes of the prince, she agreed. But Louisa almost immediately regretted it. "For the first time in my life I felt the dreadful 'trapped' sensation that I afterwards experienced so much," she wrote, "and I cried bitterly when I contrasted my position with that of other girls, who were, I imagined, not precipitated into matrimony, but were allowed a more liberal choice of a husband than a poor princess."[1]

In Dresden, Louisa came not as a queen but as a princess. Indeed, her husband was not even crown prince yet. King Albert, childless, would be followed by his curmudgeonly brother Crown Prince George, and only upon George's death would his son, Frederick Augustus, become king. Until then, Louisa was at the mercy of her father-in-law and his brother.

Louisa's in-laws were dour, humorless, and critical. Courtiers bowed and scraped and clicked their heels, then spied and plotted against various members of the royal family. Most servants were spies paid by one faction or another, taking crumpled letters out of wastepaper baskets, listening at doors, or peeping through keyholes.

To the great dismay of her in-laws, the stylish princess became immensely popular with the Saxon people. Women slavishly copied her gowns. Whenever the royal family went out in their carriages, it was hers that drew the most cheers, the greatest applause. Louisa never failed to stick her head out the window and wave, or hold up one of her children to the crowd. Her unpopular father-in-law became green with envy. "What a bid you make for popularity, Louisa," George growled.[2]

Louisa fulfilled her duties as royal brood mare. She had the great distinction of presenting Saxony with two male heirs within a single calendar year. On January 15, 1893, she gave birth to George, and on December 31 to Frederick Christian. She had a third son, Ernest, in 1896, followed by Margaret in 1900 and Maria-Alix in 1901.

Despite the joy she had in her growing nursery, Louisa was terribly unhappy in the palace. Her grumpy father-in-law pricked her daily with insinuations, insults, and the withdrawal of privileges, and in return she threw violent temper tantrums. Sputtering in fear before the anger of his father, Prince Frederick Augustus never rushed to his wife's defense. Tempestuous, rash, and volatile, Louisa had the spirit to fight her many battles, but she fought them alone.

By the late 1890s her bitterness at palace life and her disappointment at her husband's weakness had resulted in flirtations with other men, which she called "harmless friendships" in her memoirs.[3] Events proved, however, that they were far more than that.

In 1902 King Albert died, and her tyrannical father-in-law became King George. Knowing his health was poor and he would not live long, George felt his blood pressure rise at the thought of Louisa becoming queen, and he vowed to get rid of her before he drew his last breath. Louisa aided and abetted him with her temper tantrums and love affairs. In November 1902 a palace servant told Louisa that her relationship with her sons' tutor, Monsieur Giron, was noticed at court. The tutor promptly resigned and left the country. Soon after, according to Louisa, the king informed her that he would commit her to an insane asylum to prevent her from becoming queen at his death.

In the dead of night Louisa packed a bag and fled. Perhaps she would not have taken this step had she known that she was pregnant by Monsieur Giron or another lover, and her daughter would be forever tainted by the questionable circumstances of her birth. Louisa took the train first to her parents in Salzburg looking for refuge, which they refused her; then she traveled to Zurich where she met up with her lover Monsieur Giron.

If the Saxon royal family was relieved at her flight, the Saxon people were furious. As in Britain ninety years later, public opinion was firmly against the stodgy, heartless royal family and completely supportive of the beautiful, wronged princess. The press had a field day; politicians roared of the impending downfall of the unpopular royal family which had driven out the people's princess. In return King George paid some journalists to insinuate that the crown princess had gone mad. He then divorced his son from Louisa immediately.

Shortly afterward, her lover Monsieur Giron left her. Perhaps he could not stand the scandal, or perhaps her emotional outbursts repelled him. Louisa found herself penniless, exiled, alone, and emotionally distraught. Ironically, she committed herself to an insane asylum for several months. In May 1903 Louisa gave birth to a girl she named Pia Monica.

She must have been surprised when Frederick Augustus claimed Pia Monica as his own. Yet in August of 1902 when she was conceived—and a month before and afterward—the prince had been making official visits to the courts of Berlin, Vienna, and Munich without his wife. A man of relentless duty and stiff honor, Frederick Augustus wanted to avoid bringing shame on his country and his children by admitting that the crown princess of Saxony had conceived a bastard with a commoner. Every year the king sent Louisa a request for her daughter, and for several years she refused, even after her ex-husband became king in 1904.

Finally in 1906, realizing that Pia Monica would have a far brighter future as a princess of Saxony than as the illegitimate child of a fallen woman, Louisa gave her up. Frederick Augustus raised the child as if she were his own. Given the uncertain nature of his divorce, he never remarried. He was a popular king, good-natured if a bit thickheaded, and beloved by his people.

In 1907 Louisa, who had been groomed as the future queen of Saxony, irreparably demeaned herself by marrying an Italian pianist, Enrico Toselli, with whom she had a son. But though she had blamed all her difficulties on palace life, neither could she find peace and happiness in the mediocre apartment of a commoner. The couple separated in 1912, Louisa abandoning her young son. Ever restless, never satisfied, throughout her life rumors of love affairs wafted around her like perfume.

In 1911 Louisa further shocked the world with her autobiography, *My Own Story*. Like Princess Diana in her covert autobiography, *Diana: Her True Story,* penned by Andrew Morton in 1992, Louisa portrayed herself as the innocent victim of an ice-cold royal family jealous of her popularity and making noise about her mental imbalance.

She must have laughed in 1918 when the German monarchies fell, the kings and queens were exiled, and their viperous courts dismantled. Frederick Augustus lived the comfortable life of a wealthy private gentleman and died of heart disease in 1932 at the age of sixty-seven. His children married the scions of other toppled European royalty, Hapsburgs and Hohenzollerns. Even the illegitimate Pia Monica—who grew up painfully aware that she resembled her siblings neither in looks nor in temperament— married Archduke Josef Franz of Austria. Louisa, who had fleeting contact with her children over the years, slid into poverty and obscurity. Very little is known about her after she separated from Toselli. She died in 1947 in Brussels at the age of seventy-seven.

MARIE OF BRITAIN, QUEEN OF ROMANIA
"I Rejoice in My Beauty. Men Have Taught Me To"

Marie, princess of Edinburgh, was Queen Victoria's granddaughter by a younger son. When the seventeen-year-old married the bumbling heir to the Romanian throne in 1893, Marie soon found herself in a kind of prison with grouchy King Carol I, her husband's uncle, as her jailer. He forbade her to form friendships with anyone, to attend parties and balls, even to leave her rooms for days on end. Her husband, Prince Ferdinand, was too weak to stand up for his wife and visibly trembled when even thinking about the king. "When he spoke of him something like anxiety and not far removed from dread came into his eyes," Marie wrote. "One felt that a shiver ran down his spine."[4]

King Carol did permit Marie to attend the festivities celebrating the coronation of Nicholas and Alexandra in Moscow in 1896 as Romania's representative. Clad in gorgeous new gowns and dazzling jewels, the princess suddenly came alive, a magnificent butterfly bursting forth from her drab cocoon. Her large blue eyes sparkled with greater intensity than her glistening sapphires as princes, prime ministers, and generals, their strong hands tight against the back of her slender waist, took turns sweeping her around the ballroom. For twenty-one-year-old Marie this was a moment of sexual awakening, a sudden awareness of her power over powerful men. "Russians catch fire easily," she wrote years later in her autobiography, "and Slav tongues are soft."[5]

No longer the shy and awkward girl who had married the crown prince, after her success in Moscow she told an admirer, "I rejoice in my beauty. Men have taught me to."[6] Tall and slim, with a dazzling fair complexion and blond hair, Marie was described by many as the most beautiful woman they had ever seen.

Suddenly empowered with her sensuality, Marie embarked on numerous love affairs, often arranging for her lovers to work in the palace for easy access to her rooms, or meeting them while visiting health spas in Germany on trips to see her mother. Hearing the rumors, Marie's English relatives were worried sick that her scandalous lifestyle would result in divorce. In between his stern lectures to her on the subject, King Carol must have considered the possibility. After all, by 1903 the crown prince of Saxony had divorced his adulterous Louisa. But Romania's dynasty, founded in 1866, was new and fragile, whereas the house of Wettin had sat solidly on the Saxon throne for a thousand years. Moreover, while Louisa's family were dispossessed dukes of Tuscany now living on the charity of the Austro-Hungarian emperor, Marie's close relatives were the British royal family.

If her family looked with horror at her love affairs, the Romanian people admired her for them. They pointed with pride to their crown princess as the most sensual woman in Europe. And indeed, early-twentieth-century Romania reveled in a sexual equality among the aristocracy that was unheard of in other nations. A beautiful married woman who took handsome lovers was admired for her panache and sense of style, not chastised for immorality. Marie's reputation was enhanced by her amours, much as that of a virile king was gilded by his numerous fragrant mistresses.

In 1907 Marie began a love affair that would last until her death thirty years later. Two years older than Marie, Barbo Stirbey came from an ancient aristocratic family and was one of the richest men in Romania. A dapper dresser, Stirbey had a noble brow, intense brown eyes, Slavic cheekbones, and a full dark moustache that almost hid his sensual lips. Sophisticated, tall, and slender, Stirbey carried himself with quiet confidence. Despite his loving wife and four children, he was reputed to be quite a lady-killer, and many Bucharest socialites spoke dreamily of the "strange hypnotic quality" of his eyes.[7]

Stirbey was forever cool and unruffled. "No one had ever guessed what passions lay beneath his unbendable pride," Marie wrote later.[8] "His manner was unassuming, yet full of charm," Princess Anne-Marie Callimachi wrote. "He spoke little, but a gift of persuasion and instinctive psychological insight made him rarely miss his aim whenever he set himself one. Extraordinary was the way he always struck the right note."[9]

Marie visited Stirbey's estate at Buftea often, going on horseback rides with him. In 1913 King Carol, well aware of the love affair, unofficially gave it his blessing by appointing Stirbey superintendent of the royal estates. This gave the lovers an excuse to work together every day. It was rumored that Marie's fourth child, Ileana, born in 1909, was fathered by Stirbey. It was fairly certain that her last child, Mircea, born in 1913, was his.

But Stirbey was not simply her lover. It was through him that Marie first developed a serious interest in politics; from him she learned of defense, agriculture, foreign affairs, and trade. He became her chief political adviser, and even poor doddering Ferdinand grew to rely heavily on Stirbey's wisdom. Although Stirbey was one of the most powerful political figures in Romania during the first three decades of the century, he was not one to seek the limelight, preferring to play the role of gray eminence.

In October 1914 old King Carol died and Marie, who had been crown princess for over twenty years, was finally queen of Romania. She had just inherited World War I. After two years of uneasy neutrality, Romania finally sided with the Allies; within hours of the declaration, the German Kaiser sent warplanes to bomb Bucharest. Throughout the war, stammering King Ferdinand wrung his hands while Marie ran the show with Stirbey's political advice. "There is only one man in Roumania and that is the Queen," said one French nobleman.[10]

When Communists deposed and murdered Marie's cousin Czar Nicholas II of Russia in 1918, many Romanians feared the revolution would swoop down upon them. One reason it did not was because of Queen Marie's popularity; unlike the frivolous and haughty Marie Antoinette of France, unlike the stiff and stubborn Empress Alexandra of Russia, Marie wisely guided her country through the shoals of the war. Moreover, she was always available to her people; a farmer seeking justice had only to walk into the palace and ask for her.

One young guest at the palace in the 1920s carefully observed the queen and her lover, both in their early fifties. "She had a dress, a very long dress with a train in black velvet with all her magnificent pearls. She was in a corner of the throne room, and Barbo Stirbey was next to her discussing something. They were not looking at each other, they were looking at the crowd. It was an extraordinary sight. . . . They were such a magnificent pair. She was so beautiful and he was so handsome. They had such extraordinary allure and grandeur and distinction. . . . The best proof is that after more than fifty years I can still see them as if it happened last night."[11]

In the 1920s Romania's economy was booming. Bucharest became known as the Paris of the East. In 1925 Marie's oldest son, the erratic Crown Prince Carol, abdicated his rights to the throne and moved to Paris with his mistress. His father, who had been ailing, was devastated; his death eighteen months later was probably hastened by the scandal. Carol's five-year-old son, Michael, became king with Stirbey as his prime minister.

But in 1930 Carol, bored with stewing in France on little money, swooped back to Romania and proclaimed himself King Carol II. He marginalized his mother, whom he had resented for her affair with Stirbey since he first learned of it at the age of thirteen. Suddenly Marie found herself transported back forty years to the time of her imprisonment under King Carol I, restricted in her communication, her freedom of movement, and her finances. Her servants were spies who opened her mail and listened in on her telephone calls.

Stirbey, ever discreet and dignified, retired to his estates and out of Marie's life. When Carol banished him from Romania in 1934, he took his family to Switzerland. At the end of Marie's life, the loss of Stirbey afflicted her most. Since her first step onto Romanian soil in 1893 she had endured ups and downs; but since 1907 Stirbey had always been there to advise her, to help her make it through. Now he was gone.

Years earlier, Stirbey had predicted that Romania would fall to wrack and ruin under King Carol II. Casting her glance into the near future, Marie sadly agreed and saw a lifetime of work coming undone. She began to suffer from internal hemorrhaging, perhaps from a liver ailment. In 1938, her condition deteriorating, her son refused her permission to visit the world's leading expert in Dresden.

Hearing of her serious illness, Stirbey managed to smuggle a letter to her. "My thoughts are always near you," he assured her. "I am inconsolable at being so far, incapable of being any help whatsoever to you, living in the memory of the past with no hope for the future. . . . Never doubt the boundlessness of my devotion."[12]

Dying, Marie wrote one last letter to her lover. She deeply regretted that she must leave "so much unsaid, which would so much lighten my heart to say: all my longing, my sadness, all the dear memories which flood back into my heart. . . . The woods with the little yellow crocuses, the smell of the oaks when we rode through those same woods in early summer—and oh! so many, many things which are gone. . . . God bless you all and keep you safe. . . ."[13]

Then Marie turned to her other love, Romania, and wrote her final letter. "I have become yours for joy or sorrow," she wrote. "When I look back, it is difficult to say which was greater, the joy or the sorrow. I believe the joy was greater, but too long was the sorrow."[14]

ALEXANDRA OF HESSE-DARMSTADT, EMPRESS OF RUSSIA

"Rasputin Is a Messenger of God"

Aping Queen Victoria's devotion to John Brown, Empress Alexandra of Russia, wife of Czar Nicholas II, was equally devoted to a blunt-spoken peasant. But unlike her wise grandmother, the foolish Alexandra made a choice that was politically explosive. Alexandra fell in love with a sexual satyr, a con man, and a lunatic, the man who lit the spark of the Russian Revolution. His name was Gregory Rasputin.

Alexandra, a German princess, had come to Russia as a bride in 1893. Haughty, stubborn, and loudmouthed, she won the immediate dislike of many who met her. Upon hearing the news of her betrothal to the future czar, an official from her native land of Hesse whispered to a Russian diplomat, "How lucky we are that you are taking her from us."[15]

Tall and slender with rich chestnut hair and large blue-gray eyes, she completely overwhelmed her indecisive husband who signed himself "Your poor, weak-willed little hubby."[16] Nicholas's handsome features were marred by his insipid expression. His cousin Kaiser Wilhelm of Germany thought he should have been "a country gentleman growing turnips." When his tutor tried to teach him about governing a nation, Nicholas "became actively absorbed in picking his nose."[17]

Believing herself to be a political genius, Alexandra pushed her weak husband out of the way and ruled one-seventh of the surface of the globe herself. Nicholas's old tutor remarked that Alexandra was "more autocratic than Peter the Great and perhaps as cruel as Ivan the Terrible. Hers is a small mind that believes it harbors great intelligence."[18] One court official described her as having "a will of iron linked to not much brain and no knowledge."[19] She knew she was detested at all levels of society, but thought the root cause was jealousy of her intellectual brilliance and steely resolve not to change her mind merely because the Russian people objected.

Increasingly isolated as the years passed, gullible Alexandra fell prey to various charlatans and psychics. As the mother of four daughters who were not allowed to rule the Russian Empire by virtue of their gender, her main objective was to have a son. But Czarevich Alexis, born in 1904, suffered from hemophilia, a disease which always resulted in death at a very early age. Desperate for a cure, the empress agreed to meet a Siberian holy man who had come to St. Petersburg.

Gregory Rasputin had grown up on a farm and stumbled into the Russian capital to obtain sex, which he needed several times a day. Siberian farms offered a limited number of women, and many of their fathers and husbands objected to his ravishing them. But in the decadent, overripe world of St. Petersburg, he reflected, there would be countless women ready to sleep with him.

Though only of medium height, Rasputin gave the impression of being incredibly tall. He had a shaggy, dirty beard and wild unkempt hair; his teeth were black stumps. He wore silk peasant blouses of blue or red, embroidered with flowers, and baggy black pants tucked into thick high peasant boots.

Rasputin's most striking feature was his eyes. They were a gray so light that they often appeared to be white—burning white eyes, pinpricks of fiery light shooting out relentlessly from beneath a Neanderthal brow. "The eyes of a maniac," said one Russian who met him.[20] "He looked like a lascivious, malicious satyr," said another. One had the impression of being "pierced by needles rather than merely of being looked at."[21]

When Rasputin was a child, his daughter later reported, he had the unique ability to heal sore and injured farm animals. He knew when unheralded visitors would come calling, found lost objects, and predicted village deaths. At the age of eighteen, he claimed to see a vision of the Virgin which led to a spiritual awakening. Yet his fervent prayers were usually mixed with drunken debauchery and ribald orgies.

Wrapped in a heavy mantle of ancient Russian spirituality, Rasputin became a living icon, a pallid face with burning eyes, the symbol of primitive Christianity. His unique religious outlook won him many lovers, even as it outraged the Russian Orthodox Church. The only way to become close to God, Rasputin argued, was through the redemption of sin. Therefore, if one remained sinless, one could never join with God. True believers must sin—preferably sexually and with Rasputin—to become close to the Creator. Making love to him, he assured gullible women, would actually purify them of sin. One woman expressed shock at how sinful she had been; Rasputin had needed to purify her several times.

He was only attracted to pretty women. When the not-so-pretty ones thronged about him, hoping to be purified, he would say, "Mother, your love is pleasing, but the spirit of the Lord does not descend on me."[22]

With regard to Rasputin's countless affairs, his hearty Siberian wife, at home minding the farm, said, "He can do what he likes. He has enough for all."[23]

In addition to his sexual services, Rasputin had great success healing ladies of depression, hypochondria, and migraines. Hostesses fought over him as a dinner guest; he intentionally offended the cream of St. Petersburg society, and they loved it. He jeered, cursed, and pawed the women, all the while talking of barnyard sex. His table manners were revolting; he tore food into large pieces and shoved them into his mouth with dirty hands. It was certainly much more entertaining to listen to

Rasputin discussing sex as a holy sacrament than to the standard dinner conversation of war and social unrest.

Women asked for Rasputin's dirty linen as holy relics. "The dirtier the better. It's got to have sweat," they said.[24] He was novel, he was amusing, and just maybe he was sent from God.

But while Rasputin was on the rise in St. Petersburg, Russia's fortunes were declining. In 1904 Japan declared war on Russia, but Russian armed forces did as much damage to themselves as the enemy did. Russian boats fired and sank each other by mistake. Russian minesweepers were sunk by their own mines. Trade unions struck. Hundreds of peasants protesting peacefully for better conditions were gunned down on the czar's orders. "If such a government cannot be overthrown otherwise than by dynamite," wrote Mark Twain, "then thank God for dynamite."[25] Fearing for their lives, the imperial family did not venture out into public.

Two countesses, friends of the empress, knowing her interest in quacks and charlatans, brought Rasputin to the imperial palace. The empress was awestruck by the holy man. Rasputin calmed the empress's heart palpitations and, oddly, had a healing effect on the dangerous bleeding of the czarevich. Whenever the little boy fell or knocked himself against something, internal bleeding swelled him to enormous proportions; he lay moaning in agony as palace doctors trembled for his life. But when Rasputin visited him, the pain and swelling subsided.

One witness reported, "Coincidence might have answered if it happened, say, once or twice, but I could not even count how many times it happened!"[26] Rasputin probably hypnotized the boy, calming him so he could recover naturally. But the empress declared he had miraculous powers direct from God almighty.

Soon Rasputin convinced the empress, who convinced the czar, to appoint his friends to top positions in the church and government. But the political meddling of Rasputin, who possessed the tact of a cannonball and the diplomacy of a sledgehammer, was disastrous. Officials who protested the favorite's influence were soon ousted and replaced by his friends.

When it became known that the empress was meeting

Rasputin at her maid's cottage on the palace grounds, many speculated that they were having an affair. Rumors also flew that perhaps Rasputin was enjoying the favors of Alexandra's four teenage daughters. Some people, certain he was in league with the devil, reported that the Russian flag flying over the imperial palace had been transformed into Rasputin's underpants.

Yet General Alexander Spiridovich, the head of the czar's secret service who got to know Rasputin very well, said the monk behaved with "extreme decency and chastity" with the imperial family.[27]

One day Rasputin's friend Aron Simanovich cried, "It's intolerable that rumors are spread about the grand duchesses because of you. You ought to realize that everyone pities the poor girls and that even the czarina is being drawn into the dirt."

"Go to hell," Rasputin replied. "I've done nothing. People should realize that nobody fouls the place where he eats. I'm at the czar's service, and I'd never dare do anything of that sort. What do you think the czar would do to me if I had?"[28]

In 1912 letters written by Alexandra to Rasputin were stolen from his apartment and published in the newspapers. In a letter which could be interpreted as expressing sexual desire, Alexandra wrote, "My beloved and unforgettable teacher, redeemer and mentor, how weary I feel without you. It is only then that my soul is quiet and I relax, when you, teacher, are sitting beside me and I kiss your hands and lean my head on your blessed shoulder. Oh! How light I feel then. I wish only one and the same thing then. To fall asleep forever on your shoulder, in your arms. . . . Come quickly. I am waiting for you and I am tormenting myself for you. I am asking for your holy blessing and I am kissing your blessed hands. Loving you forever, M [stood for Mama]."[29]

Many felt that the appearance of the white-eyed holy man marked the end of their world. The czar's mother, who detested Alexandra, said, "My unhappy daughter-in-law does not understand that she is destroying the dynasty and herself. She truly believes in the saintliness of this rogue and we are powerless to stave off this disaster."[30] A Russian lady wrote of Rasputin's increasing power, "It became a dusk enveloping all our world, eclipsing the sun. How could so pitiful a wretch throw so vast a shadow."[31] Alarmed by Rasputin's closeness to the imperial family, the secret police followed him. The czar waved away their reports of drunken brawls and orgies. Lies and slander, he said. The empress sniffed, "How true it is that a prophet is always without honor in his own country."[32]

Premier Vladimir Kokovtsov tried to tell the czar that Rasputin was threatening the security of the throne as popular resentment focused on him as the cause of all public grievances. But Nicholas was contemptuous of the press and public opinion. "The public does not run the country," he fumed. "It is run for their benefit, and I am the one who decides what is best for them."[33]

Casting his burning white eyes toward the future, Rasputin seemed to foresee World War I. He begged Nicholas not to join the war, for he could see Russia "drowned in her own blood," and the deaths of the imperial family soon after. But in the one instance when the czar should have listened to Rasputin, he did not. As Russia lay wounded and bleeding in the First World War, revolutionary murmurs grew to a groundswell. The czar decided to fire his efficient commander in chief and lead his forces himself. The indecisive monarch, pale and trembling astride a horse, was not an inspiring sight.

Meanwhile, Rasputin was up to his old tricks. One evening in 1915 he arrived already drunk at a Moscow nightclub. When waiters heard shrieks, breaking glass, and curses coming from the private dining room, they rushed in. A woman had refused to have sex with Rasputin, and in his frustration he had smashed the mirrors. Asked to prove he was indeed Rasputin, he unbuttoned his pants, took out his penis, and waved it in the air. Called to the scene, the police reported his behavior as "sexually psychopathic." Although he cried repeatedly that he was protected by the czar, the police dragged him away "snarling and vowing vengeance."[34]

A group of conspirators led by a cousin of the imperial family, Prince Felix Yusupov, finally had enough. The prince used his wife, Irina, as a decoy for Rasputin, who had been panting after her. In the early hours of December 16, 1916, Rasputin went to Yusupov's palace, expecting Irina to be available for sex.

Rasputin was ushered into the basement, which had been fitted up as a comfortable party room with a crackling fire, a bearskin rug, and overstuffed easy chairs. He spoke jovially with the conspirators. Prince Yusupov offered Rasputin cakes poisoned with cyanide. Rasputin greedily gulped down two and washed them down with cyanide wine. According to the conspirators, after consuming enough poison to kill an elephant on the spot, Rasputin merely cleared his throat and complained of a tickling sensation. Some historians, reading details of the attempted poisoning, believe that Rasputin had steeled himself against poison by ingesting a few grains of cyanide every day, to build up resistance. Others believe the murderers exaggerated Rasputin's demonic resistance to death to justify their foul deed.

According to their story, Rasputin began to breathe with difficulty and complained of a burning in his stomach. Yet he was suddenly eager to take his friends to sing and dance with Gypsies. Felix Yusupov suddenly said, "You'd far better look at the crucifix and say a prayer." Rasputin seemed to know what was going to happen; he looked almost kindly at the prince. Rasputin started to make the sign of the cross. When Yusupov shot him in the heart, Rasputin screamed and fell on the bearskin rug.

He was examined and declared dead. Then the eyes opened up, "green viper eyes." The bloody body stood up and rushed at Yusupov. "He sank his fingers into my shoulder like steel claws," Yusupov later recalled. "His eyes were bursting from their sockets, blood oozed from his lips." The hands reached out to strangle him, the lips crying "Felix, Felix." Yusupov raced upstairs to the others, ashen faced, eyes bulging, followed by Rasputin who had climbed the stairs and was racing across the snowy courtyard. One witness said Rasputin was shouting, "I will tell everything to the empress."[35]

Vladimir Purishkevich took out his gun and fired, hitting Rasputin in the shoulder, and then in the head. Rasputin fell to his knees, but still he was not dead, and tried to rise again. Yusupov started beating him with a blackjack until he fell over.

They wrapped the body in a rug or drape, threw it in a car and drove it to a bend in the river, and dropped it in. But in their haste the conspirators had forgotten to attach weights to it that they had brought along in the car. The following day workmen found bloodstains on the parapet of the bridge, a boot on the ice below, and peering into the frigid waters, they saw the corpse. The autopsy revealed water in the lungs. Rasputin had still been alive when he had plunged into the river.

There was no trial for Rasputin's murderers; they were not the only ones who saw their bloody deed as a patriotic act, liberating their country from the clutches of a vile lunatic. Popular opinion was decidedly in favor of the assassination. But the empress suffered a nervous collapse, sitting silently in her mauve-colored rooms, contemplating a picture of the doomed Marie Antoinette. She used opium to calm her nerves and prayed at Rasputin's grave. "He died to save us," she wrote, as if Rasputin had been Christ. As the country slipped into anarchy, the empress wandered about the palace looking for Rasputin's spirit, while the czar concentrated on thrilling games of dominoes.

The unhappy Russian people began to think that if a man as all-powerful as Rasputin could so easily be removed, so could the detested imperial family. When thousands of strikers and protesters demonstrated against the government, imperial soldiers were ordered to shoot them. But they shot their commanding officers instead and joined the mob. On March 2, 1917, Czar Nicholas II was forced to abdicate; the entire imperial family was taken prisoner.

Within a week, Rasputin's body, which had been lovingly buried in the imperial palace park, was dug up, doused with gasoline, and burned. The flames consumed him even as they consumed Russia, just as he had predicted. In July 1918 Nicholas, Alexandra, and their five children were murdered by revolutionary forces, as Rasputin—visionary, healer, satyr—had foreseen.

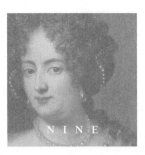

DIANA, PRINCESS OF MANY LOVERS

The chains of marriage are so heavy it takes
two to carry them, and sometimes three.

—ALEXANDRE DUMAS

❄

"THERE WERE THREE OF US IN THIS MARRIAGE," INTONED Diana, Princess of Wales, sadly in her infamous television interview, pointedly referring to her husband's mistress, Camilla Parker-Bowles, "so it was a bit crowded."[1] But the marriage was, in fact, far more crowded than Diana admitted. There were more than a dozen people in her marriage if one counted her own lovers.

It was November 20, 1995, and the stricken Diana, melancholy eyes ringed heavily with kohl, lips tragically pale, was the first royal princess ever to admit on television that she had conducted an adulterous affair.

Panorama interviewer Martin Bashir pressed her to discuss her relationship with army captain James Hewitt, who had detailed their steamy love affair in the book *Princess in Love*, in cooperation with author Anna Pasternak. "Were you unfaithful with Captain James Hewitt?" he asked. Casting her glance modestly downward, the princess murmured, "Yes, I adored him. Yes, I was in love with him."[2]

In the sixteenth century Anne Boleyn and Catherine Howard had been beheaded for adultery. In the seventeenth and eighteenth centuries Sophia Dorothea and Caroline Matilda had been locked up until their deaths. By the twentieth century execution and imprisonment were no longer accepted punishments for adulterous royal women whose battles were fought, not behind palace walls, but in the press. Diana, just like Crown Princess Louisa of Tuscany in 1902, was championed by some newspapers for her compassion and courage, and lambasted by others for her immorality and mental instability. "It's almost as if they want to put me away," she opined to a friend.[3]

And yet it had all started out so well. Wishing to avoid the scandal of men popping up in the press with lurid tales of sex with the future queen, the royal family dismissed Charles's beloved Camilla Shand from consideration as his bride. Casting about for a suitable candidate, they settled on Lady Diana Spencer, an attractive if slightly awkward teenager, young enough to be molded for her role as queen. An added advantage was the fact that Diana seemed intellectually limited; she had not managed to graduate from high school and kept failing her tests. This sweet befuddled girl, a virgin from a noble English family, would be in no position to make trouble for Buckingham Palace. She would do as she was told: wave, smile, and produce royal babies.

It is ironic that if the British royal family had picked any other woman in the world as Charles's bride, no matter what her temperament or sexual history, chances are she would not have shaken the foundations of the monarchy as Diana did. Certainly a few newspaper articles about the raucous sexual adventures of the youthful Camilla, now a discreet and supportive matron of the royal family, would not have done nearly as much damage as the virgin bride Diana.

The Princess of Wales transformed herself from a shy pudgy

teenager into a sleek, mean, and angry woman, wielding newspapers as a deadly weapon. The avenging Fury ripped moldering skeletons out of stuffy royal closets and gleefully exposed their grisly decay for all the world to see. Indeed, Queen Mother Elizabeth viewed Diana as the greatest danger to the British monarchy since the adulterous Wallis Warfield Simpson stole King Edward VIII in 1936.

As soon as her engagement was announced, Diana, worried about her fiancé's lackluster courtship, slipped into bulimia, binge eating to satisfy a hunger that could not be quelled with food, and then, repelled at her gorging, forcing herself to throw it all up. Bulimia, she said, "is like having a pair of arms around you, but it's temporary. Then you're disgusted at the bloatedness of your stomach, and then you bring it all up again."[4]

Despite her illness, Diana's sexual needs were demanding. James Hewitt said, "She couldn't get enough. She always wanted more."[5] Perhaps sex was something like bulimia, only having a real pair of arms around her. Of Charles she said, "Dead below the waist."[6] Given the revelations of his eternal passion for Camilla, perhaps we should say that Charles was dead below the waist for Diana. In 1992, while being videotaped by her speech instructor Peter Settelen as an exercise, Diana reported that even when they were first married, Charles only made love to her once every three weeks. Though a virgin, she realized his lack of ardor was odd. After about four years, she said on the tape, the royal sex fizzled out altogether. For his part, Charles reportedly told friends that the aroma of vomit wafting under layers of mouthwash and perfume disgusted him, rendering him unable to perform.

Threatened by her husband's continued friendship with his mistress and his lackluster performance in bed with his wife, Diana threw shrill temper tantrums whenever he wanted to hunt, garden, meet with friends, or attend to state duties. A single moment spent away from her seemed a painful rejection, a cruel abandonment, crystal clear proof that he didn't love her. She broke vases, slammed doors, and called him the vilest names, and when five months pregnant, she threw herself down a flight of stairs during a fiery temper tantrum. Whatever feelings he had for his bride quickly dissipated as he ran from her furious accusations into the safe and comforting arms of Camilla.

Diana told her voice coach that when she confronted her husband about Camilla, Charles replied that he refused to be the only Prince of Wales without a mistress. Undeterred, the princess took her problem directly to the queen, who said she didn't know what advice to give Diana, because Charles was hopeless.

Sex between the royal couple ceased forever soon after the birth of their second child, Prince Harry, in October 1984. According to James Hewitt, Diana told him that her former bodyguard Sergeant Barry Mannakee became her lover in 1985. Married with two children, Mannakee was an unlikely lover for a princess, a bit plump, with thinning dark hair and a blue-collar background.

The kindhearted Mannakee was deeply troubled by Diana's bouts of sobbing depression; the affair started when he began to comfort her, putting his arms around her. Before Diana and her bodyguard attended public events, Diana often pranced around her room trying on outfits for him, waiting for his compliments. "He'd tell me I looked good. Something my husband no longer did," Diana said.[7]

Mannakee quickly began to rue his involvement with the princess. Diana demanded that he remain at her beck and call twenty-four hours a day, no matter what his obligations to his wife and children. "Once it began, [Mannakee] was very distraught about being caught up with her," a friend of Charles said. "She was so intense, and he found it very difficult to handle."[8]

She often dismissed her servants and spent time alone with Mannakee at her apartment in Kensington Palace or went out with him for drives that lasted hours. Like so many princesses before her, Diana dreamed of fleeing her gilded cage hand in hand with her lover. "I was quite happy to give all this up," she told Settelen on the videotape. ". . . Just to go off and live with him."[9]

Charles, aware of her affair, was at first relieved. Diana might find some happiness with her bodyguard, and with Camilla warming his bed at night he was in no position to cast blame. "I don't want to spy on [Diana] or interfere with her life in any way," he told a friend.[10] Yet someone at the palace minded. Suddenly the detective was transferred far away from the princess. Diana was furious at the interference in her private life. When Mannakee died shortly after his transfer in a freak motorcycle accident, Diana was certain the palace had arranged his murder.

But Diana did not mourn her bodyguard for long. In 1986 at a party celebrating Sarah Ferguson's forthcoming wedding to Prince Andrew, the princess wrapped herself around a handsome financier, Charlie Carter. Shortly after midnight, according to author Lady Colin Campbell, a friend of hers went outside for a cigarette and made a shocking discovery. "I heard sounds coming from the bushes," he reportedly told Lady Campbell. "I nearly choked with astonishment when I looked over and saw Charlie Carter with the Princess of Wales. I moved away, finished my cigarette quietly, and went back inside. They didn't return for ages."[11]

Diana's most notorious love affair—the only one she admitted publicly—was with the charming Captain James Hewitt who met her at a London party in August 1986. When she heard he was a staff captain in the household division and helped run the royal stables, she confided her fear of horses after a childhood riding accident, and her wish to get back in the saddle. Hewitt gallantly offered to give her riding lessons.

During her first riding lessons Diana had her detectives in tow riding alongside her. She then began to make them ride behind her and Hewitt, and finally told them not to come along at all. Her lessons were invariably followed by coffee with her instructor. Through tears she told him of her painful marriage, her husband's neglect of her and his love for another woman. "I am surrounded by people but so alone," she cried, that ancient lament of royalty.[12] "You are not alone. You have me," he gulped, that ancient reply of a valiant knight to a damsel in distress.[13]

Diana began to phone Hewitt several times a day. Awed by her beauty and position, and unfettered by a wife and children of his own, he was flattered. She invited him to a private dinner at Kensington Palace, where she served Hewitt from the buffet with her own slender hands. Afterward, according to Hewitt, she seduced him and, lying in his arms, cried for joy and sorrow.

Diana often visited Hewitt's family in the county of Devon, accompanied by two palace detectives and watched by police in four counties as they traveled. Palace officials and members of the royal family—including Charles and the queen—must have been well aware of the love affair.

But still Diana could not find happiness. Her insecurities ran deep; when Hewitt didn't respond exactly the way she wanted, she would throw a royal tantrum, flinging bitter accusations. These emotional outbursts frightened and repelled him. "She needed constant attention and reassurance," he said. "Ten minutes after I'd left, having spent most of the time making love to her, she'd be on the phone needing to be told how much I loved her. She'd phone five, six, ten times a day, always needing to hear the same thing."[14]

Oddly, for all the tantric sex and breathless promises of eternal devotion, neither Hewitt nor Diana was sexually faithful. For much of the five-year love affair with Diana, Hewitt was involved with Emma Stewardson, whom he lamely claimed in his book was a decoy from his affair with the princess, a very convincing decoy indeed. For her part, Diana, still as needy as ever, had a series of love affairs unbeknownst to Hewitt.

Shortly after her love affair began with Hewitt, she took up with the wealthy banker Philip Dunne. Tall, virile, and witty, Dunne was darkly handsome with polished manners. The princess and the banker were seen in trendy restaurants flirting and laughing. One society lady reported having seen them playing footsie under the table. Charles, grateful for any man who could distract Diana, seemed to stamp the seal of approval on their relationship by inviting Dunne to join the royal skiing party at Klosters, Switzerland.

But the princess made a huge faux pas in June 1987 at a society wedding reception. Dancing with Dunne, Diana ran her hand through his hair and pushed her tongue down his ear. She danced wildly with him, bold sexual undulations, pressing her body against his, as an awestruck crowd looked on with mouths agape. Charles quietly left the party without her at two A.M., and Diana and Dunne danced until dawn.

The story was the sensation of the moment and made the newspapers. Philip Dunne received a call from Buckingham Palace instructing him to stop seeing the Princess of Wales. With journalists hunting him down like a pack of ravenous wolves, he went into hiding.

Having learned her lesson with Dunne, Diana was far more discreet with her next lover, David Waterhouse. A distant cousin of hers, Waterhouse was tall, dark, and handsome, and a grandson of the duke of Marlborough. He never spoke about the relationship, and little is known about it.

In the summer of 1989 Diana reconnected with a man she had flirted with as a teenager, car dealer James Gilbey, tall, handsome, and muscular. Diana visited him in his apartment building while members of the press waited in the street counting the hours until she reappeared. With time she became reckless. One morning the police stopped her for speeding at 6:45 A.M. coming back to the palace from Gilbey's apartment. Trying to keep a straight face, the palace spokesperson asserted that the princess had, in fact, been going for an early morning swim. When the story broke, a red-faced Gilbey claimed they had been playing bridge, just the two of them—but bridge requires at least three players. Unwisely, Diana had phone sex with Gilbey on a cell phone call in December of that year in which he called her Squidgey, and Diana, who had stopped sleeping with her husband, admitted her fear of getting pregnant.

The tabloid the *Sun* was given a copy of the cell phone recording, and a reporter accosted Gilbey about his voice being on it. He blanched and started to shake, confirming the reporter's suspicions. When Gilbey told Diana, she dumped him as too hot to handle for her public image. The tabloid kept the recording in a safe for three years before releasing it. When it was released in

August 1992, the newspaper carefully edited out segments of the conversation in which the lovers apparently had phone sex.

As embarrassed as Diana was about the recording, she was delighted when, in January 1993, an equally damning recording of a cell phone conversation between Charles and Camilla was released. In the recording the Prince of Wales expressed the desire to be reincarnated in his next life as Camilla's tampon. Surely that was worse than phone sex and made the Squidgey tapes look positively boring in comparison.

Serving in the Gulf War in 1991, James Hewitt received Diana's impassioned letters accompanied by presents. But an old girlfriend of Hewitt's, jealous of his passion for Diana, contacted the press. Newspaper reporters swooped down like vultures on the Princess of Wales for sending the army captain gifts and steamy missives.

An adulterous love affair, like mold, grows in dark and humid places. Confronted with fresh air and the clear light of day, it often shrinks back into nothingness. Hewitt's affair with Diana was over. He was drummed out of the army for having failed his exams by 1 percent, and, worst of all, invitations to parties stopped coming. When Hewitt's story *Princess in Love* was published in 1994, he became public enemy number one in Britain, the quintessential cad. To kiss was fine, but to kiss and tell was unforgivable. "Sometimes it seems that serial killers get a better press," he lamented, as he pocketed hundreds of thousands of dollars for his titillating revelations.[15]

When Hewitt's book first came out in 1994, Diana denied their love affair. But by then she was having her own problems with the press. In 1992, the same year she and Prince Charles officially separated, she began seeing married Islamic art dealer Oliver Hoare. The affair sometimes raced, sometimes limped, until 1994. At the start of her affair with Hoare, Diana dispensed with her personal protection—a move that certainly contributed to her accidental death in 1997—in order to enjoy her romantic adventures unencumbered by detectives watching her every move.

At forty-seven Hoare was Diana's type—handsome with melting dark eyes, flirtatious, and suave. She often had sex with Hoare at the home of her best friend, Lucia Flecha de Lima, wife of the Brazilian ambassador to the United Kingdom, and at the home of restaurateur Mara Berni. Sometimes she smuggled him into the Kensington Palace compound hidden in the trunk of her car. Diana would park in the courtyard next to her own, which happened to be owned by Queen Elizabeth's sister, Princess Margaret; there Hoare would climb out of the trunk and sneak into the rear entrance of Diana's apartment. Peering through the lace curtains of her drawing room, Princess Margaret was not amused.

Hoare's chauffeur reported that Diana would call Hoare up to twenty times a day while he was driving around London. "If she only called five or six times, we thought of it as a quiet day," the chauffeur reported. "The sheer number of calls she made used to get Mr. Hoare down. Whenever his wife was in the car, he'd carefully pull the plug out just a fraction to break the connection."[16] Unable to reach him, Diana would become frantic and start calling him at his home.

Anonymous telephone calls began in September 1992 and continued until October 1993, when Hoare's wife, Diane, asked the police to trace the calls. In January 1994 the police tracked the anonymous phone calls to Kensington Palace and Diana's cell phone.

According to the police report, "Mr. Hoare believes that the calls are being made by Princess Diana."[17] Hoare followed the police advice and, next time a call came, called Diana by name. She began to cry and said, "Yes, I'm so sorry, so sorry. I don't know what came over me."[18] But a few days later the calls started again, this time traced to phone booths in the vicinity of Kensington Palace. Still, he did not dump his possessive lover. In March 1994 a photographer caught them driving into Kensington Palace. By August 1994 the January police report leaked to the press, who had a field day.

Diana's obsession with Hoare did not preclude other lovers. She started working out regularly at the Harbour Club where her objective was not only keeping her body toned and trim. "She was definitely on the lookout for men . . . ," said a former palace adviser. "The fact that they were in shorts and vests left little to the imagination. If she saw someone she liked, she'd go right up to him, introduce herself, and ask him when he was going to ask her for coffee. She met many, many men there and had several flings. Believe me, Diana had more men than anyone will ever be able to figure out."[19] One of her Harbour Club conquests was Christopher Whalley, a tall, muscular property developer she saw for several years until shortly before her death in 1997.

In 1994 Diana met American billionaire businessman Teddy Forstmann, who flew her to the United States to wine and dine her and play tennis. Forstmann remained a friend of Diana's until her death, though details of the relationship are unclear.

Another of her conquests was Will Carling, captain of the English rugby team. Carling was easygoing, confident, and athletic. He was also very married. Tabloids reported that the princess was enjoying secret trysts with Carling at Kensington Palace. Speaking to the press, Julia Carling insisted that her marriage was strong "however much someone is trying to destroy what you have. This has happened to [Diana] before, and you hope she won't do these things again, but she obviously does."[20]

Carling promised his wife never to see Diana again. "If I had a sexual relationship with her," he remarked, "I wouldn't say I had."[21] Considering that the press had countless photographs of Carling entering and leaving Kensington Palace for late-night visits with Diana, he didn't have to say a word. "She struck me as an incredibly lonely person," he later said.[22]

The press tore Diana to shreds for having an affair with yet another married man. "Is Will Carling merely another trophy for a bored, manipulative and selfish princess?" asked *Today*. The *Sun* called her a home wrecker. The *Daily Express* asked, "Is no marriage and no man safe from the wife of the heir to the throne?"[23] Soon after the unfavorable coverage, Diana dumped Carling. She had not been in love with him and felt she was paying a high price for merely having a bit of fun. "Why can't they leave me alone?" she wailed, the innocent victim of an evil press.[24]

Why so many affairs? Diana's fitness counselor, Carolan

Brown, explained, "She was the sort of person who didn't like being out of a relationship. She didn't like being on her own because she needed constant reassurance that she was loved. That was her ultimate dream—to find the perfect husband. Have more children and settle down. She was looking for the right man."[25]

Diana's public adventure with telephone harassment resulted in even greater rumblings about her precarious mental state. "Friends, on my husband's side, were indicating that I was again unstable, sick, and should be put in a home of some sort," she said.[26] *Sun* photographer Ken Lennox agreed: "The courtiers were saying she was a mad woman, they were putting out stories at dinner parties that she was a mad woman."[27]

To vindicate herself in the eyes of the world, to present herself as a sane woman victimized by a cruel palace, in 1992 Diana authorized Andrew Morton to write a book about her travails. *Diana, Her True Story* was supposedly the product of interviews with Diana's friends who spoke with the author about the princess's atrocious treatment by the royal family. In fact, Diana herself delivered audiotapes to Morton, tapes which surfaced after her death.

In November 1995, bolder than ever, Diana agreed to a television interview with journalist Martin Bashir. She intended to vilify Charles and Camilla in the public eye and draw admiration from the public for her silent suffering. The press lambasted her performance, but according to surveys, Diana achieved her goal of winning public sympathy among her audience of fifteen million Britons, and tens of millions of viewers around the world. Treated so despicably by her philandering husband, Diana was forgiven for her love affair with James Hewitt.

But soon after the interview aired, Diana visited Argentina and was met by headlines such as "The adulteress Di arrives on a mission of charity" and "Ladies look after your husbands: the seducer Lady Di Arrives Today."[28]

After finally obtaining a divorce from Charles in August 1996, Diana remained in the headlines more than ever. She fell in love with Hasnat Khan, a Pakistani heart surgeon devoted to his work. Khan was not her usual type. Highly intelligent but somewhat rumpled, he was no tall, dark, and scintillating swain to sweep the glamorous Diana off her feet. Moreover, he hated publicity.

Costumed as a Pakistani woman in a traditional ankle-length dress over flowing trousers, a silken shawl covering her hair, Diana visited Pakistan. She helped publicize Khan's hospital and watched him perform open heart surgery. Yet the saintly martyr, who had so often had herself photographed oozing compassion by the side of a dying person, took to berating Khan for spending too much time operating on sick patients at his hospital and not enough time with her. When visiting her in Kensington Palace, Khan would sometimes call his family in Pakistan. After several minutes, Diana, impatient and aching to be the focus of his attention, would distract him by turning up her music or dancing in front of him.

Trying to force Khan's hand, Diana leaked stories about their romance to the press in November 1996. The surgeon was livid. Moreover, the same problems kept cropping up that she had had with her husband and her many lovers. Khan refused to be at the princess's beck and call twenty-four hours a day. "He saves so many lives," Diana moaned to a friend. "He makes such a difference in people's lives. It's wonderful. But he has so little time for me. It's become a problem. We're always arguing over it. He puts his work before me. If he really loved me, he'd put me first."[29]

Khan, unable to take many things about Diana, broke up with her in June 1997. The princess, once again rejected and abandoned, was devastated. She had been willing to convert to Islam and move to Pakistan to marry him. "No one wants me," she opined to a former adviser. "I come with too much baggage. Why can't I find a nice guy who loves me and wants me to love him?"[30]

But within days of losing Hasnat Khan, Diana finally found a man who *could* devote twenty-four hours a day to making her feel loved, another Muslim who would help her embarrass the stodgy Church of England royal family. A man with no job, a playboy living the life of a prince. He had much in common with Diana. Both suffered from borderline personality disorder—they teetered precariously on the edge of life even as their periodic brilliance won them the admiration of many. Both were narcissistic, volatile, and self-destructive. The name of her new lover was Dodi Fayed.

A friend of Diana's in London recalled, "I didn't think he was good-looking. But he was nicely dressed, wore lovely cashmere, nice shoes, very soigné. And he smelt nice. He loved to laugh."[31] At five foot nine, Dodi was two inches shorter than Diana and at forty-one, five years older. Charming, fun-loving Dodi was a spoiled boy who had never grown up and felt no shame at accepting a $100,000-a-month allowance from his aging father. As insecure as Diana, Dodi was outrageously generous to friends and girlfriends and went out of his way to impress, often substantially overspending his $100,000 monthly allowance. His distraught father sometimes refused to pay the balances, leaving Dodi to be sued by American Express for $106,000. But despite his generosity, Dodi couldn't keep a girlfriend for very long; he was always looking for a woman who was prettier or more famous than his current one. Diana, Princess of Wales, was the big fish. For no other woman on earth combined her beauty and fame.

When he met Diana, Dodi was engaged to a model named Kelly Fisher. After flirting with Diana on his father's yacht in July 1997, he would sneak off and make love to his fiancée, who was waiting for him on another yacht, according to Fisher, who at the time had no idea he was coming fresh from the embraces of Princess Diana. When journalists got wind of Diana's latest love affair, they were flabbergasted by her choice. On August 18 one paper wrote that Dodi was "so cynical, shallow and spoilt you feel nostalgic for James Hewitt."[32]

With regards to Diana's dating Dodi, Charles told a reporter, "I'm happy if she's happy."[33]

But Diana was not happy. No amount of food, or sex, or fame, or shopping could ever fill the gaping wound in her psyche for very long. A good friend of Diana's who spoke with her the day she died came away from the conversation with the distinct impression Diana was eager to dump Dodi, even as he was eager to propose.

It was not only with her lovers that Diana had problems.

Throughout the 1990s Diana grew increasingly suspicious of her friends and staff to the point of paranoia. She dropped most of her friends one by one, believing they had leaked stories about her to the press or had somehow profited from her friendship. She never confronted them about her suspicions and simply refused ever to talk to them again. Many women expressed shock that their good friend Princess Diana had cut them dead with no explanation.

Palace employees soon learned that working for Diana involved looking into a pair of smiling blue eyes and feeling a stiletto sink into their backs. According to her private secretary of eight years, Patrick Jephson, Diana was vindictive, paranoid, manipulative, and cruel. She often threw important memos in the trash and claimed she had never seen them. Her staff soon learned to make copies of all memos, noting down the date and time they were placed on her desk. She frequently took sudden irrational dislikes to loyal employees and refused to speak to them until they quit in frustration.

By early 1996 she was sending macabre messages to her employees' pagers, messages claiming knowledge of their disloyalty to her and of their supposed extramarital love affairs. When accused of sending the messages, the princess denied it vehemently, her blue eyes wide and innocent. Buckingham Palace, acutely aware of Diana's nasty tricks on her employees, often smoothed the path for them to find other positions by giving them glowing recommendations.

If Diana became increasingly unhinged over time, it was not because she suffered all the tribulations of earlier crown princesses; we could hardly call her alone and impoverished at a foreign court. Living in her native land, surrounded by friends and family, in close and loving contact with her children, Diana received a truly royal allowance and wallowed in luxury. Yet she suffered one ancient lament of many princess brides—her husband didn't love her, hadn't wanted to marry her, rarely slept with her, and far preferred his mistress.

In her own way, Diana was heroic, even in her self-imposed victimhood. Suffering inconceivable emotional pain, Diana did not meekly go to bed and pull the covers over her head. Bristling at perceived injustice, the awkward girl who couldn't graduate from high school rolled up her sleeves and took on formidable enemies: the royal family, the Buckingham Palace "firm," the detested Camilla, even the entire British press when they weren't cooperating with her efforts to increase her popularity or vilify her enemies. She was defiant; at all costs she would fight for what she believed to be right. On one occasion Katharine Graham, publisher of the *Washington Post,* asked Diana if she gambled. "Not with cards," came the reply, "but with life."[34]

Throughout her life, the world held a strange fascination for Diana's body: her virginity, her pregnancies, her sexuality, her bulimia, the clothes draped on her tanned, well-toned flesh. In a Paris tunnel on August 31, 1997, that body lay inert and bleeding next to the mangled corpse of Dodi Fayed, still the object of global fascination as photographers snapped away at it. She had gambled with life, and with men, and lost.

CONCLUSION
THE POLITICS OF ADULTERY

Titles are shadows and crowns are empty things.

—DANIEL DEFOE

❋

FOR NEARLY NINE HUNDRED YEARS—FROM THE DAY QUEEN
Urraca of Castile and Leon first rode into battle beside her lover
Pedro Gonzalez until the last ride of Diana and Dodi—the fates
of adulterous royal women have been as diverse as the women
themselves. The common themes among these women were unhappy marriages and empty lives. Indeed, the seeds of a queen's
adultery were sown in negotiations for her marriage to a man
unsuited in temperament and education.

"No hour of the day passes when I do not desire your death
and wish that you were hanged . . . ," the spirited Marguerite-
Louise of France wrote to her husband, the somber and melancholy grand duke Cosimo de Medici in 1680.[1]

"How fortunate you are, to marry where you wish!" sighed

Queen Caroline Matilda of Denmark, married to a stark raving imbecile, to her ladies-in-waiting in 1771. "If I were a widow, I would marry him I loved, and give up my throne and my country."[2]

"From the very threshold of your Majesty's mansion the mother of your child was pursued by spies, conspirators, and traitors . . . ," wrote Queen Caroline of Britain to her husband George IV in 1820. "You have pursued me with hatred and scorn, and with all the means of destruction. You wrested me from my child. . . . You sent me sorrowing through the world, and even in my sorrows pursued me with unrelenting persecution."[3]

Sick to death of her husband, when a queen took a lover, anything could happen—from disgrace and death to political triumph. The crucial factor was the political significance of her love affair. Liaisons that benefited the state were not only tolerated, but approved. When Queen Maria Francisca of Portugal began an affair with her brother-in-law, courtiers applauded. Their relationship allowed power factions to trade the insane and impotent King Alfonso, who had deprived them of their rights and property and dishonored the throne, for his brother Pedro, who restored everything that had been lost, including the polish to the Portuguese crown. Moreover, by keeping the bride and merely swapping the husbands, Portugal retained the treaties and dowry that Maria Francisca had brought from France. An accusation of adultery would never be made when the adultery offered so many financial and political benefits.

With her politically brilliant lover at her side, Queen Marie of Romania guided her country through a world war and the threat of Communist revolution. As ancient European thrones toppled around her like dominoes, Marie's throne stood firm. Romania's powerful elite, proud of their queen, gave her solid support. The fact that three of her five royal children were fathered by lovers, and not the king, mattered little in the face of the rich rewards she provided the nation.

Catherine the Great made Russia a world power, equal to France and Britain. The economy boomed; the rich got richer;

the poor were given free farmland in new southern territories. Catherine's people might snicker about her young lovers, but no one suggested shoving her off the throne for her lascivious immorality. Life under her rule was just too good.

But liaisons that threatened the state were swiftly and brutally punished. When Sophia Dorothea, crown princess of Hanover, began her love affair with Count Philip von Königsmark in 1690, everyone at court knew about it, including her husband, the crown prince, and his powerful father, the elector. But it wasn't until four years later when the princess planned to elope with the count and take her inheritance rights with her—threatening the power and wealth of Hanover—that she was disgraced, divorced, and imprisoned, and the count murdered. Had she remained, on the surface at least, a staunch supporter of the Hanoverian power structure, she may have been allowed to continue her love affair unhindered for years.

Many a queen was disgraced not because she threatened the state itself, but because she stood in the way of rival power factions at court jockeying for position. Seething with discontent, greedy courtiers aimed to topple the queen and all her supporters, and then grab the plum positions for themselves. Henry VIII's queens Anne Boleyn and Catherine Howard, and Caroline Matilda of Denmark, were victims, not of their own uncontrollable sexual desires, but of the ambitions of vicious courtiers.

Oddly, the innocent Anne Boleyn was beheaded for adultery by her powerful enemies while the guilty Caroline of Brunswick was legally cleared by her powerful friends. At European courts, it was the political machinations—not the sex—that caused a royal woman's downfall.

THE ENVY OF SPLENDOR

Royals, whether venerated or denigrated, are cut from the same bolt of human fabric as their subjects. Yet the grandeur of a palace serves to exaggerate the stories that take place inside its walls. Gilded magnificence lifts joy to greater heights; mocked by surrounding splendor, pain sinks to lower depths. Certainly, royal triumphs and sorrows are more visible than those of ordi-nary people. As Elizabeth I said, "We princes, I tell you, are set on stages in sight and view of all the world."[4]

Some of those stages were scaffolds, the ultimate manifesta-tion of palace politics gone awry. "Good Christian people, I am come here not to preach a sermon but to die," said Anne Boleyn on an unbearably sweet May morning. Six years later her cousin Catherine Howard, having practiced laying her neck on the block the night before, did so on the scaffold with admirable grace. And on the way to her execution, Marie Antoinette cried, "It is to live that requires courage, not to die."[5]

The tragic saga of nine hundred years of queenly adultery is punctuated here and there with comedy. Queen Juana of Spain, having endured artificial insemination with a golden turkey baster containing drops of her impotent husband's sperm, un-locks the bedroom door for her handsome lover. Queen Maria Carolina of Naples pulls on her long white gloves to enthrall her husband and make him forget her lovers. Caroline of Brunswick jolts about Europe in a carriage with her lover Bartolomeo Pergami, sound asleep, their hands resting lovingly on each other's private parts.

Whether a royal woman denied herself the pleasures of illicit love, or grasped them with outstretched arms, it is safe to say that most remained unhappy despite all the pomp and grandeur of their lives.

"The *éclat* and renown of great kings are like the machines at the opera," wrote Elizabeth Charlotte in 1701. "Seen from afar, nothing is grander and more beautiful, but if one goes backstage and takes a close look at all the ropes and wooden slats that make the machines move, they are often most ungainly and ugly."[6]

Looking around Versailles Palace in 1705, she wrote, "All of this is supposed to be fun, and yet one does not see anyone hav-ing fun and senses that there is more spite than pleasure."[7]

Dying of uterine cancer in 1837, Hortense de Beauharnais, former queen of the Netherlands, looked back on her life of magnificence and misery. "I have done right whenever I could, and I hope that God will be good to me," she sighed. "They say He is good, and yet"—she paused, summing up the single greatest theological problem of all time with great simplicity—"He lets us suffer so."[8]

Seated in her splendid Kensington Palace drawing room in 1992, Princess Diana reminisced about a day when she thought of fleeing the fame and luxury of her position. "I was quite ready to give all this up," she said.[9]

Even the most powerful woman of her time, Elizabeth I of England, told Parliament in 1601 after forty-three years as queen that "to wear a Crown is a thing more glorious to them that see it, than it is pleasant to them that bear it. . . . The cares and trouble of a Crown I cannot resemble more fitly than to . . . bitter pills gilded over, by which they are made more acceptable and less offensive, which indeed are bitter and unpleasant to take."[10]

Of all royal women, perhaps Josephine Bonaparte best summed up the emptiness of splendor. The forty-four-year-old empress was divorced by Napoleon in 1809 for infertility and replaced by an eighteen-year-old Austrian princess who gave him a healthy bouncing boy within a year.

At her estate of Malmaison outside Paris, the cast-off wife liked to bring out her astonishing collection of jewels for visiting ladies to admire. Her visitors gasped in wonder at the gems—fat lustrous baroque pearls, dazzling diamonds, exquisitely faceted rubies, sapphires, and emeralds. But Josephine insisted that jewels had little value "when you reflect how unhappy I have been, although with such a rare collection at my command. At the beginning of my extraordinary life I delighted in these trifles. . . . I grew by degrees so tired of them that I no longer wear any except when I am in some respects compelled to do so by my rank in the world. A thousand accidents may contribute to deprive me of these brilliant though useless objects. Do I not possess the pendants of Queen Marie Antoinette? And yet am I quite sure of retaining them?"

Looking at her sparkling gems, the empress sighed and said, "Believe me, ladies, do not envy a splendor that does not constitute happiness."[11]

NOTES

INTRODUCTION

1. Andrews, p. 161.
2. D'Auvergne, p. 224.
3. Troyat, *Peter,* p. 193.
4. Levin, p. 45.
5. Ibid.
6. Given-Wilson and Curteis, p. 20.
7. D'Auvergne, p. 87.
8. De Grazia, p. 140.
9. Acton, p. 656.

CHAPTER ONE: LIFE BEHIND PALACE WALLS

1. Maroger, p. 125.
2. Alexander, p. 44.
3. Forster, p. 146.
4. Ibid., p. 167.
5. Ibid., p. 170.
6. Cohen and Major, p. 463.
7. Forster, p. 246.
8. Sutherland, p. 137.
9. Rosenthal, p. 260.
10. Pevitt, p. 16.
11. Baily, p. 242.
12. Forster, p. xviii.
13. Ibid., p. xxiii.
14. Ibid., p. 80.
15. Acton, p. 134.
16. Ibid., pp. 144–145.
17. Louisa of Tuscany, pp. 73–74.
18. Pakula, pp. 68–69.
19. Bingham, vol. I, p. 325.
20. Farr, p. 56.
21. Ibid., p. 110.
22. Ibid., p. 125.
23. *Memoirs of the Courts of Sweden and Denmark,* vol. I, p. 321.
24. Ibid., p. 85.
25. Asprey, p. 87.

26. Ibid., p. 95.
27. Quinlan, p. 16.
28. Forster, p. 65.
29. Ibid., p. 78.
30. Ibid., p. 75.
31. Ibid., p. xxiii.
32. Battifol, p. 74.
33. Quinlan, p. 15.
34. Freer, vol. II, p. 39.

35. Ibid., p. 69.
36. Ibid., p. 125.
37. Forster, p. 90.
38. Ibid., p. III.
39. Ibid., p. 103.
40. Ibid., p. 7.
41. Ibid., p. 41.
42. Moote, p. 291.

CHAPTER TWO: THE QUEEN TAKES A LOVER

1. Bergamini, p. 102.
2. Chastenet, p. 18.
3. Acton, p. 690.
4. Weiner, p. 128.
5. Levin, p. 80.
6. Iremonger, pp. 204–205.
7. Ibid., p. 200.

8. Ibid., p. 192.
9. Williams, pp. 378–379.
10. Weiner, p. 167.
11. Hewitt, p. 157.
12. Cronin, *Louis XIV*, p. 82.
13. Ibid., p. 114.
14. Alexander, p. 215.
15. McKay, p. 105.

CHAPTER THREE: MEDIEVAL QUEENS, TUDOR VICTIMS

1. Kelly, p. 27.
2. Ibid., p. 77.
3. Weir, *Eleanor*, p. 65.
4. Kelly, p. 60.
5. Weir, *Eleanor*, p. 67.
6. Doherty, p. 25.
7. Ibid., pp. 82–83.
8. Ibid., p. 113.
9. Cohen and Major, p. 245.
10. Miller, p. 28.
11. Ibid., p. 66.

12. Ibid., p. 67.
13. Ibid., p. 87.
14. Liss, p. 68.
15. Ives, pp. 57–58.
16. Warnicke, p. 58.
17. Somerset, p. 132.
18. Weir, *Court*, p. 333.
19. Ives, p. 392.
20. Ibid.
21. Ibid.
22. Ibid., p. 387.
23. Ibid.

24. Ibid., p. 410.
25. Ibid.
26. Ibid., p. 411.
27. Lacey Baldwin Smith,
    p. 103.
28. Starkey, p. 669.
29. Ibid.
30. Lacey Baldwin Smith,
    p. 58.
31. Ibid., p. 59.
32. Ibid.
33. Ibid.
34. Ibid.
35. Acworth, p. 8.
36. Weir, *Henry VIII,* p. 403.
37. Lacey Baldwin Smith,
    p. 118.
38. Ibid., p. 122.
39. Ibid., p. 125.
40. Ibid., p. 146.
41. Ibid., p. 147.
42. Ibid., p. 148.
43. Acworth, p. 20.
44. Weir, *Court,* p. 449.
45. Lacey Baldwin Smith,
    pp. 168–169.

46. Acworth, p. 21.
47. Lacey Baldwin Smith,
    p. 158.
48. Ibid., p. 180.
49. Ibid., pp. 181–182.
50. Ibid., p. 182.
51. Weir, *Court,*
    pp. 445–446.
52. Starkey, p. 672.
53. Lacey Baldwin Smith,
    p. 183.
54. Ibid., p. 184.
55. Ibid.
56. Ibid., p. 185.
57. Ibid., p. 189.
58. Acworth, p. 40.
59. Lacey Baldwin Smith,
    p. 167.
60. Ibid., p. 190.
61. Ibid., p. 199.
62. Ibid., p. 142.
63. Ibid.
64. Ibid., p. 198.
65. Ibid., p. 202.
66. Acworth, p. 43.

CHAPTER FOUR: THE SEVENTEENTH CENTURY:
ESCAPE FROM THE GILDED CAGE

1. Gribble, *Portugal,* p. 66.
2. Ibid., p. 67.
3. Ibid., p. 68.
4. Ibid., pp. 66–67.
5. Rodocanachi, p. 87.
6. Ibid., p. III.

7. Ibid., p. 90.
8. Cardini, p. 92.
9. Wilkins, *Uncrowned Queen,*
    vol. I, p. 31.
10. Ibid., p. 37.
11. Ibid., p. 82.

12. Morand, p. 23.
13. Ibid., p. 62.
14. Ibid., p. 119.
15. Ibid.
16. Ibid., p. 82.
17. Ibid., p. 98.
18. Wilkins, *Uncrowned Queen,*
    vol. II, p. 470.
19. Ibid., p. 413.
20. Morand, pp. 89–90.
21. Wilkins, *Uncrowned Queen,*
    vol. I, p. 235.
22. Ibid., vol. II,
    pp. 359–360.
23. Morand, p. 113.
24. Wilkins, *Uncrowned Queen,*
    vol. I, p. 310.
25. Ibid., p. 215.
26. Morand, p. 81.
27. Wilkins, *Uncrowned Queen,*
    vol. I, p. 258.
28. Ibid., pp. 274–275.
29. Ibid., p. 260.

30. Ibid., vol. II, p. 409.
31. Morand, p. 106.
32. Ibid., p. 140.
33. Ibid., p. 156.
34. Wilkins, *Uncrowned Queen,*
    vol. I, p. 282.
35. Morand, p. 172.
36. Ibid., p. 173.
37. Wilkins, *Uncrowned Queen,*
    vol. II, p. 534.
38. Morand, p. 176.
39. Colburn, vol. I,
    p. 259.
40. Wilkins, *Uncrowned Queen,*
    vol. II, p. 540.
41. Ibid., vol. I, p. 294.
42. Morand, p. 76.
43. Ibid., p. 77.
44. Ibid., p. 233.
45. Ibid., p. 256.
46. Wilkins, *Uncrowned Queen,*
    vol. I, p. 278.

CHAPTER FIVE: EIGHTEENTH-CENTURY RUSSIA:
THE UNCHASTE EMPRESSES

1. Troyat, *Catherine,* p. 63.
2. Troyat, *Peter,* p. 255.
3. Longworth, p. 25.
4. Ibid., p. 52.
5. Ibid., p. 58.
6. Ibid., pp. 58–59.
7. Troyat, *Peter,*
   pp. 321–322.
8. Longworth, p. 59.

9. Troyat, *Peter,* p. 322.
10. Longworth, p. 158.
11. Ibid., p. 159.
12. Ibid., p. 162.
13. Ibid., p. 169.
14. Ibid., p. 182.
15. Ibid., p. 191.
16. Haslip, p. 26.
17. Troyat, *Catherine,* p. 67.

18. Erickson, *Catherine*, p. 68.
19. Haslip, p. 46.
20. Alexander, p. 21.
21. Troyat, *Catherine*, p. 69.
22. Alexander, p. 46.
23. Haslip, p. 70.
24. Ibid., p. 71.
25. Maroger, p. 199.
26. Haslip, p. 83.
27. Ibid., p. 99.
28. Ibid., p. 96.
29. Maroger, p. 246.
30. Rice, p. 207.
31. Troyat, *Catherine*, p. 136.
32. Haslip, p. 115.
33. Ibid., pp. 228–229.
34. Alexander, p. 11.
35. Maroger, p. 112.
36. Erickson, *Catherine*, pp. 236–237.
37. Maroger, p. xv.
38. Troyat, *Catherine*, p. 181.
39. Montefiore, p. 28.
40. Ibid., p. 57.
41. Ibid., p. 37.
42. Haslip, p. 176.
43. Troyat, *Catherine*, p. 170.
44. Haslip, p. 201.
45. Troyat, *Catherine*, p. 248.
46. Erickson, *Catherine*, pp. 301–302.
47. Alexander, p. 137.
48. Haslip, p. 217.
49. Ibid., pp. 225–226.
50. Ibid., p. 226.
51. Troyat, *Catherine*, p. 252.
52. Haslip, p. 233.
53. Montefiore, p. 116, note.
54. Haslip, p. 237.
55. Ibid., p. 245.
56. Alexander, p. 140.
57. Haslip, p. 239.
58. Montefiore, p. 3.
59. Troyat, *Catherine*, p. 253.
60. Haslip, p. 244.
61. Troyat, *Catherine*, pp. 191–192.
62. *Montefiore*, p. 391.
63. Ibid., p. 390.
64. Ibid., p. 355, note.
65. Ibid., p. 340.
66. Alexander, p. 207.
67. Montefiore, p. 166.
68. Ibid., p. 168.
69. Troyat, *Catherine*, p. 258.
70. Montefiore, p. 182.
71. Haslip, p. 259.
72. Ibid., p. 263.
73. Troyat, *Catherine*, p. 274.
74. Ibid., p. 291.
75. Montefiore, p. 314.
76. Ibid., p. 180.
77. Haslip, p. 300.
78. Ibid., p. 301.
79. Ibid., p. 310.
80. Ibid., p. 320.
81. Montefiore, p. 367.
82. Erickson, *Catherine*, p. 361.
83. Ibid.
84. Montefiore, p. 445.
85. Haslip, p. 332.
86. Alexander, p. 221.
87. Ibid., p. 223.

88. Haslip, p. 353.
89. Troyat, *Catherine*, p. 351.
90. Ibid.
91. Erickson, *Catherine*, p. 373.
92. Cronin, *Catherine*, p. 276.
93. Montefiore, p. 470.
94. Haslip, p. 356.
95. Montefiore, p. 8.
96. Haslip, p. 356.
97. Montefiore, p. 488.
98. Ibid., p. 478.
99. Troyat, *Catherine*, p. 362.
100. Haslip, p. 363.
101. Troyat, *Catherine*, p. 394.
102. Ibid., p. 399.
103. Maroger, p. x.
104. Montefiore, p. 61.
105. *Memoirs of the Courts of Denmark and Sweden*, vol. II, p. 96.
106. Troyat, *Catherine*, p. 165.

CHAPTER SIX: EIGHTEENTH-CENTURY EUROPE:
POWER, PASSION, AND POLITICS

1. Gribble, *Isabella*, p. 3.
2. Chastenet, p. 22.
3. Bergamini, p. 107.
4. Ibid.
5. Ibid., p. 108.
6. Acton, p. 432.
7. Ibid., p. 188.
8. Ibid., p. 564.
9. Coryn, p. 80.
10. Farr, p. 16.
11. Coryn, p. 53.
12. Ibid., footnote.
13. Farr, p. 41.
14. Ibid., pp. 41–42.
15. Ibid., p. 42.
16. Coryn, p. 64.
17. Farr, p. 62.
18. Coryn, p. 65.
19. Farr, p. 65.
20. Ibid., p. 68.
21. Coryn, p. 90.
22. Farr, p. 83.
23. Ibid., p. 93.
24. Ibid., p. 94.
25. Ibid., p. 123.
26. Ibid., p. 127.
27. Ibid., p. 142.
28. Ibid.
29. Coryn, p. 184.
30. Ibid., p. 185.
31. Farr, p. 157.
32. Ibid., p. 167.
33. Ibid., p. 166.
34. Ibid., p. 169.
35. Coryn, p. 306.
36. Ibid., p. 47.
37. Farr, p. 179.
38. Coryn, p. 238.
39. Farr, p. 196.
40. Ibid., p. 204.
41. Ibid.
42. Coryn, p. 268.

43. Farr, p. 208.
44. Ibid., p. 210.
45. Ibid., p. 219.
46. Coryn, p. 288.
47. Farr, p. 217.
48. Ibid., p. 220.
49. Ibid., p. 221.
50. Ibid.
51. Coryn, p. 300.
52. Farr, p. 221.
53. Ibid., p. 222.
54. Ibid., p. 223.
55. Ibid., p. 227.
56. Ibid.
57. Ibid., p. 231.
58. Coryn, p. 31.
59. Farr, p. 42.
60. Chapman, p. 125.
61. Ibid., p. 35.
62. Wilkins, *A Queen of Tears,* vol. I, p. 81.
63. Ibid.
64. Chapman, p. 48.
65. Ibid., p. 54.
66. *Memoirs of the Courts of Denmark and Sweden,* vol. I, p. 118.
67. Chapman, p. 54.
68. Wilkins, *A Queen of Tears,* vol. I, p. 198.
69. Chapman, p. 81.
70. Ibid., pp. 89–90.
71. Ibid., p. 90.
72. Ibid., p. 97.
73. Wilkins, *A Queen of Tears,* vol. I, pp. 340–341.
74. Chapman, p. 102.
75. Ibid., p. 114.
76. Wilkins, *A Queen of Tears,* vol. I, p. 332.
77. Chapman, p. 120.
78. Ibid., p. 125.
79. Ibid., p. 135.
80. Ibid., p. 137.
81. Ibid., p. 139.
82. Ibid., p. 140.
83. Wilkins, *A Queen of Tears,* vol. II, p. 130.
84. Ibid., p. 115.
85. Chapman, p. 147.
86. Ibid.
87. Ibid., p. 148.
88. Ibid., p. 150.
89. Ibid., p. 155.
90. Wilkins, *A Queen of Tears,* vol. II, p. 270.
91. Chapman, p. 169.
92. Ibid.
93. Ibid., p. 174.
94. Morand, p. 206.
95. Chapman, p. 206.

1. Epton, p. 45.
2. Erickson, *Josephine*, p. 158.
3. Weiner, p. 49.
4. Fraser, p. 52.
5. Ibid., p. 47.
6. Ibid., p. 48.
7. Ibid., p. 54.
8. Ibid.
9. Leslie, p. 101.
10. Fraser, p. 60.
11. Parissien, p. 77.
12. Fraser, p. 62.
13. Ibid., p. 87.
14. Ibid., p. 90.
15. Ibid., p. 156.
16. Ibid., p. 171.
17. Ibid., p. 186.
18. Ibid., p. 162.
19. Ibid., p. 259.
20. Ibid., p. 171.
21. Ibid., p. 203.
22. Ibid., p. 209.
23. Ibid., p. 251.
24. Ibid., p. 259.
25. Ibid., p. 273.
26. Ibid., p. 302.
27. Deans, p. 316.
28. Fraser, p. 423.
29. Deans, p. 353.
30. Ibid., p. 368.
31. Fraser, p. 380.
32. Deans, p. 368.
33. Ibid., p. 400.
34. Fraser, p. 404.
35. Ibid., p. 410.
36. Ibid., p. 446.
37. Ibid., p. 454.
38. Ibid., p. 7.
39. Ibid., p. 457.
40. Ibid., p. 459.
41. Ibid., p. 119.
42. Bergamini, p. 226.
43. Ibid., p. 229.
44. Gribble, *Isabella*, p. 210.
45. Aronson, p. 145.
46. Ibid.
47. Ibid., p. 147.
48. Hibbert, p. 325.
49. Ibid.
50. Aronson, p. 159.
51. Ibid., p. 159.
52. Hibbert, p. 321.
53. Ibid., p. 322.
54. Ibid., p. 441.

CHAPTER EIGHT: THE TURN OF THE TWENTIETH
CENTURY: STRUGGLE FOR EQUALITY

1. Louisa of Tuscany, p. 92.
2. Ibid., p. 162.
3. Ibid., p. 224.
4. Pakula, p. 60.
5. Ibid., p. 106.
6. Ibid., p. 107.
7. Ibid., p. 148.
8. Ibid., p. 149.
9. Quinlan, p. 23.
10. Pakula, p. 227.
11. Ibid., p. 321.
12. Ibid., p. 416.
13. Ibid.
14. Ibid., p. 420.
15. Moynahan, p. 62.
16. Ibid., p. 321.
17. Ibid., p. 64.
18. Ibid., p. 68.
19. Ibid., p. 311.
20. Ibid., p. 4.
21. Ibid., p. 133.
22. Ibid., p. 123.
23. Ibid., p. 108.
24. Ibid., p. 248.
25. Ibid., p. 87.
26. Ibid., p. 118.
27. Ibid., p. 104.
28. Ibid., p. 286.
29. Ibid., p. 157.
30. Ibid., p. 161.
31. Ibid., p. 3.
32. Ibid., p. 288.
33. Ibid., p. 167.
34. Ibid., p. 216.
35. Ibid., p. 337.

CHAPTER NINE: DIANA, PRINCESS OF MANY LOVERS

1. Morton, p. 196.
2. Hewitt, p. 5.
3. Morton, p. 28.
4. Beatrix Campbell, pp. 213–214.
5. Colin Campbell, p. 93.
6. Ibid., p. 125.
7. Ibid., p. 139.
8. Sally Bedell Smith, p. 161.
9. "Videotape Reveals Body- guard Affair," *The Age,* December 8, 2004.
10. Sally Bedell Smith, p. 162.
11. Colin Campbell, p. 143.
12. Pasternak, p. 44.
13. Ibid., p. 45.
14. Colin Campbell, p. 145.
15. Hewitt, p. vi.
16. Sally Bedell Smith, p. 258.
17. Ibid., p. 259.

18. Ibid.
19. Colin Campbell, p. 231.
20. Sally Bedell Smith, p. 282.
21. Ibid., p. 283.
22. Morton, p. 126.
23. Sally Bedell Smith, p. 283.
24. Colin Campbell, p. 220.
25. Morton, p. 124.
26. Beatrix Campbell, p. 214.

27. Ibid., p. 222.
28. Sally Bedell Smith, pp. 288–289.
29. Colin Campbell, p. 236.
30. Ibid., p. 237.
31. Sally Bedell Smith, p. 339.
32. Ibid., p. 352.
33. Spoto, p. 160.
34. Sally Bedell Smith, p. 367.

CONCLUSION: THE POLITICS OF ADULTERY

1. Cardini, p. 92.
2. Chapman, p. 125.
3. Fraser, p. 410.
4. Levin, p. 129.
5. Coryn, p. 300.
6. Forster, pp. 129–130.
7. Ibid., p. 160.

8. Wright, p. 398.
9. "Videotape Reveals Bodyguard Affair," *The Age*, December 8, 2004.
10. Marcus, p. 342.
11. Epton, p. 200.

BIBLIOGRAPHY

Acton, Harold. *The Bourbons of Naples.* London: Prion Books Limited, 1998.

Acworth, M. W. *The Unfaithful Queen.* London: St. Catherine Press, 1962.

Alexander, John T. *Catherine the Great: Life and Legend.* New York: Oxford University Press, 1989.

Andrews, Allen. *The Royal Whore: Barbara Villiers, Countess of Castlemaine.* Philadelphia, New York, London: Chilton Book Company, 1970.

Anonymous. *Relation des Troubles arrivez dans la cour de Portugal en l'année 1667 & en l'année 1668.* Amsterdam, 1674.

Aronson, Theo. *The Heart of a Queen: Queen Victoria's Romantic Attachments.* London: John Murray Ltd., 1991.

Asprey, Robert B. *Frederick the Great: The Magnificent Enigma.* New York: Ticknor & Fields, 1986.

Baily, F. E. *Sophia of Hanover and Her Times.* London: Hutchinson & Co., 1936.

Battifol, Louis. *Marie de Médicis and the French Court in the XVIIth Century.* New York: Charles Scribner's Sons, 1908.

Bergamini, John D. *The Spanish Bourbons: The History of a Tenacious Dynasty.* New York: G. P. Putnam's Sons, 1974.

Bingham, The Honorable Captain D. *The Marriages of the Bourbons.* 2 volumes. New York: Scribner and Welford, 1890.

Campbell, Beatrix. *Diana, Princess of Wales: How Sexual Politics Shook the Monarchy.* London: The Women's Press, 1988.

Campbell, Lady Colin. *The Real Diana.* New York: St. Martin's Press, 1998.

Cardini, Franco, ed. *The Medici Women.* Perugia: Gramma, 1996.

Chapman, Hester. *Caroline Matilda, Queen of Denmark.* New York: Coward, McCann & Geoghegan, Inc., 1972.

Chastenet, Jacques. *Godoy, Master of Spain 1792–1808.* London: Batchworth Press, 1953.

Cohen, M. J., and John Major. *History in Quotations: Reflecting 5000 Years of World History.* London: Cassell, 2004.

Coryn, M. *Marie-Antoinette and Axel de Fersen.* London: Thornton Butterworth Ltd., 1938.

Cronin, Vincent. *Catherine, Empress of All the Russias.* New York: William Morrow, 1978.

———. *Louis XIV.* London: Collins, 1964.

D'Auvergne, Edmund B. *Some Left-Handed Marriages, Misalliances, Irregular and Secret Unions of Royalty.* New York: J. H. Sears & Co., circa 1900.

Deans, R. Storry. *The Trials of Five Queens.* London: Methuen & Co., 1909.

De Grazia, Sebastian. *Machiavelli in Hell.* Princeton, NJ: Princeton University Press, 1990.

Doherty, Paul. *Isabella and the Strange Death of Edward II.* New York: Carroll & Graf Publishers, 2003.

Epton, Nina. *Josephine: The Empress and Her Children.* New York: W. W. Norton & Company, 1976.

Erickson, Carolly. *Great Catherine: The Life of Catherine the Great, Empress of Russia.* New York: St. Martin's Griffin, 1994.

———. *Josephine: A Life of the Empress.* New York: St. Martin's Press, 1998.

Farr, Evelyn. *The Untold Love Story: Marie Antoinette and Count Fersen.* London: Allison and Busby Ltd., 1997.

Forster, Elborg, trans. *A Woman's Life in the Court of the Sun King: Letters of Liselotte von der Pfalz, Elisabeth Charlotte, Duchesse d'Orléans, 1652–1722.* Baltimore: Johns Hopkins University Press, 1984.

Fraser, Flora. *The Unruly Queen: The Life of Queen Caroline.* Berkeley: University of California Press, 1997.

Freer, Martha Walker. *Elizabeth de Valois, Queen of Spain.* London: Hurst and Blackett, 1857.

Given-Wilson, Chris, and Alice Curteis. *The Royal Bastards of Medieval England.* London: Routledge & Kegan Paul, 1984.

Gribble, Francis. *The Royal House of Portugal*. Port Washington, NY, and London: Kennikat Press, 1970.

——. *The Tragedy of Isabella II*. Boston: Gorham Press, 1913.

Haslip, Joan. *Catherine the Great*. New York: G. P. Putnam's Sons, 1978.

Hauptstaatsarchiv Hannover. *Die Briefe von Kurprinzessin Sophia Dorothea von Hannover und Graf Philipp Christoph von Königsmark*.

Hewitt, James. *Love and War*. London: Blake Publishing, 1999.

Hibbert, Christopher. *Queen Victoria: A Personal History*. New York: Basic Books, 2000.

Iremonger, Lucille. *Love and the Princesses: The Strange Lives of Mad King George III and His Daughters*. London: Faber and Faber Ltd., 1958.

Ives, Eric W. *Anne Boleyn*. Oxford: Basil Blackwell, 1986.

Kelly, Amy. *Eleanor of Aquitaine and the Four Kings*. Cambridge: Harvard University Press, 1950.

Leslie, Anita. *Mrs. Fitzherbert*. New York: Charles Scribner's Sons, 1960.

Levin, Carole. *The Heart and Stomach of a King: Elizabeth I and the Politics of Sex and Power*. Philadelphia: University of Pennsylvania Press, 1994.

Liss, Peggy K. *Isabel the Queen: Life and Times*. New York: Oxford University Press, 1992.

Longworth, Philip. *The Three Empresses: Catherine I, Anne and Elizabeth of Russia*. New York: Holt, Rinehart & Winston, 1972.

Louisa of Tuscany, Ex–Crown Princess of Saxony. *My Own Story*. New York: G. P. Putnam's Sons, 1911.

Marcus, Leah S., Janel Mueller, and Mary Beth Rose, eds. *Elizabeth I: Collected Works*. Chicago and London: University of Chicago Press, 2000.

Maroger, Dominique, ed. *Memoirs of Catherine the Great*. New York: Collier Books, 1961.

McKay, Derek. *The Great Elector*. London: Pearson Education, 2001.

Memoirs of the Courts of Sweden and Denmark during the Reigns of Christian VII of Denmark and Gustavus III and IV of Sweden. 2 volumes. Published for the Grolier Society, Boston, circa 1910.

Miller, Townsend. *Henry IV of Castile*. Philadelphia and New York: J. B. Lippincott Co., 1972.

Montefiore, Sebag. *Prince of Princes: The Life of Potemkin*. New York: Thomas Dunne Books, 2000.

Moote, A. Lloyd. *Louis XIII, The Just*. Berkeley: University of California Press, 1989.

Morand, Paul. *The Captive Princess: Sophia Dorothea of Celle.* New York: American Heritage Press, 1972.

Morton, Andrew. *Diana: In Pursuit of Love.* London: Michael O'Mara Books Ltd., 2004.

Moynahan, Brian. *Rasputin: The Saint Who Sinned.* New York: Random House, 1997.

Pakula, Hannah. *The Last Romantic: The Life of the Legendary Marie, Queen of Roumania.* New York: Simon & Schuster, 1984.

Parissien, Steven. *George IV.* New York: St. Martin's Press, 2001.

Pasternak, Anna. *Princess in Love.* New York: Signet, 1995.

Pevitt, Christine. *Philippe, Duc D'Orléans, Regent of France.* New York: Atlantic Monthly Press, 1997.

Quinlan, Paul D. *The Playboy King: Carol II of Romania.* Westport, CT: Greenwood Press, 1995.

Rice, Tamara Talbot. *Elizabeth Empress of Russia.* New York: Praeger Publishers, 1970.

Rodocanachi, E. *Les Infortunes d'une Petite-Fille d'Henri IV, Marguerite d'Orléans, Grande-Duchesse de Toscane, 1645–1721.* Paris: Ernest Flamario, circa 1890.

Rosenthal, Norman, ed. *The Misfortunate Margravine: The Early Memoirs of Wilhelmina, Margravine of Bayreuth, Sister of Frederick the Great.* London: Macmillan & Co., 1970.

Smith, Lacey Baldwin. *A Tudor Tragedy: The Life and Times of Catherine Howard.* London: Jonathan Cape, 1961.

Smith, Sally Bedell. *Diana in Search of Herself.* New York: Random House, 1999.

Somerset, Anne. *Ladies in Waiting: From the Tudors to the Present Day.* London: Weidenfeld and Nicolson, 1984.

Spoto, Donald. *Diana: The Last Year.* New York: Harmony Books, 1997.

Starkey, David. *Six Wives: The Queens of Henry VIII.* New York: HarperCollins, 2003.

Sutherland, Christine. *Marie Walewska: Napoleon's Great Love.* London: Robin Clark Ltd., 1979.

Troyat, Henri. *Catherine the Great.* New York: E. P. Dutton, 1980.

———. *Peter the Great.* New York: E. P. Dutton, 1987.

Warnicke, Retha M. *The Rise and Fall of Anne Boleyn.* Cambridge: Cambridge University Press, 1989.

Weiner, Margery. *The Parvenu Princesses: The Lives and Loves of Napoleon's Sisters.* New York: William Morrow & Co., 1964.

Weir, Alison. *Eleanor of Aquitaine.* New York: Ballantine Books, 1999.

——. *Henry VIII: The King and His Court.* New York: Ballantine Books, 2001.

——. *The Six Wives of Henry VIII.* New York: Grove Press, 1991.

Wilkins, W. H. *The Love of an Uncrowned Queen, Sophie Dorothea, Consort of George I, and Her Correspondence with Philip Christopher Count Königsmarck.* 2 volumes. London: Hutchinson & Co., 1900.

——. *A Queen of Tears, Caroline Matilda, Queen of Denmark and Norway and Princess of Great Britain and Ireland.* 2 volumes. New York and Bombay: Longmans, Green & Co., 1904.

Williams, H. Noel. *Queen Margot, Wife of Henry of Navarre.* London: Harper & Brothers, 1907.

Williams, Robert Folkstone. *Memoirs of Sophia Dorothea, Consort of George I.* 2 volumes. London: Henry Colburn Publisher, 1845.

Wright, Constance. *Daughter to Napoleon: A Biography of Hortense, Queen of Holland.* New York: Holt, Rinehart & Winston, 1961.

INDEX